COMPUTER LITERACY THROUGH APPLICATIONS

Dr. Barbara L. Kurshan
Alan C. November
Jane D. Stone

HOUGHTON MIFFLIN COMPANY Boston
Atlanta Dallas Geneva, Ill. Lawrenceville, NJ Palo Alto Toronto

Authors

Dr. Barbara L. Kurshan, Hollins College, Hollins, Virginia

Alan C. November, Lexington Public Schools, Lexington, Massachusetts

Jane D. Stone, Houston Independent School District, Houston, Texas

Editorial Advisor

Dr. David Moursund, University of Oregon, Eugene, Oregon

Teacher Consultants

Ihor Charischak,
Board of Cooperative
Education Services,
Ardsley, New York

Judith J. Daley,
Claremont Unified
School District,
Claremont, California

Irwin Hoffman,
Denver Public Schools,
Denver, Colorado

1989 Impression

Printed in U.S.A.

ISBN: 0–395–36605–4

IJ–V–H–943210

CONTENTS

CHAPTER OPENER PHOTOS

Cover Photo Computer chips with thousands of integrated circuits are photographed on top of computer wires.

Chapter 1 Managers of baseball teams are using computers to keep track of batting and fielding records and to generate team line-ups.

Chapter 2 A microcomputer contains thousands upon thousands of integrated circuits contained on chips.

Chapter 3 As the price of home computers goes down, more people will own computers, allowing them to perform a variety of tasks for work, school, and leisure time.

Chapter 4 Babbage's Analytical Engine was never completed due to a lack of technology, but it is considered to be a forerunner of the modern computer.

Chapter 5 Programs direct the computer to perform a wide range of tasks. For example, this young man is composing with a music software program.

Chapter 6 A computer-controlled robot is programmed to play board games.

Chapter 7 Computer literacy programs are an important part of many schools' curriculums. These students are learning BASIC programming.

Chapter 8 Many people are beginning to depend on word-processing software to help them write, edit, and print everything from letters to books.

Chapter 9 Computers with data-base management software are replacing traditional card catalogues in libraries.

Chapter 10 Electronic spreadsheets have had a major influence on the growth in the number of microcomputers being used in business today.

Chapter 11 Scientists can use the graphics capabilities of computers to analyze data such as the heat patterns in a solar eclipse.

Chapter 12 By connecting a microcomputer to a modem, people can communicate with other computers and tap into data banks of information.

Chapter 13 A scientist is testing a computer that will convert voice input into written text.

Chapter 14 One of the most exciting and rapidly expanding fields of computer technology is robotics.

CREDITS

Cover: photography by Joel Gordon.
Chips courtesy of Intel Corporation and Arrow Electronics.
Software provided by American Micro Media.

Chapter 1 10: © Tom Zimberoff/Gamma-Liaison. 12: © Erich Hartmann/Magnum. 13: © Tom Zimberoff/Gamma-Liaison. 14: t. © Lonny Kalfus/International Stock Photo; b. © Enrico Ferorelli/DOT. 15: IBM Corporation. 18: © 1984 Cameramann International, Ltd. 21: l. © Peter Tenzer/Wheeler Pictures; r. "Photo courtesy of Hewlett Packard Company." 23: © Dan McCoy/Rainbow. 24: Michal Heron.
Chapter 2 28: © Christopher Springmann/SFO. 30: Michal Heron. 31: IBM Corporation. 33: © Roger Tully/Black Star. 34: RCA. 37: t. © Phillip Harrington/Peter Arnold; b. © James A. Sugar/Black Star. 41: t. © Viewdata Corporation of America; b. IBM Corporation. 43: "Photo courtesy of Hewlett Packard Company". 45: Michal Heron.
Chapter 3 50–52: Michal Heron. 57: © Enrico Ferorelli/DOT. 59: © John McGrail/Wheeler Pictures. 60–63: Michal Heron.
Chapter 4 68: © Bill Pierce/Rainbow. 70: t. © Loren McIntyre/Woodfin Camp; b. The Computer Museum, Boston, MA. 71: The Science Museum, London. 72: The Computer Museum, Boston, MA. 74: Harvard University, Cruft Laboratory, Photographic Dept. 76: U.S. Navy. 77: The Moore School of Electrical Engineering/University of Pennsylvania. 78: © Dan McCoy/Rainbow. 80: © Will Blanche/DPI
Chapter 5 90–103: Michal Heron
Chapter 6 108: © Dan McCoy/Rainbow. 110–121: Michal Heron.
Chapter 7 126: © 1983 Joel Gordon. 130: Michal Heron. 142: The Science Museum, London.
Chapter 8 150: Michal Heron. 155: The Granger Collection. 156: Michal Heron. 161: © Joel Gordon.
Chapter 9 168–170: Michal Heron. 171: © 1986 Cameramann International, Ltd. 172: © John McGrail/Wheeler Pictures. 173–178: Michal Heron.
Chapter 10 184: Michal Heron. 187: "Courtesy of Apple Computer Inc." 188: The Granger Collection. 190: Michal Heron. 196: l. Robin Schwartz/International Stock Photo; r. Michal Heron. 198: Michal Heron.
Chapter 11 200: © Dan McCoy/Rainbow. 207–210: Brighter Image. 211: © Roger Tully/Black Star. 212: © Joe McNally/Wheeler Pictures. 213: © Dan McCoy/Rainbow. 214: "Photo courtesy of SubLogic Corporation."
Chapter 12 224: Michal Heron. 226: © Sepp Seitz/Woodfin Camp. 227: Culver Pictures. 229: © Scott Thode/International Stock Photo. 233: © CompuServe Information Service. 235: © Sepp Seitz/Woodfin Camp. 236: © Dan McCoy/Rainbow.
Chapter 13 240: © Hank Morgan/Rainbow. 242: © 1983 James A. Sugar/Black Star. 243: © Dan McCoy/Rainbow. 244: © Cameramann International, Ltd. 246: © Roger Ressmeyer/Wheeler Pictures. 247: © 1982 Brian Payne/Black Star. 249: © Viewdata Corporation of America, Inc. 250: © James Balog/Black Star. 251: Vioujard/Gamma-Liaison. 253: © John McGrail/Wheeler Pictures.
Chapter 14 258: © Roger Ressmeyer/Wheeler Pictures. 260: © Christopher Springmann/SFO. 261: © Eric Preau/Sygma. 263: © Dan McCoy/Rainbow. 267: © 1984 Camermann International, Ltd. 269: © Dan McCoy/Rainbow. 273: © Michael Tcherevkoff/The Image Bank.

UNIT ONE

COMPUTERS IN YOUR LIFE

One of best known early electronic computers, named ENIAC, was built in 1946. It was one hundred feet long and weighed thirty tons. It cost half a million dollars. A team of technical experts was required to make ENIAC work.

Today, there are computers that are light enough to carry in your arms. These machines work faster and are more powerful than ENIAC, yet cost no more than a stereo set. And ten year olds can operate them easily.

Welcome to the Computer Age: a time when the same technology that sent astronauts to the moon is used daily in offices, stores, banks, schools, hospitals—and in our homes. A time when electronic *beeps* are as familiar to us as the sound of raindrops in spring.

In this unit, you'll learn about the computer: what it is, how it works, and how it came to be. You'll see why this powerful tool is playing a role of growing importance in your life.

CHAPTER

13 14 1 2 3

INTRODUCTION TO COMPUTERS

Hi. C'mon in. . . .

Welcome to the home of the Dawson family: Joseph and Linda; their fifteen-year-old daughter, Jane; and their thirteen-year-old son, Tod. It's a nice home, probably a lot like the house or apartment in which you live.

You wouldn't know it on first glance, but the Dawson home is filled with computers. No, the Dawsons aren't computer programmers. As a matter of fact, there's only one desktop computer in the house. All the other computers are invisible. Well, not exactly invisible. . . .

Take a look at the hallway wall over there. See that little rectangular box? It's a thermostat. It controls the heating and air-conditioning systems. Inside the box there's a **microprocessor**—a computer "brain." You'll learn more about microprocessors in the next chapter. For now, just think of them as tiny computers.

The microprocessor lets the Dawsons program, or preset, the thermostat to whatever temperatures they want. In winter, for example, the Dawsons keep the daytime temperature at 68 degrees. At night the temperature is lowered—automatically—to 60 degrees. Then, in the morning, the thermostat causes the temperature to rise to 68 again. The tiny computer inside the thermostat does all the work. The Dawsons had only to set it once.

The microprocessor in the thermostat is only one of many computers in the Dawson home. Let's go into the living room. The television set in the corner there contains a microprocessor to control channel selection. So does that bright-red digital clock on the shelf and the stereo set against the wall.

Next stop, the kitchen. Linda Dawson just got home from work, and she's cooking dinner using a microwave oven, which contains a microprocessor also.

In Jane's room there are microprocessors in her pocket calculator, in her night-table radio, and even in the new camera she just bought with the money she earned baby-sitting. In Tod's room next door, there's a microprocessor inside the electronic typewriter that he got for his last birthday.

Down the hall is the Dawsons' master bedroom. Right now Joseph Dawson is sitting at the desk, typing away at the one recognizable computer in the house. It's a **personal** or **home computer**, which consists of a keyboard, a television-type screen, and a boxlike unit containing—you guessed it—a microprocessor.

Mr. Dawson is using the computer to complete some work he didn't finish at the office. He knows he'd better use the family computer now, because after dinner Jane and Tod will no doubt be using it—unless Mrs. Dawson gets to it first.

Since they bought it last month, all the Dawsons have been enjoying their new computer. They use it to play games, to do financial calculations, and for various other purposes. Later in this book you'll read about the many ways that a personal computer can be put to both practical and enjoyable use.

COMPUTERS ALL AROUND US

Invisible or not, computers are playing a role of growing importance in all our lives. Today computers are used in many

This tiny microprocessor, magnified many times, is the computer's "brain."

car engines, telephone systems, industrial robots, home appliances, even toys and games. Students are studying computers in school—as you are now—and workers are learning how to use them on the job. Computers are used in hospitals, banks, airports, factories, sports arenas, even farms. Artists draw with them, writers write with them, and musicians use computers to compose music. More and more supermarkets are using computerized scanners to check out your purchases electronically. And the personal computer, which is fast dropping in price, will soon become as common as the pocket calculator.

Hard to believe: Less than fifty years ago there were *no* electronic computers in the world. In fact, the word *computer* didn't even refer to a machine. It meant a person who did computing, or calculating, for a living. Today there are *millions* of computers—and they're all around us.

UNDERSTANDING THE COMPUTER

When you hear the word *computer*, what's the first thing you think of? A small desktop machine that hooks up to a television set? Or maybe you think of a huge metal box with blinking lights, like the computers shown in many science-fiction movies. Maybe you think of video games with colorful graphics and loud sound effects.

Computers create different images in our minds, some good, some not so good. When a computer helps us perform a task more easily or quickly, we smile and say, "Aren't they great!" But when a department store computer sends us a bill for an item we didn't buy, we groan and complain that computers are driving us crazy.

Well, few things in life are *all* good or *all* bad, computers included. An important purpose of this book is to help you understand exactly what computers are, how they work, how they help people solve problems, and what they can—and can't—do. Such knowledge won't eliminate department store computer errors, of course. But it will help you get the most from the countless computers around you.

WHAT *IS* A COMPUTER?

A computer is a machine in many ways similar to other machines. It runs on electricity. It contains a number of parts that work together. It's designed to perform certain tasks.

So far we could just as easily be describing a hair dryer, a power drill, or an electric lawnmower as a computer. What is it that makes the computer special?

Several things. First, computers are fast. Not sixty-miles-per-hour fast. *Blink-of-an-eye* fast. Think about this: A "slow" computer can add hundreds of thousands of numbers in *one second.* More powerful computers can add *millions* of numbers per second. In fact, when computer users discuss computer speed, they often don't even use the word *second.* They talk in terms of **microseconds** or **nanoseconds**. How small a unit of time do these terms refer to? Well—a second contains one million microseconds . . . or one *billion* nanoseconds.

Besides being incredibly fast, computers are also extremely reliable. The average person using a pencil and paper to do arithmetic might make one or more mistakes in an hour. After several hours of work, the person would get tired and probably make more mistakes. By comparison, a computer can do arithmetic more quickly and more accurately, and it can continue working for hours or days at a time. Long after any human would have fallen asleep at his or her desk, the computer would still be calculating

Computers at a baseball game? Here a computer is being used to track the team's performance during a major league game.

This ground station depends on computers to track satellites high above the earth.

along—without so much as a yawn!

A third feature of computers that makes them unique machines is that they can receive, store, and use information and instructions that you give them. What other machines can you think of that are able to do all that? (Careful, now—don't include machines containing microprocessors!) Can an ordinary mechanical typewriter, for example, remember tomorrow the letter you type today? A computer can—and, at your command, it can reproduce that same letter ten times, addressed to ten different people!

THE INFORMATION THAT COMPUTERS HANDLE

Every day your brain deals with new information. You read books and magazines. You learn the words to a new song. Someone gives you directions to his home. You listen to the weather report. You study current events in school. The constant daily flow of information is enormous, but the amazing human brain can handle it easily.

Computers, too, deal with large amounts of information. Even though they're sometimes called "electronic brains," they can't think the way you do. Nevertheless, their capacity to handle different kinds of information is remarkable.

Processing data. When information is put into a computer, it's *processed*. That is, the computer handles or manipulates it in some particular way. For example, a computer may add a column of numbers, or it may arrange a series of names in alphabetical order. The computer is *processing* those numbers and names.

Without computers, air traffic controllers could not direct the many planes at this airport.

The pieces of information that a computer processes—numbers, words, facts—are called **data**. *Data* is a general term that may refer to anything from sports statistics (numbers) to a list of the top records (words) for the last five years.

Give Me One Datum, Please . . .

Data is actually the plural form of the word *datum*. *Datum* comes from Latin and originally meant "something given." However, you'll rarely hear anyone refer to "one datum." In fact, the word *data* has become so much more common that it's now treated as either singular or plural, as in: "Medical data is/are kept in the patient's file."

When computers sort, add, rearrange, or otherwise manipulate information, that's called **data processing**. Many large businesses have a special data-processing department set up to handle information, keep records, and take care of accounting. Such a department may contain millions of dollars' worth of computer equipment.

Storing data. You read a moment ago that one of the features that makes computers unique is that they can store information. Computers have **memory**. Their memory is electronic. They store data in electronic circuits. The data stored in a computer's memory can be recalled, erased, or changed.

A microprocessor "brain" and electronic memory are the two most important parts of a computer. Working together, they enable the computer to use the data that it receives. If the computer couldn't remember numbers and letters, it wouldn't be able to process them, just as you couldn't form words if you couldn't remember the letters of the alphabet. You'll read more about computer memory in Chapter 2.

Data is stored on memory chips like the one shown on the left. The chip is magnified even more on the right, showing part of the circuits.

"A Memory Like an Elephant"

Have you ever heard someone say, "Boy, you've got a memory like an elephant!" That expression is commonly used to describe someone who can remember many facts for a long time.

Computers have impressive memories too. Depending on how powerful the computer is, it can remember thousands or millions of **characters** —letters, numbers, or symbols (like "!" or "$"). The amount of data that a computer's memory can store is known as its *memory capacity*.

The memory capacity of a computer is measured in **bytes**, **kilobytes**, and **megabytes**. A byte is equal to one character (a letter, a number, a symbol, or a space.) A kilobyte is equal to 1024 bytes. And a megabyte is equal to about one million bytes.

A typical home computer may have a memory capacity of 64 kilobytes, abbreviated 64K. How much memory capacity is that? Sixty-four kilobytes is equal to about thirty-two double-spaced typewritten pages.

In other words, a home computer with 64K of memory can store in its memory more than thirty pages' worth of typed characters. Seems like a lot, doesn't it? It is—for a machine. But think how much data is stored in *your* memory:

- the names, addresses, phone numbers, and birthdays of friends and relatives
- all the words in your vocabulary
- the titles of books, movies, songs, and plays
- the names of streets, cities, states, and countries
- facts about history, science, math, and numerous other subjects

And much more. In fact, the human brain can store *trillions* of characters in its memory. Quite likely, in years to come, the computer will be able to match that. But for now, humans are still the champs. . . .

Key Points

- Computers are playing a role of growing importance in all our lives. They're used in homes, offices, stores, schools, banks, hospitals, and countless other places.
- Computers are electronic machines that operate with remarkable speed and reliability. In addition, they are unique in that they can receive, store, and use information and instructions that the user gives them.
- A microprocessor "brain" and electronic memory work together to enable the computer to process data.

Review Questions

1. "Computers are secretly invading our homes." Explain this statement, citing specific examples.

2. In some ways, computers are similar to other machines. In other ways, though, they're unique. Explain.

COMPUTERS AS TOOLS

What do the following items have in common?

a carpenter's hammer
a scientist's microscope
a gardener's hoe
a plumber's wrench
a dentist's electric drill
an accountant's computer

If you answered that they're all tools, you're correct. Did the last one make you stop and think? Many people find it hard to view the computer as a tool. But that's really what it is.

Tools are devices that people use to perform specific work tasks. Tools enable the user to work more quickly, easily, or efficiently. The carpenter uses a hammer to drive nails. The plumber uses a wrench to tighten pipes. Similarly, the accountant uses a computer to do complex mathematical calculations.

The carpenter, the plumber, and the accountant all could do their jobs without their tools, but the work would take longer and be harder to accomplish. Tools save both time and effort. Bear in mind, though, that it's *people* who use and control tools. The finest hammer and the most powerful computer are equally worthless unless a person has the skill and knowledge to use them.

AN ALL-PURPOSE ELECTRONIC TOOL

While computers share basic similarities with other tools, they also have some important differences. You've already read about some of these differences: the computer's amazing speed, for instance, and its ability to store information. Another key difference is the computer's ability to serve many purposes.

Would you use an artist's paintbrush to paint a house? Of course not. Like other tools, brushes are designed to serve certain specific purposes.

Computers, however, have a vast range of uses. As you'll see in later chapters, the computer is an all-purpose electronic tool that can be used to

manipulate numbers
keep records
prepare letters
draw pictures
operate machines
teach
entertain
communicate
. . . and do a thousand other things!

CONVERSING WITH YOUR COMPUTER

In addition to their speed, memory, and versatility, computers have another feature that sets them apart from other tools: They're interactive. Let's see exactly what that means.

When you use a power tool or other machine, communication is generally one way. You communicate your instructions by flipping a switch or turning a dial. Except perhaps for the hum of a motor, the device won't answer you in any way.

Computers, on the other hand, allow for interactive, or two-way, communication. You communicate with the computer. The computer responds. You communicate again. The computer responds again. And so on. Here's an example.

Let's suppose you work in the office of a sales company. Your boss has asked you to use a desktop computer to assemble a list of customer names and telephone numbers. Your "conversation" with the computer would go something like this:

• Through the computer keyboard, you communicate both data and instructions. That is, you type in the names and phone numbers of the customers. Then you instruct the computer to put those names in alphabetical order.
• The computer does as told. In a moment an alphabetized list of names and phone numbers appears on your screen.
• You study the list. Then you decide that all you really need right now is a list of those customers whose area code is 555.
• You instruct the computer to read the list and pull out the 555 customers.
• In a flash, the computer displays the revised list of 555 customers only.

Like you, these students are gaining valuable skills learning about computers in their school's computer center.

Each time you communicate with the computer, you receive a response—the computer communicates back in some way. This back-and-forth process is called **interactive** communication. The computer's responses are known as **feedback**.

Sometimes the computer may even ask you questions. For example, the computer's screen might look like this:

```
WHAT TASK DO YOU WANT TO DO?
TYPE THE NUMBER OF YOUR CHOICE.
   1. ADD NEW INFORMATION.
   2. CHANGE INFORMATION.
   3. TRANSFER INFORMATION
      TO ANOTHER FILE.
```

You would type in a number, and the computer would carry out your instructions. Even though the computer is asking you questions, it's still *you* who are in control.

The interactive nature of computer communication is pretty amazing when you think about it. After all, when was the last time some other tool or machine asked you a question?

KINDS OF COMPUTERS

How many of the following terms do you recognize?

jeep	hardtop
convertible	pickup truck
sedan	tractor-trailer
station wagon	van

You probably know most or all of them. These words all refer to kinds of cars and trucks.

There are a wide range of motor vehicles, each unique in some way: size, power, structure. Although all motor vehicles share some common features, each is best suited for certain specific purposes. A station wagon, for example, is great for taking a large family on a picnic. But if that family wanted to move its furniture and belongings across the country, a moving van would better serve the purpose.

In a way, computers are like motor vehicles. There are many different kinds, each particularly well suited for certain purposes. Let's take a look at the diverse world of computers.

ANALOG COMPUTERS AND DIGITAL COMPUTERS

Although all computers make calculations, they don't all make them in the same way. **Analog computers** work by measuring, while **digital computers** work by counting.

Analog computers. An analog computer calculates by measuring the continuous change in some physical quantity. To understand what this means, picture a weather thermometer. As temperature increases, the liquid inside the thermometer's glass tube expands. As the liquid expands, it rises in the tube. The higher the temperature, the longer the line of liquid in the tube. The scale of numbers alongside the tube translates the temperature change into degrees.

Next time you're riding in a car, you might see a kind of analog device in action—the car's speedometer. In effect, it computes speed in miles per hour by measuring how fast the car's wheels are rotating. As the car goes faster, the movement of the speedometer needle shows you the computed speed.

The first analog computer was built more than fifty years ago by Vannevar Bush, an American scientist. Today analog computers are used mainly for scientific and engineering purposes.

Digital computers. A digital computer calculates not by measuring, like an analog computer, but by counting. The great majority of computers used in business and science today are digital computers.

To solve problems, a digital computer counts numbers. In a way, the computation that a digital computer does is like the calculation you do in your head to make change for a dollar. Both the computer and you apply basic arithmetic—addition, subtraction, multiplication, and division. The computer, of course, can work much faster—especially if it's $987,438,761.51 to be made change for instead of just one dollar. Also you would use the ten-digit decimal system to make your calculation. Digital computers use the special two-digit *binary* system, which you'll read about in Chapter 3.

While many cars' speedometers are analog, newer models often have digital speedometers.

Key Points

• The computer is a versatile electronic tool that enables its user to perform a wide range of tasks quickly, easily, and efficiently.
• Computers allow for interactive, or back-and-forth, communication.
• There are different kinds of computers, each particularly well suited for certain purposes.
• Analog computers work by measuring. Digital computers work by counting.

Review Questions

1. Why may the computer rightfully be called a "tool"?
2. One feature that sets computers apart from other tools is that they're interactive. What does this mean? Why is this feature important?

MAINFRAMES, MINIS, AND MICROCOMPUTERS

Nearly all the computers you'll read about in this book are electronic digital com-

An analog speedometer (top) displays a continuous change in speed. A digital speedometer (bottom) displays the change of speed in intervals.

puters. Although they all have certain characteristics in common, they vary greatly in size, power, and cost.

Generally speaking, large computers are called **mainframes** and small computers are known as **microcomputers**. In between the two are medium-sized computers called **minicomputers**. Keep in mind, though, that these are just basic labels. Not every computer fits neatly into one of these three groups.

For example, some small computers are more powerful than some midsize ones. One reason for this is that as technology has advanced, scientists and engineers have been able to fit more computer power into less and less space. As a result, some modern desktop computers have as much power as the *room*-size computers built several decades ago.

Mainframe computers. Large, powerful, and expensive, mainframes are used in business, science, and government. These computers can store vast amounts of data and perform many tasks at the same time. Want to buy one? You'd better start saving: Mainframes are generally priced between $100,000 and $10,000,000!

Minicomputers. Smaller than mainframes are the minicomputers. These computers, too, can store large amounts of information and perform more than one task at once. Their power, however, is not as great as that of mainframe computers. That's why they're "inexpensive"—ranging in price from about $5,000 to $80,000.

Microcomputers. The smallest computers are the microcomputers. You may have heard them called by a variety of names.

home computer	portable computer
personal computer	briefcase computer
desktop computer	lap-top computer

All these terms refer to microcomputers. Take another look at the list. These six names tell a lot about what microcomputers are and why they've become so popular.

Some microcomputers are so small and lightweight that they're easily portable. In fact, there are microcomputers that will fit into a briefcase or rest comfortably on your lap. Nevertheless, despite their small size, microcomputers have enough power and storage capacity to meet the personal needs of many different users, ranging from business owners to professionals to students. And in recent years more and more families have bought them for home use.

Were the prices of mainframes and minicomputers out of your range? If so, a microcomputer might be more in line with your budget. Some microcomputers cost less than $100. With prices that low, it's no wonder that we're in the midst of a "personal computer revolution."

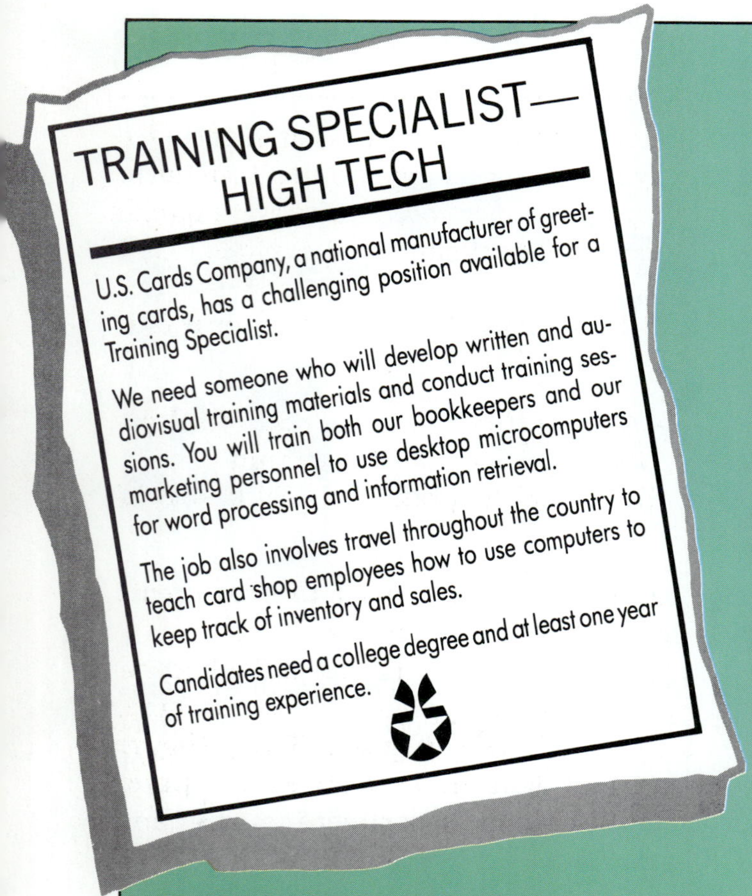

TRAINING SPECIALIST—HIGH TECH

U.S. Cards Company, a national manufacturer of greeting cards, has a challenging position available for a Training Specialist.

We need someone who will develop written and audiovisual training materials and conduct training sessions. You will train both our bookkeepers and our marketing personnel to use desktop microcomputers for word processing and information retrieval.

The job also involves travel throughout the country to teach card shop employees how to use computers to keep track of inventory and sales.

Candidates need a college degree and at least one year of training experience.

THAT'S MY JOB

Jay Hutton, a training specialist for a greeting card company, says:

"People are initially pretty nervous about using the machines—of high technology in general. As they start to work on the computer and become familiar with the vocabulary, however, I can see them become more and more comfortable. I like knowing that I play a part in that shift.

"Sometimes I get tired of being asked the same questions, but I don't let it show. You really need good interpersonal skills in this job, and that includes a big dose of patience."

MORE INFORMATION

The demand for training specialists is expected to grow steadily.... Computer manufacturers and companies that are large users of computers will continue to be the main employers of training specialists.... This is a good career area for people interested in teaching.

This lap computer is so small it can be easily taken anywhere, even on vacation.

GENERAL-PURPOSE AND SPECIAL-PURPOSE COMPUTERS

Besides their size, power, and cost, computers may also be distinguished from one another by the purposes they serve.

General-purpose computers are machines that can do a variety of tasks. With a home computer, for example, you can play games, write letters, draw pictures, or solve mathematical problems.

Special-purpose, or **dedicated, computers** are designed for one particular purpose. A special-purpose computer might, for example, be used in the navigational system of an atomic submarine. A professional writer may use a **dedicated word processor**, a computer built specifically to work with pages of text. Inside an automobile, a tiny microprocessor may serve to control the car's fuel system.

Both general-purpose and special-purpose computers are common today. Together they meet the needs of individuals and families, businesses, schools, government, and numerous other users.

COMPUTERS AND YOU

There's no denying it: Computers are playing an increasing part in all our lives. They're in our homes and cars, in banks and supermarkets, in hospitals, and schools.

Do you like movies? How about these:

Superman III	*Star Trek II*
Star Wars	*Tron*
Return of the Jedi	*Futureworld*

Computers were used to help create every one of these movies.

Sometimes it seems as though computers are popping up everywhere, doesn't it? Well, they are. Today they're sold not just in specialized computer stores but in department stores and hobby shops. They're constantly written about in newspapers and magazines. They're advertised on television and radio. Bookstores are overflowing with computer guides, and mailboxes are filled with computer-generated letters. In schools students are taking computer-related courses—just as you are now.

YOUR NEED FOR COMPUTER LITERACY

Do you know the meaning of the word *literacy*? It means the ability to read and write. Being literate is essential to success in school, at work, and in life in general.

In recent years another kind of literacy has also become important: **computer literacy**. Computer literacy means knowing about computers: understanding their usefulness as tools and knowing how to use and control them. It also means being aware of both the computer's benefits *and* its drawbacks.

The book you are reading now will help you become *computer literate*. It will help you learn to use one of the most powerful tools of our time: the computer.

A computer makes a good tutor—it can even teach you how to use . . . a computer!

"Don't You Trust Me?"

Nowadays people routinely feed data into a computer and accept the computer's calculations without question. But it wasn't always so.

One of the earliest computers was the UNIVAC—the *Univ*ersal *A*utomatic *C*omputer. The first UNIVAC was built in 1951, but many other models were made and sold in subsequent years. CBS Television used one of these computers to predict the results of the 1952 presidential election between Dwight D. Eisenhower and Adlai E. Stevenson.

After the computer had been fed huge amounts of data, it calculated that Eisenhower would win a landslide victory. UNIVAC made this prediction after a mere 7 percent of the votes had been counted! The engineers operating UNIVAC couldn't believe what the computer was telling them. Political experts had predicted a close election, not a landslide. The computer must have made a mistake, they decided.

Before long, though, the engineers realized it wasn't UNIVAC that had made the mistake. Eisenhower received nearly five times as many electoral votes as Stevenson. He won—by a landslide. In fact, UNIVAC had predicted the outcome of the election within 1 percent of the actual vote count!

REVIEW & APPLICATION

SUMMARY

- Computers are versatile electronic tools that can store information and instructions and process data with remarkable speed and reliability.
- Unlike other tools and machines, computers allow for interactive, or two-way, communication.
- Analog computers calculate by measuring the continuous change in some physical quality. Digital computers calculate by counting numbers.
- Mainframe computers are large, powerful, and expensive. Minicomputers are smaller than mainframes and not as powerful.
- Microcomputers, the smallest computers, are also known as personal computers, home computers, and desktop computers.
- General-purpose computers can perform a variety of tasks. Special-purpose, or dedicated, computers are designed for one particular purpose.

VOCABULARY

Match each item in the left column with the correct item on the right.

a. microprocessor	1. information that a computer processes
b. digital computer	2. calculates by measuring
c. data	3. unit for measuring storage capacity
d. home or personal computer	4. computer "brain"
e. kilobyte	5. microcomputer
f. analog computer	6. calculates by counting

REVIEW QUESTIONS

1. What are the three main types of digital computers? Why can't some computers be classified easily?
2. What is a byte? How many bytes in a kilobyte? In a megabyte?
3. Why is computer time measured in microseconds or nanoseconds?
4. How are analog and digital computers different from each other? Give examples of uses for each type.

DISCUSSION QUESTIONS

1. Describe some ways in which computers can save people time and effort. Include specific examples.
2. What ways do you think you could use a computer to help you with your schoolwork?
3. Why is it important for a person growing up in the 1980's to be computer literate?

PROJECTS

There are two ways to start your computer. A **cold start** is when you turn on the machine. Sometimes a faulty program can cause the computer to malfunction. When this happens, a **warm start**—resetting the computer without turning it off—is preferable to turning the machine off and on. Both will give you a cursor. (See page 33.)

APPLE IIe—Cold Start

1. Insert a DOS disk into Drive 1.
2. Turn on computer and display screen.
3. Wait for] prompt.

APPLE IIe—Warm Start

1. Make sure DOS disk is in Drive 1.
2. Type PR#6 and press RETURN.

COMMODORE 64–Cold Start

1. Turn on disk drive and peripherals.
2. Turn on computer and display screen.

COMMODORE 64—Warm Start

Hold RUN/STOP key down while pressing RESTORE key.

IBM PCjr—Cold Start

1. Turn on disk drive and peripherals.
2. Turn on computer and display screen.
3. The PCjr will perform a self-test, and then ask for the date and time. Press ENTER twice.

IBM PCjr—Warm Start

1. Make sure DOS disk is in Drive A.
2. Press CTRL key, ALT key, and DEL key at same time. The PCjr will not run BASIC (a computer language you will learn more about later) unless told to do so. To start IBM BASIC, type BASIC, and press ENTER.

TRS-80 Model III—Cold Start

1. Make sure disk drives are empty.
2. Turn on computer.
3. Wait until disk drives stop.
4. Insert DOS disk into Drive 0.
5. Press orange RESET button.
6. The computer will ask you to enter the date using this format: MM/DD/YY. (January 2, 1987, would be entered as 01/02/87.) Then press ENTER.
7. The computer will ask you to enter the time. Press ENTER.
8. Wait for "TRS DOS Ready" to appear.

TRS-80 Model III—Warm Start

1. Make sure DOS disk is in Drive 0.
2. Press RESET key.
3. Follow steps 6 and 7 above. To start TRS-80 BASIC, type BASIC, then press ENTER. The computer will then ask, "How many files?" Press ENTER. It will then ask, "Memory size?" Press ENTER again. The BASIC prompt 〉 will appear.

Further Practice

On an index card, outline the instructions for starting your school's computer(s).

Enrichment

List all the computers that you can find in your school. Don't forget hidden ones like the thermostat!

CHAPTER TEST

Write your answers on a sheet of paper numbered 1 through 10.

MATCHING

1. Match each term to its definition.

a. nanosecond	1. one character
b. process	2. one billionth of a second
c. byte	3. sort, add, or rearrange
d. feedback	4. computer response

MULTIPLE CHOICE

2. The original meaning of the word *computer* was:
   a. a kind of telescope
   b. someone who wrote books
   c. a ship's navigator
   d. someone who did calculations
3. A feature that is unique to computers is the fact that they:
   a. can be used as tools
   b. can receive, store, and use data
   c. require special training to use
   d. run on electricity
4. In order for a computer to be able to process data, it needs to be able to:
   a. store numbers and letters
   b. give feedback to the user
   c. convert analog to digital data
   d. recognize the human voice
5. Once stored in a computer's memory, data *cannot* be:
   a. recalled
   b. erased
   c. heard
   d. changed
6. The characters that can be recognized by most computers consist of:
   a. dates, places, and times
   b. letters, numbers, and symbols
   c. words, sentences, and letters
   d. bytes, snacks, and morsels
7. A memory capacity of 64K in a computer is enough to store about:
   a. 64 double-spaced typewritten pages
   b. 12 double-spaced typewritten pages
   c. 128 double-spaced typewritten pages
   d. 32 double-spaced typewritten pages
8. A computer is a versatile tool that can be used to:
   a. draw pictures
   b. manipulate numbers
   c. entertain
   d. all of the above
9. An example of an analog device is:
   a. a calculator
   b. a clock without hands
   c. a speedometer with a needle
   d. an adding machine
10. Which of the following could be a desktop computer?
    a. a microcomputer
    b. a mainframe
    c. a minicomputer
    d. all of the above

CHAPTER

14 1 2 3 4

THE PARTS OF A COMPUTER

Sabrina's guitar teacher is explaining how to play certain chords. Sabrina listens carefully, absorbs the information, and then puts it to use by playing the chords correctly.

Alan is watching an exercise show on television. He memorizes the routines that are being taught and later goes through them on his own.

These actions are so familiar and natural that you may not think much about them. If you do stop to think about them, though, you will notice that Sabrina and Alan each went through three distinct steps. They are the same three steps that a computer goes through in handling information: input, processing, output.

PROGRAMS—TELLING THE COMPUTER WHAT TO DO

On a simple level, a computer works in much the same way as your brain. A computer, like your brain, receives, stores, compares, changes, and manipulates information. There is one major difference, though. A computer is a mechanical device and has to be told what to do. In fact, a computer has to be told *exactly* what to do. Once it has received its instructions, it goes ahead and carries them out. Then it shows you the results of what it has done.

How is a computer told what to do? It is given a set of instructions called a **program**. You can create your own computer programs, or you can buy programs that are ready-made. Thousands of packaged programs are available for computers—everything from space adventures to math drills to financial management programs to typing tutors.

When a computer follows the instructions in a program, it is said to "run" the program. How is a computer program developed in the first place?

Usually someone types the instructions into the computer. The program may be easy to create or very complex, depending on how much the computer will be required to do. A few simple instructions can make a computer display the words "HI, THERE!" But thousands of instructions are needed to produce a game like Zork I.

Imagine having to type in thousands of instructions each time you wanted to play your favorite computer game. Fortunately, that isn't necessary. Once a program is written, it is usually saved on a magnetic disk or tape. That way it can be used again.

A computer program is called **software**. Software is the set of instructions that tells the computer what to do. Most computers can run hundreds of different programs. Chapter 3 discusses software in more detail.

Hardware is the physical equipment of a computer. A Commodore 64, a TRS-80, an Apple IIe, and an IBM-PC are all hardware. So are any of the devices that can be attached to them. This chapter deals mainly with hardware.

THREE BASIC STEPS

Sabrina and Alan, you will recall, went through three steps in handling information, just as a computer does. The three steps are input, processing, and output. Let's look at each of them more closely.

Computer programs, along with instructions for their use, may be purchased at a store.

INPUT

A program provides the basic instructions the computer must follow in order to do a specific job. Like the basic rules of a game, the program is only the beginning, however. In order to do a job, the computer and the program must also have **input**. Input is the data and additional instructions you give to a computer to enable it to do a specific job. The input may be in the form of numbers, letters, words, or pictures.

The computer may receive input through a **keyboard**, which looks very much like the keyboard on an ordinary typewriter. It may also receive input from a disk or cassette. Until a computer receives input, it can do nothing.

PROCESSING

What does a computer do with the information it receives? Like the human brain, it sorts information, puts it into usable form, and does calculations. This step is called processing.

OUTPUT

Finally, the computer does something with the information it processes. It usually displays the results, often on a screen or on paper. The product of computer processing is called **output**. Output is the information the computer produces as a result of its work.

You are likely to see this three-step process—input, processing, output—in many day-to-day activities, such as when you use a pocket calculator. In a calculator the input consists of numbers that you press on its keypad—let's say the numbers 3 and 7. The processing occurs after you tell the calculator what you want it to do for example, multiply. The output—21—appears on a little screen at the top of the calculator.

The calculator can process the same information in different ways. You might have asked it to add the two numbers, in which case "10" would have appeared on the screen. Or you might have asked it to find what percentage 3 is of 7. The answer to that is 42.857142 percent. Remember: The output depends on what kind of processing is done.

Let's look at these three steps in a larger computer, such as one at the local library. More and more libraries are using a computer to keep track of books, because it handles the job efficiently.

Suppose you have a library card in such a library, and you want to borrow two books. You present your card to the person at the circulation desk, who runs a bar code reader (which looks like a small flashlight) across a number on your card. Immediately words appear on a display screen: your name, address, even the fact that you have a book checked out that is overdue. You had forgotten about that book, but the computer hadn't.

The computer remembered because each time you checked out books, the librarian ran that "flashlight" not only over the numbers on your library card, but also across numbers on labels inside the books. This stored information on titles, authors, and due dates was ready to be displayed whenever the computer received your card number as input.

Key Points

- A computer receives, stores, compares, changes, and manipulates data.
- A computer program is a set of instructions that tells a computer what to do. A program is also known as software.
- There are three basic steps in handling data: *input*—entering data and instructions that enable the computer to do a specific job; *processing*—sorting data and doing calculations; and *output*—sending the results of processing to a storage or display device.

Review Questions

1. What is the difference between software and hardware?
2. Describe the three information-handling steps as they might occur in a pocket calculator.

The output is a picture on the computer screen, but the output could also be printed on paper.

INPUT DEVICES

You have seen two ways of creating input. The calculator received input through a miniature keyboard, and the library's computer received input through a device that looked like a small flashlight. Let's look at other input devices.

THE KEYBOARD

Nearly every computer you see will have a keyboard. Most computer keyboards have plastic keys similar to those on a standard typewriter. Some, however, have what are called **membrane keys**. Membrane keys look as if they were printed on a flat surface. Unlike regular keys, they don't have to be pushed; they

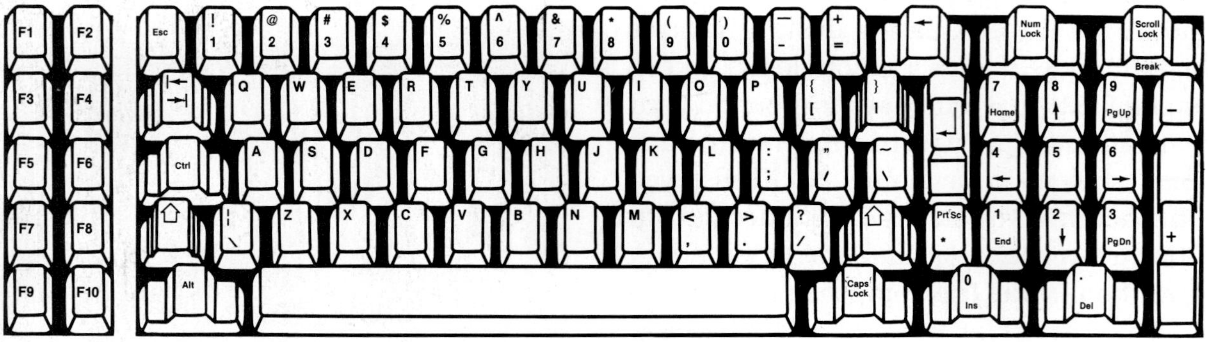

merely have to be touched.

A computer keyboard, like a typewriter keyboard, has numbers and letters. Most of the keys are arranged like those on a typewriter. This is sometimes called the **QWERTY layout.** "QWERTY" refers to the sequence of letter keys at the far left just below the number keys.

Most computer keyboards have more keys than typewriter keyboards. Some have many more. These extra keys are of three basic kinds.

Function keys. A **function key** on a typewriter is any key that does not produce a letter, number, or special symbol. On an electric typewriter, the tab key, return key, and shift key are all function keys. They make it possible to arrange letters, numbers, and other symbols on paper in an orderly way.

Most computers have function keys too, but many of these keys operate differently from those on a typewriter.

Many computers have a reset key to tell the computer to forget the current program and start over. On many machines the clear key tells it to take the displayed text or graphics off the screen. When using any computer, you have to learn what its function keys do.

Numeric keypad. On some computers a **numeric keypad** is located off to one side of the basic cluster of keys. It looks very much like the keys on a pocket calculator. And no wonder—it serves the same purpose: to input numbers for the computer to use in calculations.

Locate keys. The purpose of locate keys is to enable the user to move quickly from point to point on the display screen. On many computers the locate keys are four keys with arrows. One arrow points up, one down, one right, and one left. Computer users call these directions "north," "south," "east," and "west," respectively.

OTHER INPUT EQUIPMENT

In addition to the keyboard, other devices are available to enter information into the computer. These devices are called **peripherals**. A peripheral is any hardware device that is connected to a computer in order to make the computer easier to use or to extend the computer's capabilities. Peripherals provide input to or accept output from the computer.

A great many kinds of peripherals have been invented to provide input to a computer. Here are a few of the most common ones.

Joystick. If you have played computer games, you have probably used a **joystick**. A joystick is a device that permits you to move a picture, line, word, or cursor from point to point on a display screen. (A **cursor** is a spot of light on the screen that indicates the exact place at which you are entering data or giving commands.) You operate a joystick by moving it in various directions. It carries out the same functions as the locate keys on the keyboard. But it is faster, and it lets you move in eight directions instead of four.

Graphics tablet. A **graphics tablet** lets you draw a design just as you might do on paper. You use a special pen or your finger to do the drawing on a flat, tabletlike surface. Your drawing appears immediately on the display screen.

Light pen. The **light pen** looks almost like an ordinary pen, but its tip is a light-sensitive detector. When you touch the tip of the pen to the display screen, the computer locates what are called the *X-Y* coordinates of that point. By touching the screen at various points, or by moving the pen across the surface of the screen, you can write and draw.

Mouse. The computer age has brought a new meaning to the word **mouse**. As an input device, a mouse is a small box with one or more buttons. It usually sits on a

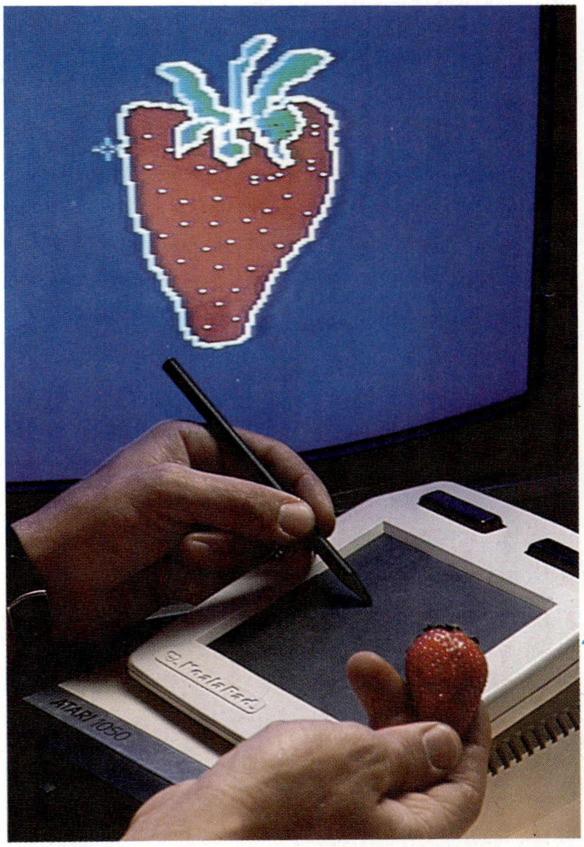

This artist is using a graphics tablet to produce the image on the computer screen.

desk, although some mice go on the floor. When the box is moved around, the cursor on the screen also moves. Mouse software has menus that appear on the screen. (A **menu** is a list of operations the computer is able to perform in relation to a specific program.) You choose the operation you want by moving the mouse, which in turn moves the cursor to that item. You press a button on the mouse, and the computer will perform the operation you have chosen.

OCR (optical character reader). An **OCR** scans a typewritten or printed page and converts the letters or numbers into electronic signals. These signals can then be recorded on a magnetic tape or disk.

Some OCR's require that the pages they scan be prepared in a special kind of type. More expensive machines, however, will read a variety of standard type styles. These OCR's are particularly useful to commercial printers. Some printers use an OCR to read typewritten manuscript, convert the text to electronic signals, and then send it directly to a machine that sets the text in the kind of type you see in magazines, newspapers, and books. This procedure eliminates complete retyping of the copy, which used to be required.

Voice-recognition device. Suppose you could just talk to a computer and have it follow your directions. That would be an easy input method, wouldn't it? In fact, **voice-recognition devices** are available. While now most of them recognize only a few words—although some recognize hundreds—their ability is being improved all the time.

A convertor changes analog input into a digital series of zeros and ones.

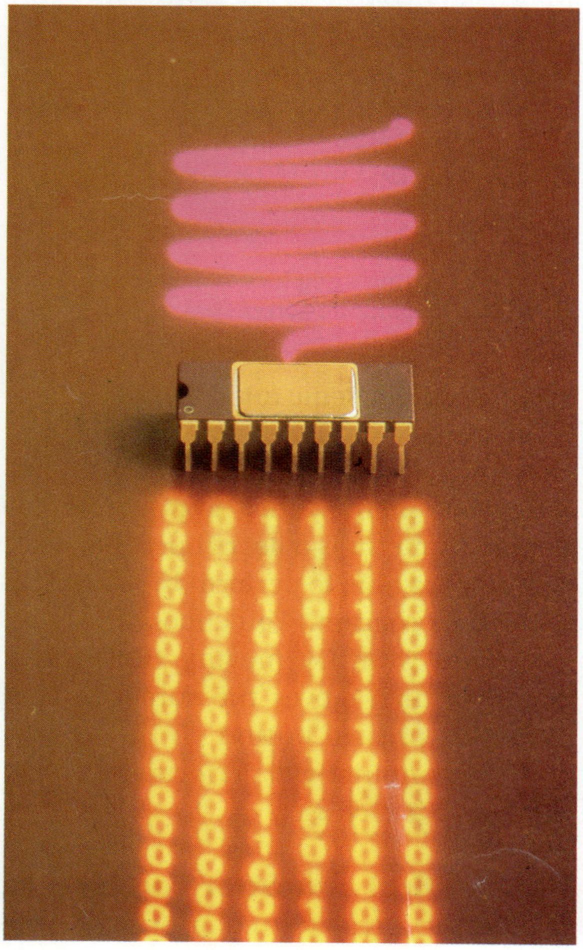

CONNECTING PERIPHERALS TO COMPUTERS

A peripheral is connected to a computer by means of an electric cable or wire. Each piece of equipment has a **port**, or jack, which allows the necessary connection to be made.

Very often the peripheral can't be connected directly to the computer, however. There are two reasons for this. The first is that many different kinds of computer equipment are being made by many different manufacturers. Not all of it works together. Just as you can't install a Ford muffler on a Chevrolet, neither can you always connect one company's peripheral to another company's computer.

The other reason some peripherals can't be connected directly to computers is that analog equipment, which you learned about in Chapter 1, can't be directly attached to digital equipment. First, analog signals must be "translated" into digital signals or vice versa.

To link two incompatible pieces of

hardware, you need an **interface unit**. An interface unit supplies the connections to make the two kinds of hardware work together.

THE "BRAIN" OF THE COMPUTER

You have seen that there are quite a few ways to get information into the computer. Once the information is there, what does the computer do with it? You already know the answer: The computer processes it. But how?

Instructions from the keyboard and from other forms of input—such as a program—go to the **central processing unit**, or **CPU**. The CPU interprets and follows instructions, and sends the results of its work to the user, to the computer's memory, or to both.

The CPU is the "brain" of the computer and its traffic cop. Located inside the computer's case, its work involves arithmetic, logic, and control. Arithmetic and logic are handled by one unit of the CPU, control by another.

ARITHMETIC/LOGIC UNIT

Suppose you want the computer to multiply 563 × 442. How do you think the computer goes about it? The computer *adds*. It adds 563 to 563 to 563, and keeps right on adding 442 times. Slow? Surprisingly, no. The answer—248,846—appears on your screen in a split second. Whether a computer is or isn't smart, it certainly is fast—*very* fast.

A computer can also make logical decisions with astonishing speed. It does this by the process of comparison. For instance, if you want to know whether one number is less than, greater than, or

When the control unit of the CPU receives input, it determines which process the arithmetic/logic unit should perform.

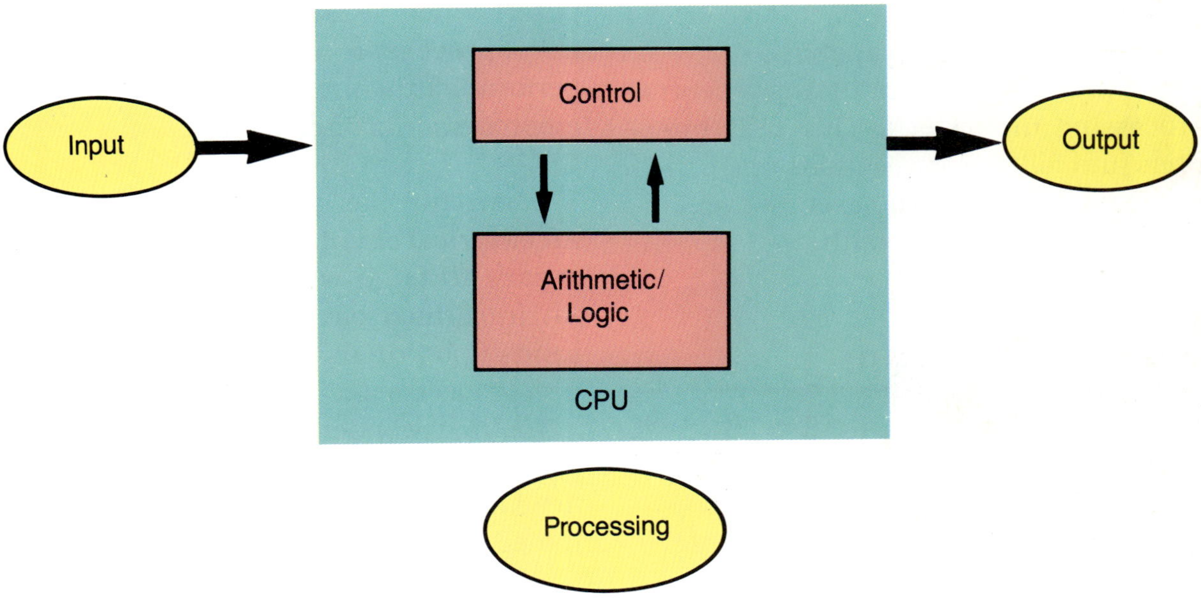

equal to another number, the arithmetic/logic unit will give you the correct answer instantly.

CONTROL

In the two examples just given, the CPU's control unit determined whether the arithmetic/logic unit would add, subtract, or compare the numbers it was given. While this is about all the control unit can do, as you have seen, it can produce very significant results indeed.

Key Points

- Most computer keyboards resemble typewriter keyboards.
- Some of the extra keys on the computer keyboard are function keys. A function key tells the computer how to handle certain information. Some computers have a numeric keypad similar in look and function to a calculator.
- A peripheral is a hardware device that is connected to a computer. A peripheral makes the computer easier to use or extends the computer's capabilities.
- The brain of the computer is a central processing unit (CPU). This unit interprets and follows instructions and sends results of its work to the user, to the computer's memory, or to both.

Review Questions

1. Describe two input devices and tell what each one does.
2. Explain the function of an interface unit.

CHIPS, CIRCUITS, AND MEMORY

Since the CPU is so important, and its speed is so remarkable, you might picture it as being very large. In fact, it can be tiny. The CPU in a microcomputer may be no larger than a thumbnail! And since it requires so little space, it is often included in the same case as the keyboard. In a mainframe or minicomputer, the CPU is located in a separate unit. It is this unit that people in a data-processing department are talking about when they refer to "the computer."

CHIPS AND CIRCUITS

A **chip** is a thin wafer, about a quarter of an inch square, that plugs into a board in the computer. Most chips are made of silicon, which is a common, nonmetallic element found in the earth's crust, most often in sand. Because of this, they are frequently called **silicon chips**.

A single silicon chip can be the entire central processing unit of a microcomputer. When it is, the CPU is called a **microprocessor**. Even if several chips perform all the processing, the word *microprocessor* is often used to refer to the CPU.

Each chip has an **integrated circuit**. An electrical circuit, as you may know, is a path through which electricity flows. An integrated circuit consists of thousands upon thousands of tiny, interconnected electrical circuits.

You may wonder how all those circuits get on a wafer not much bigger than the head of a thumbtack. The answer is contained in a big word: **miniaturization**. An integrated circuit is first designed by an engineer using a computer. The circuit is then printed in very large scale on a piece of paper. Next it is reduced photographically to fit on a silicon chip.

An integrated circuit is more than just a tiny photograph, of course. The chip on which the photo goes must be a **semiconductor**. A semiconductor is a material that will conduct electricity in some circumstances but not in others. This is exactly the kind of material silicon becomes after a tiny amount of iodine and other substances are added to it.

The miniaturized photo serves as a kind of screen through which light passes in a pattern. The parts of the chip that are exposed to light become hard, and the rest of the chip is removed. This process is known as "etching the chip." After the chip is etched, thousands of fine metal wires, or conductors, are added, creating the integrated circuit.

Making an integrated circuit is a very delicate process since each wire on the chip is no more than a few microns thick. (A micron is a millionth of a meter, and a page of this book is about twenty microns thick.) The slightest flaw in the procedure can ruin a chip. The finished chip, a marvel of modern technology, can conduct electricity along all those thousands of circuits. Its ability to do so, as you will see in the next chapter, is what makes the computer work.

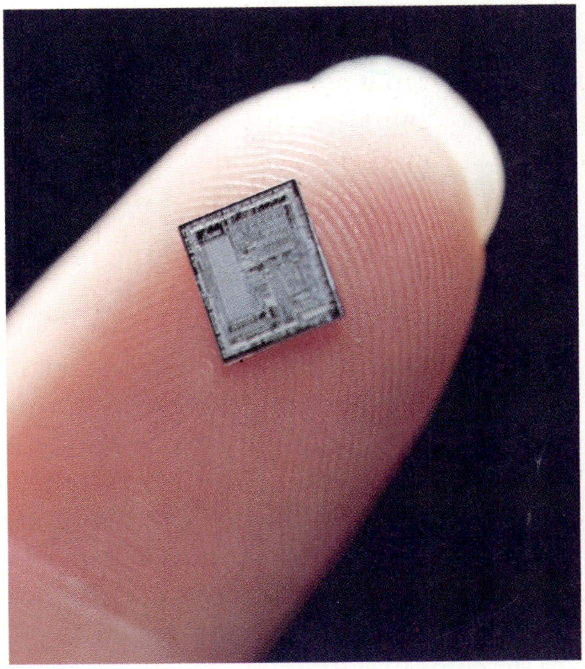

The process of miniaturization enables people to fit thousands of electronic circuits on a little chip that is smaller than your fingerprint. The tiny silicon chip is the "brain" of the computer.

ROM: read-only memory	**RAM:** random-access memory
permanent	temporary
not affected when computer is turned off	information is cleared from it when computer is turned off
instructions can be "read" from it but cannot be "written" to it	instructions can be both "read" and "written" to it

COMPUTER MEMORY

If you go to a picnic, you later have memories of it. You may remember the taste of the food, the excitement of the games, and the names of friends who were there. With the passage of time, however, you will probably forget some of the details.

A computer's memory is different. No matter how you program it, the computer cannot remember such things as the taste of food or the feeling of excitement. But it can remember names. Your computer will easily keep track of the names of everyone who attended the picnic.

Of course, the computer doesn't already know the names. You have to tell it the names of the picnickers. Once you supply it with that input, the computer's memory, unlike yours, will never forget. The list will always be complete and always correct—as long as the computer is turned on. When you turn it off, the list disappears. Why does this happen?

The computer has two kinds of memory. One kind is called **read-only memory**, or **ROM**, and it is not affected when you turn off the machine. ROM is *permanent* memory. The second kind of memory is called **random-access memory**, or **RAM**, and this is the kind of memory in which your list of picnickers was stored. RAM is *temporary* memory.

ROM (read-only memory). A computer has to have a built-in set of instructions. It has to know what to do when it is turned on. Different computers have different kinds of instructions in ROM, but some instructions are standard and necessary for all computers. For example, all computers have to know how to do various mathematical computations.

The instructions built into ROM are there permanently. The computer can "read," or follow, the instructions in ROM, but it cannot change them or add to them. That's why the memory is called "read only."

RAM (random-access memory). RAM is the memory that holds the software and other input data while you are working on them. When you used the keyboard to enter the names of the picnickers, you put the names in RAM. This kind of memory is called **random access** because you can instantly go right to any part of the stored data or program. You do not have to run through all the data stored up to the part that you want to see.

You can easily change input data that is stored in RAM. For instance, you can add a missing name or correct a misspelling. However, many commercial software producers write their programs in such a way as to make it very difficult for you to change them.

RAM is temporary memory. When you turn off the computer, everything that has been stored in RAM disappears. If you want to save data that is stored in RAM, you have to store it externally—that is, outside the computer. As you know, you can store programs and data on disk or tape.

The amount of RAM varies from one computer model to another. But no matter how much RAM your computer has, it is not unlimited. At some point, the memory will be filled. When that happens (or even before it happens) you will need to transfer data from the filled internal storage to some form of external storage, such as a disk or tape.

Key Points

- When a single silicon chip serves as a computer's CPU, that chip is called a microprocessor.
- ROM is memory that is built into the computer.

Input can be stored in the computer's memory to be retrieved later, or it can be processed and displayed as output.

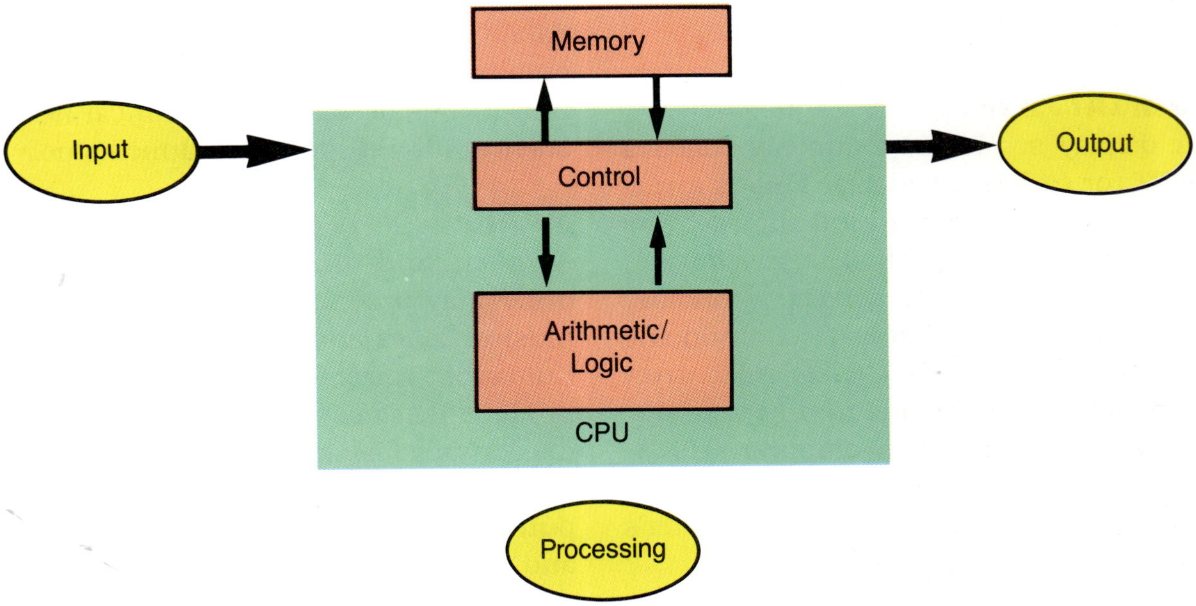

• RAM is temporary memory.
• The amount of RAM in a computer is not unlimited. At some point the user will have to make a copy of some of the data in RAM and store it externally.

Review Questions

1. What is the difference between ROM and RAM?
2. What advice would you give someone who is just learning to use a computer, has been working all day on a program, and is ready to turn off the machine and go home?

OUTPUT DEVICES

You have seen how data and programs are entered as input in a computer, and you have seen how they are processed and stored. The next step is output. Just as there are a number of ways to get data into a computer, there are also a number of ways to get data out of a computer. The most common way is by means of a display screen.

DISPLAY SCREEN

A display screen is commonly called a **CRT**, or cathode-ray tube. This is a vacuum tube—the same kind that delivers the picture on an ordinary television set. Recent advances in screen technology have introduced other ways of producing images, but the term CRT is still correct for most of the screens now in use.

Sometimes a microcomputer will be attached to a television set. The television screen then becomes the computer's display screen.

There are also special, or dedicated, display screens built to be used with computers. They are called **monitors**. They look like television sets, but they aren't. Their only purpose is to function as an output device for a computer. Like television sets, some monitors display only monochrome (one-color) images, while others display color images.

A screen can produce two major kinds of output: text and graphics.

Text. Output that consists of letters or numbers is called **text** or **copy**. The screen, as an output device, allows you to see the data you are working with. You are likely to be reading, changing, correcting, or deleting text on the screen.

Graphics. When you manipulate data in the form of pictures, you are using **graphics**. Once an image appears on the screen, it can be changed, corrected, or deleted as easily as text can.

Perhaps the most familiar kinds of graphics are those of computer games, but there are other kinds of pictorial data. Graphics in the form of charts and graphs are becoming increasingly important in business and in technical fields such as aircraft design and medicine.

SOUND

Another kind of output that the computer may produce is sound, including musical tones and melodies and even a humanlike voice. How does the computer produce these sounds? A program on a disk or tape may include instructions for producing an audio signal. In most computers, the unit that contains the CPU and keyboard also contains a small speaker, or else it might be in the monitor. When the computer reads the audio instructions on the disk or tape, it sends a set of signals to a small amplifier and then to the speaker.

You are probably familiar with an instrument called a *synthesizer*. A synthesizer is a musical keyboard, such as you'd see on a piano or organ, but the sound it produces is created by a computer built into the instrument. The instrument is in fact a kind of computer whose input device is a musical keyboard and whose output is sound.

The process of producing sounds that imitate the human voice is known as **voice synthesis**. At this time only a few computers can produce these sounds. The output of most computers is in the form of text and graphics.

HARD COPY

The text and graphics that appear on a screen are called **soft copy**. Soft copy is not permanent; it can be changed or corrected; it can also be erased forever.

Hard copy is text or graphics printed on paper. Hard copy is sometimes called a **printout**. When computer output must be read by many different people, the most practical way to accomplish this is through a printout.

You have probably seen many kinds of printouts. Most of the bills, checks, form letters, invoices, and personalized advertising pieces that arrive in the mail are forms of computer printouts or hard copy, including the printed labels on which the recipient's name and address appears.

Hard copy is produced by one of two peripherals—a **printer** or a **plotter**.

Soft copy—output on computer screens—when printed on paper becomes hard copy.

PRINTER

A printer is a mechanical device containing elements that allow it to produce text such as you might see on a typewritten page. Most printers, however, are extremely fast—much faster than even the fastest human typist. Some printers produce whole pages of text in seconds.

PLOTTER

Although a regular printer can create certain kinds of graphics, the device that produces the best graphics is a plotter. A plotter is an output unit that controls the movements of a pen—or several pens—

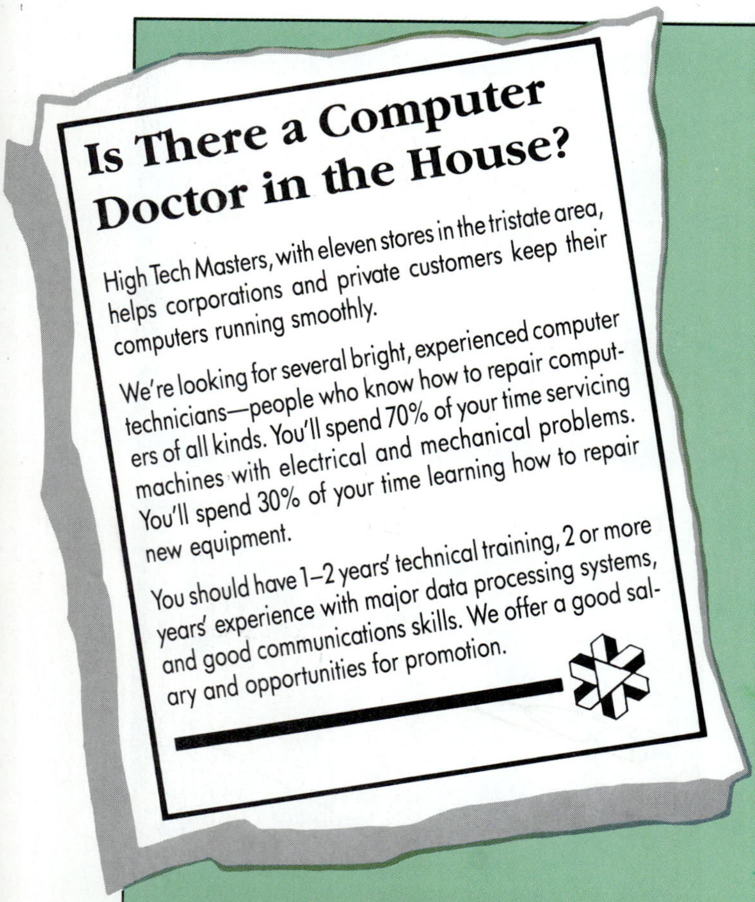

THAT'S MY JOB

Here's what Pearl Neuman, field engineer, says about her work:

"Computers need repair just like other machines; then people call on me. I really like dealing with people and tinkering with the machinery to find out what's wrong. I feel like a doctor—except that my patients are computers, not people.

"Of course, sometimes I get a little annoyed when I get phone calls from customers at midnight. But that comes with the job. The pay is good and those midnight calls don't happen that often.

"Someday I may go into selling. After all, I know quite a bit about different computer systems."

MORE INFORMATION

Service technicians are also known as customer engineers, field engineers, or service engineers.... They generally install and keep computer systems running and test machinery to make sure it performs efficiently.... Service technicians may provide training to computer users.... This is a fast-growing field.

over a piece of paper. It can produce accurate and intricate hard-copy drawings. A plotter is highly useful to engineers, architects, physicians, and others who need detailed drawings in their work.

INPUT/OUTPUT DEVICES

It's easier to separate input and output in a textbook than it is in actual use. Certain kinds of peripherals can carry out both input and output functions. These are called **input-output (I/O)** devices. Two such devices are the touch-sensitive screen and the modem.

Touch-sensitive screen. In a way, the **touch-sensitive screen** goes one step beyond a light pen. Instead of pointing a mechanical device at the touch-sensitive screen, you use your finger to touch it. By simply touching the screen, you can move text or graphics to a new location, or you can instruct the computer to carry out certain commands.

Modem. The purpose of a **modem** is to make it possible to connect one computer with another computer by means of telephone lines. Why not simply connect the computer directly to the telephone lines? Here's the reason: Modern computers, as you know, are digital devices. The telephone is an analog device. The two can work together only with an interface device. The modem serves as that interface.

If a computer in Los Angeles is to communicate with a computer in Dallas, the Los Angeles computer's digital signals are changed into analog signals by the modem and sent out on telephone lines. In Dallas, another modem changes the analog signals back into digital signals that can be received by the Dallas computer there. This process of changing signals is known as *modulating* and *demodulating*, and the word *modem* comes from these two terms.

A modem is an I/O device because it allows input to be sent to another computer and also allows output to be received from another computer. Modems are vital to electronic communications. Their uses will be discussed in detail later in the book.

Key Points

- One of the main output devices for a computer is a display screen.
- Two kinds of output are text and graphics. Text, also known as copy, is made up of letters and numbers. Graphics are data in the form of pictures, charts, and graphs.
- An input/output (often referred to as I/O) device is one that carries out both input and output functions.
- A modem serves as an interface unit between computers and telephones.

Review Questions

1. How does a computer monitor differ from a television?
2. What is the difference between soft copy and hard copy? What output devices are used for each?

Just point to what you want and a touch-sensitive screen lets your finger become an input device.

STORAGE METHODS

As you have learned, you lose any program and data stored in RAM when you turn off the computer. The only way to save a program and data is to store them externally—that is, outside the computer. The two main forms of external storage are disk or tape. Once you've stored data externally, you can load it back into RAM. In this way the storage medium—disk or tape—is also a form of input.

Programs and data are stored on disks or tape in the form of magnetic impulses. When you load a program or data into the computer, these impulses are "read" and the data is sent into RAM. The procedure is somewhat like playing a record. When you put a record on your turntable, the grooves are "read" by the stylus and the impulses are sent to the system's amplifier and speakers. The grooves containing the music remain on the record; they do not have to be recaptured and stored again.

CARTRIDGE

A **cartridge** is a small plastic box that contains a permanent program, somewhat like ROM. The box, about the size of a pocket calculator, plugs into a slot in a microcomputer. Cartridges are often called *ROM cartridges* because they have read-only memory. As a user, you cannot store anything new on a cartridge. You can only use what is put there by the manufacturer.

Cartridges are fully enclosed and sturdy. For that reason, computer games are often put on cartridges. Not all microcomputers accept cartridges.

CASSETTE

A **cassette** is a small reel of magnetic tape in a plastic case—exactly like a music cassette but containing a computer program instead of music. By attaching a simple, fairly inexpensive cassette recorder to some microcomputers, cassette tapes can be used to store programs and data.

Since information must be stored in sequence on the tape, the material stored at the end of the tape can be reached only by running through the whole tape up to that point. Consequently, a cassette recorder is called a **sequential-access** device.

The main advantage of a cassette over other kinds of storage is its comparatively low cost. The main disadvantage is that there is slower access to data with a cassette than with some other storage devices. Cassette recorders also sometimes lose data through accidental erasures or mechanical problems. Because of their drawbacks, cassette recorders are not as popular as storage devices as they once were.

FLOPPY DISK

By far the most common storage device used with microcomputers is the **floppy disk**, or **diskette**. A floppy disk looks like a 45-rpm phonograph record in a sealed black protective jacket. The jacket has a couple of small openings (in addition to the large spindle hole in the center) that permit the storage unit to "read" the contents of the disk. A disk is much thinner than a record—in fact, thin enough to be flexible, or "floppy." The disk is made of silver metallized polyester, a kind of plastic, and is magnetically coated rather than grooved the way records are.

A floppy disk usually allows **random** access. You will remember that the letters RAM stand for "random-access memory." Just as RAM offers random access to stored data, a floppy disk allows direct access to any data stored on it. Unlike sequential access, random access does not require you to go through everything previously stored.

Floppy disks come in three sizes. Many microcomputers use disks that are 5¼ inches in diameter. Others use an 8-inch diskette. And some newer equipment uses 3½-inch disks.

In order to load the data on a disk into RAM, you need to insert the disk into a **disk drive**. A disk drive may be built into the computer, or it may be separate from it. The disk drive spins the floppy disk at a high speed. A "head" located inside the disk drive does one of two things. It either "reads" information already recorded or it "writes" new data onto the disk. Because the head performs both of these functions, it is often called a **read/write head**.

Single disk drives, dual disk drives, and even multiple disk drives are available. One advantage of having more than one disk drive is the increase in storage capacity. You can work with more information at the same time. Another advantage is convenience: You have to do far less inserting and removing of disks than with a single disk drive.

A disk drive costs more than a cassette recorder, but it is worth the price difference for these reasons:

- Floppy disks store much more information than cassettes.
- Random access makes floppy disks faster and more efficient than cassettes.
- Although disks sometimes fail, they are considerably more reliable than cassettes.

The biggest drawback to using floppy disks is that the disks require very careful handling. Dust, dirt, fingerprints, scratches, stacking, moisture, heat, magnetism—all are hazardous to floppy disks.

Floppy diskettes must be handled with care or the information stored on them might be damaged.

HARD DISK

A **hard disk** is a round, pancake-shaped, permanently sealed magnetic storage device. Sizes vary, but one common size is about the diameter of a 33⅓ rpm record. Hard disks accept a great deal of information. A single hard disk can store many more times as much material as a 5¼-inch floppy disk.

Since hard disks are encased in rigid plastic, they are less likely to be damaged than are the somewhat fragile floppies. Hard disks are used mainly with mainframes and minicomputers although they can be used with many microcomputers. Their biggest advantage is their great storage capacity. Hard disk drive units, as you might expect, are expensive but, as with all computer hardware, their price is going down.

Key Points

- The two main forms of external storage are disk and tape. Programs and data are stored on disks or tape in the form of magnetic impulses.
- The floppy disk is by far the most popular form of external computer storage for microcomputers.
- A hard disk about the size of a 33⅓ rpm record holds much more data than a 5¼-inch floppy disk.

Review Questions

1. Explain why sequential access is not as desirable as random access.
2. Explain the function of a read/write head in a disk drive.

Seven Tips on Caring for Hardware

1. Read the instructions. Don't ignore the manual even if you're sure you know how to operate your computer.
2. Put the computer in a safe, dry, clean area. Pets, water, and snacks can harm computers.
3. Turn the computer off before inserting cartridges. Failure to do so could cause severe damage to the cartridge.
4. Avoid using the computer during lightning storms. Unplug it until the bad weather passes.
5. Keep the monitor clean, reflection-free, and clear of clutter. Don't put disks on or near the monitor.
6. Put cables where they cannot be tripped over. Make sure they aren't so tight as to strain the connectors.
7. Use care when putting disks into disk drives. Never remove or insert a disk when the drive is operating.

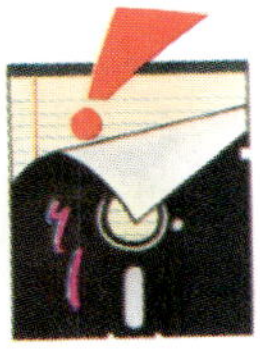

REVIEW & APPLICATION

SUMMARY

- Software is the set of instructions that tells the computer what to do. Hardware is the physical parts of a computer, including peripherals.
- A computer receives your input through the keyboard, disk drive, and other parts that you use to give it data or instructions.
- Processing includes sorting, calculating, and other steps involved in following your instructions.
- The information that results from the processing is called output. The computer displays output on its screen and can print the output or store it on tapes or disks.
- The central processing unit, or CPU, is the computer's "brain." It has a control unit and an arithmetic/logic unit. The control unit determines whether the arithmetic/logic unit will add, subtract, or compare the numbers it was given.
- A single silicon chip can be the entire CPU of a microcomputer. A chip contains thousands of tiny, interconnected electrical circuits.
- A computer's ROM is not affected when you turn off the computer. ROM includes built-in instructions that tell the machine what to do when you turn it on and how to perform calculations.
- RAM is a temporary memory that holds your input while you are working with it.

VOCABULARY

Match each item in the left column with the correct item on the right.

a. program	1. text or graphics on a display screen
b. function key	2. a set of instructions for a computer
c. plotter	3. thousands of tiny, interconnected circuits
d. integrated circuit	4. a device using pens that produces graphics
e. soft copy	5. doesn't produce a character

REVIEW QUESTIONS

1. Do you have to write a program each time you want to use a computer?
2. How is a typical computer keyboard different from a typewriter keyboard?
3. How do a CPU's control unit and arithmetic/logic unit work together to solve an arithmetic problem?
4. Where is your input stored in the computer while you are working with it, and what happens when you turn off the computer?
5. What two methods might you use for storing programs or data externally?

DISCUSSION QUESTION

How is a computer like a person's brain? How is it different?

PROJECTS

C Initializing, or formatting, a disk must be done before a disk can be used for the first time. Before initializing a disk, be sure that the write-protect notch (page 55) is not covered. IMPORTANT: Initializing a disk erases any information that may be on it.

APPLE IIe

1. Wait for the] prompt.
2. Remove any disk from drive.
3. Insert a blank disk in Drive 1.
4. Type NEW, then press RETURN. This will erase the memory.
5. Type INIT HELLO and press RETURN.

COMMODORE 64

1. Wait for prompt.
2. Insert blank disk into drive.
3. Type OPEN 15,8,15 and then press RETURN.
4. Type PRINT#15,"NO:MY DISK,A1", and press RETURN.

IBM PCjr

1. Wait for "A>" prompt. (If "OK" is displayed, type SYSTEM, and press ENTER.)
2. Put DOS disk in Drive A.
3. Type FORMAT/S and press ENTER.
4. The computer will tell you to remove DOS disk and insert disk to be formatted. Do this, then press ENTER.
5. The computer will ask, "Format another disk? (Y/N)". Type N for no; Y for yes.

TRS-80 Model III

1. Put DOS disk in Drive 0.
2. Wait for "TRSDOS Ready" prompt.
3. Type FORMAT and press ENTER.
4. The computer will ask, "Format which drive?" Type 0 and press ENTER.
5. Remove DOS disk and replace with disk you wish to format.
6. The computer will ask, "Diskette Name?" Type MYDISK and press ENTER.
7. The computer will ask, "Master Password?" Type PASSWORD, and press ENTER.
8. After one to two minutes the message "00 Flawed Tracks" will be displayed, followed by "Writing System Information". Then the computer will ask you to "Insert SYSTEM diskette ⟨Enter⟩." Remove formatted disk and replace it with DOS disk. Then press ENTER.

Further Practice

D Is a computer more than the sum of its parts? Design a chart entitled "The Parts of a Computer." List input, output, and storage devices. Describe each device and how it is used.

Enrichment

D *Peripheral* means "of secondary importance." But computer peripherals are essential. Research a computer peripheral and write an explanation of how it works.

CHAPTER TEST

Write your answers on a sheet of paper numbered 1 through 18.

MATCHING

1. Match the term to its definition.

a. output	1. sorting data
b. input	2. programs and data
c. hard copy	3. result of processing
d. processing	4. CPU on a chip
e. light pen	5. printed output
f. microprocessor	6. input device

FILL-IN

2. A ____________ is the computer's "brain."
3. A program provides the ____________ that a computer must follow to perform a task.
4. A computer usually has a ____________ similar to that of a typewriter.
5. The numeric keypad on a computer looks very much like the set of keys on a small ____________.
6. A ____________ is an attachment that extends a computer's capabilities or makes it easier to use.
7. To enter a page of a typed manuscript into a computer's memory without retyping it, you might use a peripheral called an ____________.
8. The part of a CPU that compares one number with another to see if one is larger is the ____________ unit.
9. Most computer chips are made of ____________.
10. The computer can read the instructions that are in its ____________, but it cannot change them or add to them.
11. Everything that you have stored in a computer's ____________ will disappear when you turn off the machine.
12. A computer's ____________, as its display screen is often called, is like the picture tube of a television.
13. A plotter is a special kind of ____________ for producing graphics.
14. A floppy disk usually allows ____________ access to the data that is stored on it.
15. In order to load the data on a disk into RAM, you need to insert the disk into a ____________.

MULTIPLE CHOICE

16. To give a computer your input, you might use:
    a. a keyboard
    b. a mouse
    c. an OCR
    d. any of the above
17. A joystick is a:
    a. program
    b. printer
    c. peripheral
    d. chip
18. The diameter of a floppy disk can be:
    a. $5\frac{1}{4}$ inches
    b. 8 inches
    c. $3\frac{1}{2}$ inches
    d. any of the above

CHAPTER 3

HOW a COMPUTER WORKS

Suppose you're walking down the street. You may be thinking about nothing in particular, but information is being sent to your brain constantly. Nerve cells note the coldness of the air, the grayness of the sky, the diesel odor of a truck's exhaust. Electrochemical impulses carry this information to your brain. Your responses are determined by which of the pathways—among billions of possible pathways—that these impulses take. Perhaps you shiver and walk faster. Those are simple physical actions, but the activity in the brain that led to them was far from simple.

Just as your brain supervises and controls the functions of your body, the central processing unit (CPU) controls the functions of a computer. Suppose you instruct your computer to display the name *Linda*. That seems easy enough, but the instruction will set off quite a bit of activity in the electrical conducting paths of the microprocessor. Let's see why.

USING BINARY NUMBERS

Throughout your years in school you have been using the decimal system in mathematics. The decimal system is based on 10's, and it works very well for human computations. But a computer uses a different system—the **binary number system**.

The binary number system is based on only two numbers, 0 and 1. Because computers work electrically, binary numbers are ideal for them. A current of electricity either flows through an electrical circuit or it doesn't. If it does, the current is on. If it doesn't, the current is off.

In a computer, the binary numbers, 0 and 1, make use of the off/on nature of electrical circuits.

The CPU operates on that simple principle. All input is translated into 0's and 1's. A *zero* turns a circuit off. A *one* turns a circuit on.

BITS AND BYTES

Those two numbers, 0 and 1, are called **bits**. The word is a short form of the term *binary digit*. A bit is either a 0 or a 1. It cannot be anything else.

If your computer is to understand the *L* in *Linda*, it has to have a way to translate those two digits, 0 and 1, into letters of the alphabet. Since 0 and 1 by themselves could handle only two letters—*A* and *B*, perhaps—how does the computer deal with *L*?

The answer is that it does so by using bytes. A byte is usually a group of eight bits. You may see references to an "eight-bit" computer. That is because data is stored and processed in eight-bit chunks. By combining the eight 0's and 1's in various ways, it is possible to represent the twenty-six letters of the alphabet. In the binary system, the letter *L* is 01001100.

When you press the letter *L* on your keyboard, the central processing unit receives instructions for eight circuits. The instructions are these: off-on-off-off-on-on-off-off.

That may seem like a hard way to produce the letter *L*, but that's how the computer does it. Because the computer is so fast, the process takes almost no time at all.

There are 256 possible combinations for the eight bits that make up a byte—far more than enough for the alphabet. These extra combinations are needed because bytes are needed for other purposes as well. Each of the ten decimal numbers has its own sequence of binary digits. The number 7, for example, is 00110111. A byte is needed, too, for each mark of punctuation and even for a blank space. A comma is 00101100, and a blank space is 00100000.

KILOBYTES AND MEGABYTES

A computer's memory is measured in bytes. Each byte, as you have seen, can be a character—that is, a letter, a number, a space, a mark of punctuation, or some other symbol. The number of characters that a computer can accept in RAM varies widely, depending on the computer make and model.

Memory, although measured in bytes, is usually expressed in kilobytes. The word *kilobyte* means "1000 bytes." (The Greek prefix *kilo-* means "thousand.") Actually, a kilobyte is 1024 bytes. A computer with 64K of RAM can store 64 × 1024 characters, or 65,536 characters.

The first microcomputers had as little as 2K of memory. But most have at least 16K, and many have 64K. Some microcomputers, particularly models used in offices, have 128K, 256K, or even 512K.

Large computers have memories measured in millions of bytes, or megabytes. A mainframe with 10 megabytes of memory can store approximately ten million characters.

WHAT IS SOFTWARE?

No matter how much RAM your computer has, it won't be able to accomplish much without software, or programmed instructions. Software comes in different forms. The most visible kind is packaged software, which you can find in brightly colored boxes at local stores. These packages contain programs; some are games and some are intended for educational or

Many computer stores carry a variety of educational, business, and entertainment software.

business uses. The programs may be on floppy disks, magnetic tapes, or cartridges. When you buy one of these programs, it's ready to run as soon as you unpack it.

Another kind of program that needs no work on your part is the kind that is built into your computer as ROM. Some computers have much more built-in programming than others. A dedicated computer—one designed for a particular job—may have a great deal of software included as part of the machine itself. For example, a word processor is really a dedicated computer. The word-processing software is built into it. Because of this, you can't use it for computing—only for word processing. But a word processor is ready to do its job as soon as it is turned on. It doesn't need outside software to tell it what to do.

The third kind of software is the kind you write yourself. Some people program simply for the pleasure or the challenge it provides. Others learn programming so that they can develop software geared to their own unique needs. Many computer users have never written a program of their own and probably never will. They will use the computer's built-in software, and they will run programs that someone else has written. On the other hand, many users will learn to write original programs. Later in this book you will learn how to write your own programs.

Your school system may have all three kinds of software mentioned. There might be a word processor in the main office. The system probably owns a variety of packaged programs that fit its courses of study. And it probably has programs created by teachers or students.

Key Points

- A computer uses the binary number system, with "1" representing on and "0" representing off to the electrical circuits in the computer's CPU.
- Computers process information in bits, which are 1's or 0's, and bytes, which are groups of eight bits that represent characters or spaces.
- A computer's memory is usually expressed in kilobytes (K), which means "thousands of bytes." Many microcomputers have memories of 64K or more.
- In addition to memory, a computer needs software, which may be packaged, specially written by you or another programmer, or built into the machine.

Review Questions

1. Why is the binary number system ideal for computers?
2. How many bits are required to represent the word *student* to a computer's CPU? Explain how you arrived at your answer.

SYSTEM SOFTWARE

You have seen that the binary number system is the basis of the computer's capabilities. In a way, though, binary numbers are *too* simple. The computer needs some way to use its basic 0-and-1 system to go on to more complicated tasks. When the computer is first turned on, it has to have instructions on how to proceed.

OPERATING SYSTEMS

An **operating system** provides the basic instructions that tell the computer how to handle certain tasks necessary for it to work. The operating system of a large computer can be very complicated, because it has to control so many functions. A microcomputer's operating system is simple by comparison.

Suppose you had a computer with no operating system. (Yes, there are such machines.) You would have to write a program—a very complex program—in order to get the computer to do anything. Among other things, you would have to explain in your program how the computer should interpret the pressing of each key. Such a computer provides good training for a computer scientist, but it is of little value to most ordinary users.

An operating system gets you over that hurdle. It consists of a set of prewritten instructions. The operating system is the program that makes it possible for you to run all other programs that are available or can be written for your computer. The operating-system program may exist just in ROM, or it may exist partly in ROM and partly on a disk or tape.

DISK OPERATING SYSTEMS

A **disk operating system**, or **DOS** (pronounced *dahs*) is a program that controls the storage of information on disks. DOS also makes it possible for the computer to use various programs that are already stored on disks. Most packaged programs for computers are available on disks, and the DOS is what gets these programs started. Obviously, the system requires a disk drive.

With a disk operating system, some instructions are in ROM, but not very many. As a rule, ROM has just enough information to be able to "read" the rest of the operating system from a **system disk**. The instructions on this system disk go into RAM. Once they're in RAM, the computer is ready to run whatever program you wish.

The process of putting operating instructions into RAM goes by two names. One is **loading**. The other is **booting**. The word *booting* comes from *bootstrap*, suggesting that the computer is lifting itself by its own bootstraps in order to begin to function.

Storing information on a disk. A disk drive, as you will remember, has a read/write head. When you use a packaged or stored program, the head "reads" the instructions from the disk. When you want to store information yourself, the head "writes" the information on the disk.

The computer uses the same binary number system to store information as it does to process it. But instead of using electrical impulses, as the CPU does, the read/write head uses magnetic fields. Rather than using the CPU's on/off method, the head uses a left/right scheme, based on the polarity (opposing forces) of a magnetic field.

When the disk rotates inside the disk drive, the head creates a series of individual magnetic fields, one for every binary digit. Each of these bits represents a 0 or a 1, and it takes eight bits (a byte) to record a character. Therefore, if you typed *Linda* on the keyboard, the head would create forty magnetic fields to record it (5 letters × 8 bits) on eight-bit computers—

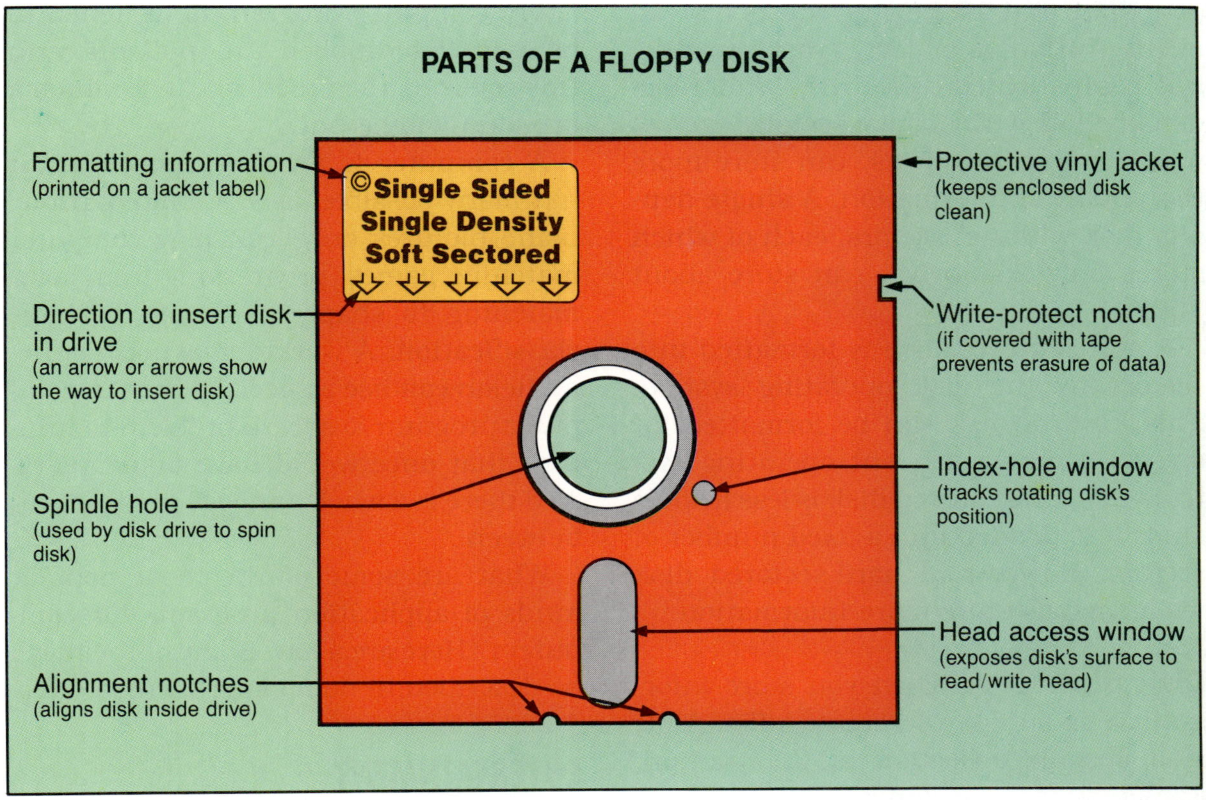

computers with CPU's that can process eight bits of information at a time.

This process is lightning fast. The head can create 125,000 magnetic fields a second, which means it could store *Linda* 3125 times every second.

Formatting a disk. Not all floppy disks are the same, even if they are the same size. Some disks can store much more information than others. The differences are based on **formatting**. Formatting means setting up the way in which information will be stored on a disk.

The disk operating system divides a disk into tracks and sectors. A **track** is one of thirty-five to eighty circles, arranged like those on a phonograph record, but not grooved. A **sector** is one of ten to sixteen fan-shaped areas radiating out from the spindle hole.

If you look at the label on a floppy disk, you will probably find a note like the following: "double-sided, double-density, soft-sectored." Each of these features has to do with the formatting of the disk.

A **double-sided disk** is designed for a disk drive with two read/write heads, one for each side of the disk. Usually, a double-sided disk can store or read twice as much information as a **single-sided disk**—designed for a disk drive with one read/write head.

A **double-density** disk works with a

disk drive that uses eighty tracks instead of the thirty-five or forty tracks read by less sophisticated disk drives. A double-density disk with sixteen sectors, each of which stores 512 bytes, can store more than 500K of information. A **single-density** disk with ten sectors, each of which stores only 256 bytes, can store about 100K.

A **soft-sectored** disk is formatted into sectors by the disk operating system. This kind of disk can be formatted for use with many different operating systems. A **hard-sectored** disk is less flexible since it is divided into a fixed number of sectors. However, a hard-sectored disk will generally store more information.

Disk directory. When you store information on a disk, you create a **file**. A file is a specific collection of information. Each disk may contain a number of files. Most computers automatically maintain a **disk directory** as the user creates files on a disk.

This disk directory is an index that shows file names, starting sectors, number of sectors used, and sectors still remaining on the disk. The directory is useful to both you and the computer. It shows you what the disk contains, and it directs the read/write head to the correct sector for finding an old file or creating a new one.

APPLICATION SOFTWARE

As you have seen, the purpose of system software is to get the computer operating. The purpose of **application software** is to get the computer to do a specific job. Every computer program is designed to be used, to be applied. An *application*, in this sense, is the practical use to which a program will be put.

A computer is an all-purpose tool; it has many possible uses. A child of three, using pictures only, can play computer matching games, progressing from color matching to shape matching to shape classification. A world-renowned mathematician can use a specially written computer program to solve a problem in minutes that once would have taken years. And there is a whole range of programs in between.

What are some of the most popular kinds of application programs for computers? Here are a few. Some of them will be described in detail later in the book.

ENTERTAINMENT

The computer is a great game machine. Hundreds of games have been devised for it, and new ones keep appearing all the time. Games can be classified in various ways. Some common categories are strategy games, adventure games, sports games, role-playing games, and action games.

WRITING AND EDITING

Word processing is a computer application that resembles typewriting but is far more versatile. Word processing accounts for at least half of the total use of personal computers. There are more than 300 word-processing programs on the market. In addition, there are programs that check spelling, others that check punctuation, and still others that teach typewriting.

Computer games can be educational and fun to play at the same time.

BUSINESS

Application programs are available for almost anything that needs to be done in the office except emptying the wastebaskets. Dozens of programs make it easier than ever before to prepare budgets, keep track of inventory, and handle mailing lists. Even owners of the smallest businesses find computers helpful, while large businesses literally could not operate in today's world without them. Although many programs for large businesses are specially written for the company, others are the same programs that small businesses and even homeowners use.

EDUCATION

The computer is a powerful teaching tool. Mathematics might seem to be its best subject, and, indeed, programs for arithmetic, algebra, and problem solving are widely used. But there are excellent programs in many other areas as well. Good software is available for reading, spelling, vocabulary, and grammar. Science programs cover such topics as volcanoes and dinosaurs to high-school chemistry and college optics. Programs also exist for music, map reading, and history.

HOW TO LOAD A PROGRAM

Suppose you've just acquired a new program to help you improve your spelling, and you want to try it out. If it's a "total load" program, as most are, you don't have to insert the DOS disk before loading. You use only the application disk. What steps do you take to get started?

First of all, if you haven't used your disk drive before, you should read the manual or some printed instruction. That's important, because all computer systems are somewhat different, and any general set of instructions may not be accurate in every detail. With that said, let's begin.

1. If your disk drive has a separate power switch from the computer, turn it on. It may have a light on it that has to go off before you proceed. If so, wait.
2. Turn on the monitor or television set.
3. Remove the program disk from its protective paper sleeve. Be careful not to touch any part of the disk except its sealed jacket.
4. Open the door to the disk drive.

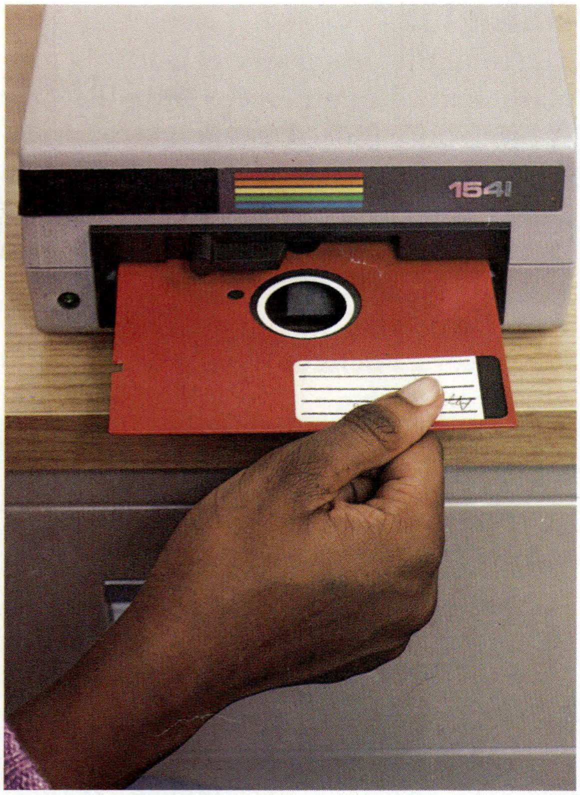

To avoid damaging a software disk, insert it into the disk drive carefully.

5. Be sure that the arrow or arrows on the disk point in the direction indicated. Then carefully but firmly insert the disk into the drive.
6. Close the disk drive door.
7. Turn on the computer.

The program will load automatically. Just as with the DOS disk, to *load* means to "read" the program into RAM. While the program is loading, the display screen remains blank. As soon as loading is complete, an image appears on the screen. Let's say that for your new spelling program, this image is a title, resembling a movie title or the title page of a book.

After a fixed amount of time, the title will disappear. With a game program, the game would appear immediately. Let's say, however, that with your spelling program the next image on the screen is a menu. The menu lists the tasks the program can perform. The spelling program gives you three choices: playing a word-unscrambling game, using a flash-card technique, or creating a personal word list. To make your choice, you move the cursor to the proper spot on the menu, or else you press a corresponding number.

The next image on the screen may be the task you chose, or a **submenu**. A sub-

After choosing an activity from the main menu, a submenu displays additional choices.

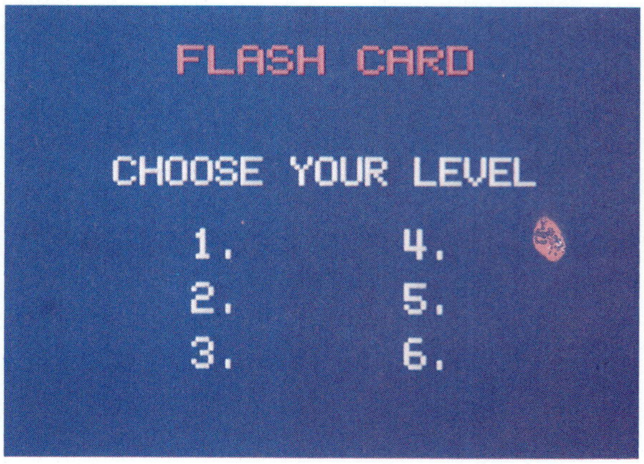

menu is a list of further choices for you to make. Suppose that on the main menu, you had chosen the flash-card technique. The submenu might give you a choice of the level of difficulty of the words.

There may be more than one submenu, but at some point you're ready to proceed with the content of the program. If you have read the **documentation**—the "how-to" printed material that came with the disk—you should have no trouble running the program.

In addition to the printed documentation, other help may be available in the software itself. Some programs, especially complicated business programs, have special built-in **help screens**, which you can refer to at any time. Sometimes just typing in a question mark will bring an on-screen explanation.

Key Points

- System software, or an operating system, gives a computer the basic instructions it needs in order to function.
- A disk operating system controls the storage of information on disks and enables a computer to use programs that are stored on disks.
- Application software enables the computer to perform a specific task, such as preparing a budget or playing a game.

Review Questions

1. Where is a computer's operating system located?
2. In a computer program, what is the function of a menu?

CHOOSING HARDWARE AND SOFTWARE

When a large company is considering the purchase of computers, it goes through a step-by-step process called **needs assessment**. The object is to find out if and why computers are needed, how they will be used, and what their effects will be.

Anyone who is choosing hardware and software should go through a similar process. It doesn't have to be complicated, but it should ask four questions:

1. Why do you need a computer? By now you have a good idea of what computers can accomplish. For someone who

Determine your computer needs, then consider such factors as memory, software, and price.

needs these capabilities, a computer will undoubtedly be useful. But not everyone needs them. An average family does not need a computer to balance a checkbook or file recipes. But if family members do a lot of writing, have complicated finances, or believe in the value of educational software, then a computer may be a useful purchase.

2. What software is available for your needs? If you think you need a computer, the next step is to find out what programs are available for the job you want done. Notice that you look at software *before* you look at hardware. It doesn't make sense to buy a computer and then find there is no suitable program for what you expect it to do. Even if you intend to write your own programs, you will want to know that packaged programs are available for your computer.

3. What computer has the capabilities you need? Computers differ widely in what they can do. After looking at the available software, you will want to look at the amount of RAM computers have. For a personal computer, 64K is now about average. But if the software you want to buy requires 128K, you will obviously need a computer with a minimum of 128K.

Look carefully at the monitor (assuming you're not using a television set). Ideally, a monitor will display at least twenty-four lines of eighty characters each on a screen that measures nine inches or more diagonally.

Consider the method of storage—disks or tape. What size disk does the software you want to buy come on? Do you need the greater capacity of hard-disk storage? Find out how easy it will be to add the peripherals you will need—and how much the peripherals will cost.

4. Where can you find out what you need to know about hardware and software? There are many sources of information. Books and magazines about computers can be helpful. Some of these are very technical, but others are aimed at less experienced users. Many are intended for users of specific computers. User groups and computer clubs, which exist in almost every part of the country, can provide valuable information. These user groups often specialize in a particular computer. The best way to find out about user groups in your area is to inquire at a local computer store.

Computer magazines are a good source of information on hardware and software.

EVALUATING SOFTWARE

Finding the right software can be a challenge. Dozens of programs exist for each of the most popular applications. Until recently, not much comparative information could be found. Now a number of magazines, catalogues, and directories review and rate software. You may want to consult one or more of them when choosing a new program.

If possible, you should also review a program yourself before buying it. Since programs are expensive, you will want to try hard to make the best possible choice. When you are looking for a program, consider the following points.

DOCUMENTATION

As noted earlier, documentation is the "how-to" printed material that comes with software. Even though the best pro-

Help!
We need an Analyst.

Our chain of department stores, Great Buys, wants to update its computer system, adding new customer services and devising more efficient methods for staff use. We have an immediate opening for a Systems Analyst to help us accomplish these goals.

You will analyze our current system; interview computer-sales and customer-service personnel; design and implement an improved system; manage the system; and design updates as needed.

To be a candidate, you need at least 3 years of programming experience (preferably in retail sales), and a college degree in accounting, computer science, or mathematics.

THAT'S MY JOB

Here's what systems analyst Bruce T. Paddock says about his job:

"It's very challenging. Many of the problems I'm asked to solve are large and complex. I spend a lot of time investigating and designing different system set-ups. I work closely with computer market representatives and with programmers. The systems I design have to work and work well; they also have to be easy to use.

"I'd say it's good not to become too specialized in this job. The more problems you're able to solve, the more valuable you are to a company."

MORE INFORMATION

Positions for systems analysts are expected to grow by 120%—to 400,000 through 1990.... Most systems analysts work in urban areas for a variety of firms including government agencies, banks, insurance companies, data-processing service firms, and manufacturers.... Salaries and benefits are very good.

grams are clear and well organized, you still need documentation to learn what the program offers and how to go about using it. Programs are often so versatile, with so many features, that it could take you weeks to discover some important capabilities by using only the software. Even after you're familiar with the program, you may still find it easier and quicker to check a manual than to seek help through the computer.

Good documentation is complete. It covers everything you need to know about the program and assumes you have no prior knowledge of the program or how to use it. It is well organized. Explanations are presented in a logical order. If you have a question, you should be able to find the answer easily. Indexes and quick-reference cards can be useful. The documentation should be clearly written and not too technical. If you have trouble understanding it, you may also have trouble using the program.

APPROPRIATENESS FOR THE JOB

If all you intend to do is keep a mailing list of your friends' names and addresses, you can choose a very simple file-manager program. It would be a mistake to choose an expensive program that was designed for organizing information in a good-sized office.

That is a fairly obvious choice, but it isn't always easy to tell how appropriate a program will be. If you know people who are using programs of the kind you want, ask them about the programs. An experienced user of a program will know the kinds of jobs it can do. On the other hand, that person may know nothing about other programs that are equally good or better. The choice of appropriate software can involve research. Explore all possible sources of information.

EASE OF USE

You may have seen or heard the term **user-friendly**. A program that is user-friendly has clear and simple instructions. Some programs are easy to use because they have so few features—they can do so little. As more capabilities are added to a program, it can become increasingly hard to keep things simple for the user.

VERSATILITY

The best programs are easy to use and also have a great many capabilities. A program with many capabilities is versatile, which means that the program will do just about everything you want it to. Such a program is often said to be "powerful." As a rule, the more powerful a program is, the harder it is to learn and use. In order to get the best program possible, you may have to make a compromise between a variety of features and ease of use.

REASONABLE PRICE

A program on a single 5¼-inch floppy disk may cost $495 or even more. Other programs have a list price of $10 or less. What causes such startling differences? How closely does price correspond to quality in application programs?

The answers are not easy to find. One point to keep in mind is that writing a good program often takes thousands of hours. A person who buys a program is therefore getting more than meets the eye. A high-priced program may well be worth its cost. On the other hand, many times a low-priced program will outperform a more costly one. Don't assume that price equals quality.

USABILITY

Before saying "Wrap it up," a buyer should ask three more questions:

1. *Is it written for my computer?* If it isn't, it won't run on it. Many of the best-selling application programs, however, are produced for more than one brand of computer.

2. *Is it available on a storage medium I can use?* If a particular program is available only on a 3½-inch disk and your disk drive uses 5¼-inch disks, you won't be able to run it. Some programs are produced only on cartridges or cassette tapes, although here, too, a best-seller is likely to be available on more than one storage medium.

3. *Does my computer have enough memory to run the program?* Many application programs require 64K or 128K of RAM. If your computer falls short, it will be unable to load the program.

Assuming that you have answered "Yes" to these three questions—and have taken all the other points into consideration—you've probably made a wise software choice. That's quite a feat when you consider that there are about 40,000 application programs on the market.

Once you have assembled the right hardware and software for your needs, your computer can become a helpful tool.

Ten Tips on Caring for Software

1. Label disks and tapes carefully. When labeling disks, don't write directly on them. Write on the sleeve or on a self-adhesive label that you can affix to the disk jacket. Always use a felt-tip pen.
2. Never leave cassettes or disks in the drive when they aren't being used.
3. Avoid exposing tapes or disks to magnetic fields. Keep them away from telephones, televisions, and other electrical appliances.
4. Be careful not to record over material you want to keep.
5. Don't touch the surface of a disk. Never remove a disk from its plastic jacket.
6. Keep extra copies of important disks.
7. If possible, store disks in storage boxes. If disks are kept in binders, store the binders upright.
8. Keep disks and disks in plastic boxes out of direct sunlight.
9. Remove disks from the drive before turning the power off.
10. Don't try to clean disks with any kind of liquid.

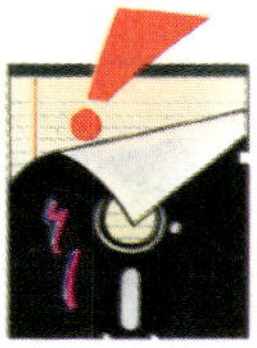

REVIEW & APPLICATION

SUMMARY

• When you use a keyboard to give input to a computer, the CPU receives it as a series of bits, or on/off instructions for its electrical circuits. Each character or space in the input requires one byte, which is eight bits.

• Many people use computers without writing their own programs. Instead, they use the computers' built-in programs along with packaged software.

• A computer's operating system consists of prewritten instructions that make it possible for the computer to run application software and accept input from you.

• To store information on disks, a computer uses the 1's and 0's of the binary system to represent the opposing forces of a magnetic field.

• Even among floppy disks of the same size, some can hold more information than others. A disk operating system formats a disk by dividing it into tracks and sectors.

• Before choosing either hardware or software, you should assess your needs carefully and determine which products can best meet them.

VOCABULARY

Match each item in the left column with the correct item on the right.

a. bit	1. 1 or 0
b. kilobyte	2. practical tasks performed by computers
c. character	3. putting operating instructions into RAM
d. applications	4. 1024 bytes
e. booting	5. letter, number, or symbol
f. sector	6. fan-shaped area on a computer disk

REVIEW QUESTIONS

1. How is the size of a microcomputer's RAM expressed? How is the RAM size of a mainframe expressed?
2. What three forms of software are available to a computer user?
3. What is the difference between system software and application software?
4. What is the difference between a hard-sectored floppy disk and a soft-sectored one?
5. What four basic questions should a needs assessment include?

DISCUSSION QUESTION

Why do you suppose computers and software packages usually come with documentation? Could the computer display all of the instructions for the user on its screen so that printed materials would not be necessary?

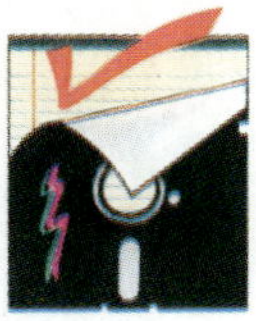

PROJECTS

You will need to know certain commands to work with disk drives. For instance, suppose you want to see a listing of what is on a disk. First, make sure your computer is on and in BASIC. Next put that disk in the drive. Then:

APPLE IIe
Type CATALOG and press RETURN.
COMMODORE 64
1. Type LOAD"$",8 and press RETURN.
2. Type LIST and press RETURN.

IBM PCjr
Type FILES and press ENTER.
TRS-80 Model III
Type CMD "D" and press ENTER.

A list of the programs on that disk should appear on the screen (other information also shows up on the screen, but don't worry about that for now). What if you want to use one of these programs? First you have to load it into the computer's memory. To do this, make a note of the name of the file—or its FILENAME.

APPLE IIe
Type LOAD FILENAME and then press RETURN.
COMMODORE 64
Type LOAD "FILENAME",8 and press RETURN.
IBM PCjr
Type LOAD "FILENAME.EXT" and press ENTER.
TRS-80 Model III
Type LOAD "FILENAME/EXT" and press ENTER.

Let's say you want to save that file on a different disk as back-up. Take a formatted disk, place it in drive, and then:

APPLE IIe
Type SAVE FILENAME and then press RETURN.
COMMODORE 64
Type SAVE "FILENAME",8 and press RETURN.
IBM PCjr
Type SAVE "FILENAME.EXT" and press ENTER.
TRS-80 Model III
Type SAVE "FILENAME" and press ENTER.

Further Practice

List the hardware and software available for your use at school. Include peripherals and storage media.

Write a short essay explaining why or why not your family needs a home computer.

Enrichment

If you can think binary, you have an idea of how a computer operates. Do research to find out more about binary numbers. Then write these numbers in binary: 1, 2, 7, 9, 1256.

CHAPTER TEST

Write your answers on a sheet of paper numbered 1 through 14.

MULTIPLE CHOICE

1. To a computer's CPU, a bit is:
   a. a letter of the alphabet.
   b. an on or off instruction for a circuit.
   c. left or right in a magnetic field.
   d. a blank space.
2. A byte can be:
   a. a letter of the alphabet.
   b. a single on or off instruction.
   c. an eight-letter English word.
   d. none of the above
3. A mainframe computer with 10 megabytes of memory can store:
   a. up to ten type-written pages.
   b. up to 10 million bits of data.
   c. about 10 million characters.
   d. up to 10 thousand bytes of data.
4. Packaged software may be on:
   a. floppy disks
   b. cartridges
   c. magnetic tape
   d. any of the above
5. Before a computer can run a program, its DOS must be:
   a. stored on a disk
   b. loaded into ROM
   c. loaded into RAM
   d. rewritten
6. Computer application software includes programs for:
   a. business
   b. education
   c. entertainment
   d. all of the above
7. A menu lists:
   a. the parts of the computer
   b. the CPU's operating instructions
   c. the tasks that a program can perform
   d. none of the above

MATCHING

8. Match each item with its function.

a. DOS	1. turns on CPU circuit
b. 1	2. formats disks
c. byte	3. represents one character
d. 0	4. turns off CPU circuit

FILL IN

Write the word or phrase that completes each sentence.

9. A ____________ is to a computer what a brain is to a human body.
10. The word ____________ is a short form of the term *binary digit*.
11. A computer with ____________K of RAM can store about 10 thousand characters.
12. A computer's ____________ tells it how to interpret the pressing of a key.
13. A file is a specific collection of ________ on a disk.
14. A ____________ is an index that shows file names, starting sectors, numbers of sectors used, and sectors still remaining on the disk.

CHAPTER
2 3 4 5 6

COMPUTER HISTORY

Suppose you're appearing on a television quiz show. So far, you've answered every question correctly. Now, here is your $10,000 jackpot question:

Who invented the computer?

Did you say Einstein? Or maybe you guessed that it was APPLE.

Sorry, but that's not the answer. If the question stumped you, though, don't feel bad. It's actually kind of a trick question. You see, *no one* invented the computer.

No *one* person, that is. The computer evolved gradually, over hundreds of years, spurred by people's growing need to perform fast, accurate calculations. During that evolution, many people contributed their ideas to the development of more and more sophisticated computing machines.

As you read, keep in mind that the computer's evolution is still continuing. Just as black-and-white television opened the door for color television, so are today's computers paving the way for the more advanced computers of tomorrow.

BEGINNINGS

Long before machines existed, people found ways to calculate. They counted on their fingers or arranged stones in piles or rows. They made scratches on the ground, cut notches in sticks, or tied knots in string in order to keep track of quantities of things.

As their need to calculate increased, people sought tools to help them. The oldest known *mechanical* aid for calculating is the **abacus**. The abacus is a portable device that consists of beads strung on wires or wooden rods. Using an abacus, someone can rapidly and accurately add, subtract, multiply, or divide large numbers.

No one is sure exactly when the first abacus appeared. Historians agree, though, that the device is between 2000 and 5000 years old and that it had its origins in ancient China, Egypt, and Greece. The abacus is still used in some parts of the world today.

MACHINES TO SAVE TIME

For hundreds of years, the devices that people used to help them calculate stayed as simple as the abacus. But as civilization advanced, people's need to perform a wide range of calculations increased. By the seventeenth century, mathematics had taken on a key role in business, trade, and science. Moneylenders, for example, had to compute interest on loans. Scientists had to perform complex calculations in physics and astronomy. The need for more advanced computing tools was becoming clear. Some sort of calculating *machine* would help people handle the growing volume of calculations quickly and accurately. Such a machine would make counting easier. It would also save valuable time.

EARLY CALCULATING MACHINES

It was a nineteen-year-old French mathematician named Blaise Pascal who invented the first mechanical calculating machine, in 1642. Pascal's invention consisted of a combination of interlocking wheels and gears. Printed on the wheels were the numbers 0 to 9. When the first wheel made a complete turn from 0 past 9, it automatically caused the second wheel to advance to the next

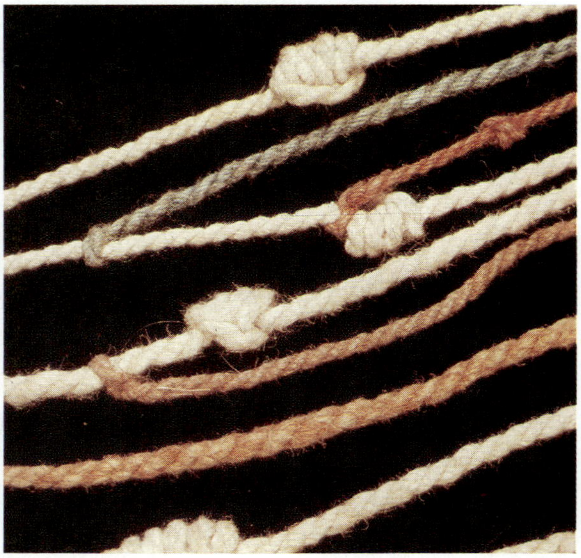

The Incas used knotted cords to help them perform calculations.

number. When the second wheel moved past 9, it caused the third wheel to turn, and so on. The Pascaline, as the machine was called, could be used only to add and subtract.

More than fifty years passed before anyone invented a calculating machine more advanced than the Pascaline. During that time, scientists' need to do complicated calculations continued to grow. Instruments such as the abacus and the Pascaline helped, but they were too limited in capability. As a result, some experiments were never finished. Others were finished, but only after months or years of tiring calculation.

A German mathematician, Gottfried Wilhelm von Leibnitz, understood the problem. He set out to build a better mechanical calculator. He knew that such a machine would save much time, enabling the scientists to concentrate on their studies rather than on the calculations. He also knew that a machine that improved on the Pascaline would help not only scientists, but anyone who used mathematics in his or her work: merchants, bookkeepers, craftspeople, geographers, navigators, and many others.

In 1694 Leibnitz completed his machine. While the Pascaline had used gears and wheels, Leibnitz's Stepped Reckoner used cylinders. These cylinders were marked with numbers and contained nine rows of pegs, or teeth. The first row had one peg; the second, two;

In 1642, nineteen-year-old Blaise Pascal invented the first mechanical calculating device. The Pascaline was only able to add and subtract.

and so on up to nine. The machine also came with movable pegs, which were placed in various cylinders by the operator. Much more complex than the Pascaline, the Stepped Reckoner was able to do more. Pascal's machine could only add and subtract, but Leibnitz's could also multiply, divide, and find square roots.

Even though the Stepped Reckoner could do more than the Pascaline, it couldn't keep up with the ever-growing need to do mathematical tasks. Less than a century later, people were again seeking a better calculating machine.

Although the Analytical Engine was never completed, many of its features are used in modern computers.

NINETEENTH-CENTURY ADVANCES

The next important stage in the evolution of the computer occurred in the nineteenth century. This was a time that was notable for its mechanical inventions. People in fields ranging from science and mathematics to manufacturing and printing used both old ideas and new theories to build new machines. These machines performed tasks faster and more easily than people could.

One of the most creative thinkers of this time was the Englishman Charles Babbage. He is considered by many to be the father of the modern computer. Like Pascal and Leibnitz, Babbage also was a mathematician. And he, too, wanted to build a machine that could perform difficult calculations accurately and quickly.

Babbage had more success in designing machines than in building them. In fact, it was Babbage who envisioned and designed the first programmable computer in the 1830's. He worked on this idea for most of his life. Unfortunately, though, he was never able to complete a working model.

Babbage called his planned machine the Analytical Engine. According to his design, this would have been a steam-powered mechanical computer. It would have been able to receive instructions, perform calculations, and produce printed output.

Programs for the Analytical Engine would be coded and punched into cards. The concept of punched cards was not new, but Babbage was the first person to apply it to a computing machine. Babbage borrowed the idea of punched-card input from Joseph Jacquard, a French weaver. In 1801 Jacquard had devised a way to use patterns of holes punched into cards to control the operation of a loom as it wove cloth. Different cards with different patterns of holes produced different woven designs. Although he didn't know it, Jacquard had come up with an idea that later would be used for processing information on computers.

Unfortunately, the Analytical Engine was too advanced for the technology of its time. Babbage was not able to make and assemble the many precision parts he needed for his machine. Nonetheless, his invention was an important one. Many later inventors used Babbage's innovative design ideas, much as he had used Jacquard's.

One person who recognized the importance of the Analytical Engine from the start was Lady Ada Augusta Lovelace, daughter of the English poet Lord Byron. Lovelace was a mathematician and a long-time supporter of Babbage. It was she who persuaded Babbage to use the binary number system for his invention instead of the decimal system. She also thought of ways to program the machine so that it would repeat the same set of instructions and carry out instructions if certain conditions existed. These techniques are still used today to make computer programs more efficient. Because of her work, many consider Lovelace to be the first programmer.

4-72

Jaquard's punched cards were later adapted for computers.

Key Points

• No one person invented the computer. The computer evolved gradually, over hundreds of years. Many people contributed to its development.

• As the need to calculate increased, people sought tools to help them. Such tools made calculating easier and saved time.

• Charles Babbage conceived of the first programmable computer in the 1830's. But the idea was too advanced for the technology of the time. He was not able to build a working model.

Review Questions

1. As civilization has become more complex, why have people needed increasingly advanced calculating devices and computers?
2. How did Joseph Jacquard contribute to the evolution of the computer?

PUNCHED-CARD PROCESSING

Charles Babbage may have been the first to link punched cards and computers, but it was Herman Hollerith who put the cards to practical use. Hollerith invented a machine to help the U.S. Census Bureau count the population.

The need for such a machine was clear. Every ten years the government conducts a **census**—a count of the population. Nowadays, computers make it possible to take the census in a matter of months. In the 1800's, though, a census was a long and drawn-out process. In fact, even though the population in 1880 was only about one fifth of what it is today, it took about *eight years* to tabulate the results of the 1880 census. By the time the government had finished counting, it was nearly time to begin again!

Obviously, a faster means of counting was needed. The Census Bureau certainly didn't want to wait until 1900 to find out what the population in 1890 was. Thanks to Hollerith's tabulating machine, it didn't have to. Quite the contrary: the 1890 census was completed in less than three years. This was particularly impressive considering that the population had grown by over twenty-five percent since the previous census.

How did Hollerith's machine accomplish this feat? It used punched cards and electricity—this was the first time electricity was used for computing. Hollerith's machine coded population data on cards, using one card for each person. The data was coded in the form of columns and rows of punched holes. For example, a hole punched in column three, row four might mean that a person was married. Similarly, other holes would indicate whether the person was male or female, family size, years of education, and so forth. All this data was then "read" by machine. As each card—about the size of a dollar bill—moved through the machine, needles pushed against it. Wherever there was a hole, the needle would pass through and touch a metal surface beneath it. This contact would complete an electrical circuit, automatically adding one to the count.

Hollerith's punched-card methods represented a big step forward in the development of faster and more accurate machines. Some seventy years later, of course, magnetic tapes and disks would begin to replace punched cards for data processing. Nevertheless, even today billions of punched cards are still made and used every year. And the code used to record data on these cards is called—you guessed it—the Hollerith Code.

THE FIRST COMPUTERS

It was during the first half of the twentieth century that the first true computers appeared. These machines were more than mechanical calculators that could add, subtract, and multiply. These were electronic machines capable of solving complex problems.

The computers that evolved in the twentieth century had two key features that the early calculating machines did not. One, they could be programmed to carry out a sequence of calculations or to perform several kinds of tasks. And two, they could store information in memory.

THE DIFFERENTIAL ANALYZER

The first calculating machine that crossed over the line to become a true computer was built by American scientist Vannevar Bush in about 1930. (For this reason some people say that Bush, not Babbage, is the real father of the

The first digital computer—the Mark I—was developed to meet the needs of the United States military forces during World War II.

modern computer.) Bush's machine was called a differential analyzer. It was the first analog computer.

As you remember, analog computers compute by measuring the continuous change in a physical quantity—air pressure or temperature, for example.

Bush's invention was a significant accomplishment. It could solve complex mathematical problems very quickly. It ran on electricity, and it used vacuum tubes (like those inside old radios) to store information.

Like other early computers, though, the differential analyzer was a far cry from today's desktop machines. As a matter of fact, Bush's machine had so many parts that it filled an entire room. As you can imagine, anything that big wasn't exactly lightweight either. Indeed, a later model of the differential analyzer that was built in 1942 weighed 200 tons!

THE MARK I

The need for fast, accurate computing increased during World War II (1939–1945). The military had many complex calculations to make for which a computer would be very useful.

What sorts of calculations did the military want computers for? One of the most important needs was to aid research in ballistics—the study of how artillery shells and other projectiles move toward a target.

For a shell to be correctly aimed, many factors must be considered. How far away is the target? What kind of shell is being used in what kind of artillery? How should the shell be directed so as to clear any obstacles? How dense is the air that the shell will pass through? Even the air temperature and the hardness of the ground beneath a cannon can have an effect. If such factors aren't considered, the shell will be fired too far or not far enough.

To help them aim their weapons, the artillery corps referred to *firing tables.* These mathematical tables told the gunners how to fire under a wide range of conditions. As you can imagine, preparing firing tables was extremely complicated work. Even though the army had over one hundred people doing nothing but calculating these tables, one table could take as long as two months to make. Calculating machines and the differential analyzer helped, but more advanced computers promised greater speed and accuracy.

One of the first machines to meet the growing need for computer power was the "Automatic Sequence Controlled Calculator"—known simply as the Mark I. It was completed in 1944 by Harvard University professor Howard Aiken.

The Mark I was the first digital computer. Digital computers solve problems by counting numbers. Of course, analog computers use numbers, too. But, as you remember, an analog system measures continuous change, while a digital system measures at specific intervals.

In developing the Mark I, Aiken blended twentieth century technical know-how with Hollerith's punched-card method. The result was an automatic computing machine that could accept input coded on punched cards or punched tape. The Mark I was not fully electronic in operation, however. It was electromechanical. That is, it used electronic signals in combination with mechanical gears, switches, and wheels.

Aiken's machine was huge. It was over 50 feet long and 8 feet high, and it had more than 750,000 parts. The amount of wire that the Mark I contained could stretch from New York to Maine!

The Mark I was an impressive machine. It could multiply two 23-digit numbers in four seconds and do six month's worth of manual calculation in a single day. It had the greatest storage capacity of any machine to date. It also had the most advanced programming capability. Nevertheless, a few years later, the Mark I was all but obsolete.

ENIAC

About the time that Howard Aiken was developing the Mark I, an Iowa State University physics professor named John Atanasoff was working on a machine of his own. Atanasoff's machine did not become as well known as the Mark I. However, many of his design ideas were used to build the first completely electronic digital computer, ENIAC.

ENIAC (Electronic Numerical Integrator and Calculator) was completed in 1946 by a team of engineers led by John Mauchly and J. Presper Eckert. The machine was built for (and paid for by) the United States Army, which used it for almost ten years.

Why did the army want an electronic computer? In 1943, when work began on ENIAC, the Mark I was not yet finished. But the war effort had accelerated. American factories were producing more weapons, and more Americans were going overseas to fight. The need for fast, accurate data processing was growing. The military had many complex calculations to make for firing tables, supply schedules, and aircraft designs. Any machine that could help to perform these calculations would be helping to end the war sooner.

ENIAC made the Mark I look like an old jalopy. It could do an amazing 5000 additions or 300 multiplications *per second.* That made it many hundreds of times faster than any other machine in use at the time. In fact, ENIAC could do prob-

Getting the Bugs Out

The term **bug**, as in "get all the bugs out of it," has been around for a long time. But it has a special meaning in the field of computers.

In September of 1947, the navy's Mark II computer (the successor to the Mark I) suddenly stopped running. After much investigation, Captain Grace Hopper located the problem. A moth had been crushed to death in one of the machine's large relays. Captain Hopper removed the moth and started the computer up again. Then she taped the moth into her log and wrote next to it, "First actual case of bug being found."

Over the years several specific terms based on the word *bug* have come into use. A *hardware bug* is a mechanical flaw in a computer system. A *software bug* is an error made by the programmer in writing the program. And the process of tracking down and fixing problems is known as *debugging*.

Since 1944, Grace Hopper has been a major force in the development of computer languages.

lems in a few hours that fifty engineers would need an entire year to solve.

ENIAC was even more enormous than the Mark I. It was 100 feet long and occupied 3000 cubic feet of space. It weighed about as much as four African elephants—30 tons. Instead of the thousands of mechanical parts that the Mark I contained, ENIAC used 18,000 vacuum tubes. These tubes enabled the computer to store and process data electronically rather than mechanically.

Using ENIAC to perform calculations was much more complicated than using a modern computer. Programming instructions had to be given manually by plugging in hundreds of wires. Once a program was carefully wired in, the order of instructions could not be changed until the whole program had run. Each new program required another new wire combination. As a result, creating and running even simple programs took far longer than it does today.

ENIAC's vacuum tubes presented problems of their own. So many thousands of tubes not only took up a lot of space but also generated a great deal of heat. A special cooling system was needed. More important, vacuum tubes aren't nearly as reliable as today's electronic components. For example, it wasn't unusual for six or seven tubes to fail in a single hour. Nevertheless, ENIAC demonstrated the potential of *electronic* computers. And though it's hard to believe, only forty years later all the power of the giant ENIAC would be contained in computers no bigger than a suitcase.

Key Points

- Herman Hollerith's tabulating machine combined the punched-card input with the use of electricity.
- The computers that evolved in the twentieth century had two key features that early calculating machines did not: they could be programmed, and they could store information.
- The first completely electronic digital computer was ENIAC, built in 1946. ENIAC used vacuum tubes to store and process data.

Many hours were needed to plug in the hundreds of wires in order to program ENIAC's circuits.

Review Questions

1. Why was using ENIAC to perform calculations much more complicated than using a modern computer?
2. In the late 1940's the most advanced computers were built with vacuum tubes. But vacuum tubes had several disadvantages. Explain.

STORED-PROGRAM COMPUTERS

One of the people who helped develop ENIAC was an American mathematician named John von Neumann. Von Neumann's most important contribution, though, was a design concept that he came up with after working on ENIAC.

Von Neumann originated the idea of storing programs in computer memory. A stored-program computer represented a big step forward from ENIAC and other earlier machines. Such a computer did not need to be manually rewired for each new task. In addition, a stored-program computer could process its instructions in more than one order. As a result, stored-program computers were not only faster but also more flexible than earlier computers.

The first stored-program machine was the EDSAC (Electronic Delay Storage Automatic Calculator). It was completed at Cambridge University in England in 1949. Today, all computers are stored-program computers.

After John Mauchly and J. Presper Eckert built ENIAC, they formed their

Not only was the transistor smaller than the vacuum tube, it was more reliable.

own company and began work on a stored-program computer. In 1951 they completed the UNIVAC (Universal Automatic Computer). The first UNIVAC was sold to the Census Bureau. After that, many other models of the UNIVAC were made and sold to businesses. Thus, UNIVAC became the first commercial computer. It was also the first computer to use magnetic tape for input instead of punched tape or cards.

GENERATIONS OF COMPUTERS

Computers such as ENIAC and UNIVAC represented only the first wave of electronic computers. In the following decades more advanced machines were built. In fact, the computers of the second half of the twentieth century rapidly made the earlier machines obsolete. This may seem hard to believe. After all, those first machines were—for their time—very impressive. Before long, though, even more powerful computers became available. Large companies, banks, and other institutions bought these new machines. They used them for information processing and for accounting. Within ten years after UNIVAC was built, 5000 stored-program computers were already in use in the United States. A mere six years later, the number of computers had quadrupled.

Why did so many companies buy computers? They bought computers for much the same reason that you might buy an electric typewriter to replace an old manual: for better performance. A company executive might think this way: "At present we can process this much data in one day. But with that new Superduper Computer, we could do the same job in one *hour.* That would save our company time and money. Let's buy it. . . . "

Furthermore, computers were popular with American business because they helped companies run more efficiently. And the more efficiently a company ran, the better it could withstand foreign and domestic competition.

SECOND-GENERATION COMPUTERS: THE TRANSISTOR

In a way, the first electronic computers were the grandparents and great-grandparents of all the computers that followed. That's why you'll hear people talk about "generations" of computers. The huge, vacuum-tube computers of the 1950's made up the first generation. As technology progressed, new and better electronic circuitry was developed. These improvements in circuitry created new generations of computers, each more advanced than the one before.

The second generation of computers began about 1960, when transistors replaced vacuum tubes. Invented in 1948, the transistor could do everything the vacuum tube could. But it was only a fraction of the size, and it used much less electricity.

Most people first heard about transistors in connection with radios, not computers. Transistor-powered radios became very popular in the late 1950's. Thanks to the tiny transistor, these new radios were smaller and lighter than the vacuum-tube radios.

The transistor offered these same advantages to computers. In addition, transistors cost less, generated less heat, and were more dependable. Thus, the transistor made possible computers that were smaller, less expensive, and more reliable.

Furthermore, one transistor could do the work of forty vacuum tubes—and do it at higher speed. As a result, second-generation computers were much more powerful and ten times faster than first-generation computers. They also had more memory capacity.

At the same time that transistors were replacing vacuum tubes, improved storage methods were being developed. Magnetic-tape storage, first used in UNIVAC, became common for computer input and output. By the mid-1960's disk storage had become popular.

THIRD-GENERATION COMPUTERS: INTEGRATED CIRCUITS

Just as transistors led the way to a second generation of computers, so did integrated circuits open the door to a third generation. An integrated circuit—also called an IC or a chip—is a miniature electronic circuit that is etched on a piece of silicon about a quarter-inch square. Think about that. A quarter-inch is about the diameter of a pencil eraser!

Integrated circuits were introduced about 1964. They were first used in spaceships and electronic military equipment. Today, you'll find integrated circuits in everything from cars to home appliances. And, of course, integrated circuits form the "brain" of computers.

The development of the integrated circuit revolutionized the computer scene. A single IC could take the place of *thousands* of transistors. (And remember that each transistor already equalled forty vacuum tubes.) Thus, one tiny, complex chip offered about as much computing power as the 30-ton ENIAC!

Third-generation computers were more reliable and far more powerful than second-generation machines. Moreover, they could do one hundred times as many calculations per second. And they were smaller—*much* smaller.

Picture the size difference this way: In 1950 computer makers could fit about 1000 circuits in one cubic foot of space. In 1960 they could fit 100,000 circuits in that same cubic foot. By 1970 that

Rows of chips containing thousands of circuits make up a modern computer board.

number had grown to 10 *million.* Today, *billions* of circuits per cubic foot are possible.

Third-generation computers were also cheaper to make than previous machines. As a result, more companies could afford computers. This, in turn, led to a growing demand for general-purpose computers—machines that could do a variety of tasks. Most earlier machines were special-purpose computers, designed for one particular purpose. Today, both general-purpose and special-purpose computers are common.

Key Points

- Stored-program computers represented a big step forward from earlier machines. They were not only faster but also more flexible.
- As technology progressed, better electronic circuitry was developed. Improvements in circuitry created new generations of computers, each more advanced than the one before.
- Just as transistors led the way to a second generation of computers, so did integrated circuits open the door to a third generation.

Review Questions

1. Why did so many companies in the 1950's and 1960's buy computers?
2. What were the advantages of the transistor over the vacuum tube? Why were transistors eventually replaced by integrated circuits?

FOURTH-GENERATION COMPUTERS: LARGE-SCALE INTEGRATED CIRCUITS

Mechanical parts were replaced by vacuum tubes. Transistors gave way to integrated circuits. You'd think that technology had about reached its limit. What could possibly be next?

The answer came in the early 1970's: large-scale integrated circuits. If one integrated circuit could be put on a silicon chip, scientists said, why not more than one?

Why not, indeed? Before long, microtechnology made it possible to squeeze *thousands* of integrated circuits onto a single tiny chip. Instructions and data in the form of electrical currents zipped through these microscopic electronic pathways at incredible speed.

By 1980 the microprocessor of a small computer could have its entire CPU fit on one quarter-inch-square chip. Desktop computers that were more powerful than

COMPUTER GENERATIONS

FIRST	SECOND	THIRD	FOURTH
1946–1960	1960–1964	1964–1970's	1970's–1980's
Vacuum tubes	Transistors	Integrated circuits	Large-scale integrated circuits
Hundreds of computers in use	Thousands of computers in use	Tens of thousands of computers in use	Millions of computers in use
1000 circuits per cubic foot	100,000 circuits per cubic foot	10 million circuits per cubic foot	Billions of circuits per cubic foot
ENIAC, EDSAC, UNIVAC		Minicomputers developed	Microcomputers developed
	10 times faster than first generation	100 times faster than second generation	10 times faster than third generation
	Magnetic-tape storage	Disk storage	Floppy disks

ENIAC and UNIVAC were now affordable by small businesses, schools and universities, and even individuals. The microcomputer revolution was under way.

When you stop to consider, it's hard to believe how far and how quickly computer technology has advanced. Microcomputers using large-scale integrated circuits calculate more rapidly than early inventors dreamed possible.

Just how fast is the modern microcomputer? It's 10 times faster than third-generation computers using integrated circuits; 1000 times faster than second-generation computers using transistors; and 10,000 times faster than first-generation computers using vacuum tubes.

Furthermore, less than forty years ago computers like UNIVAC sold for about $2.5 million. Today, a machine that's faster, more powerful, more reliable, much smaller, and easier to use costs under $2000. Two years from now, the price will probably be half that. No invention in history has fallen in price as rapidly as the computer.

WHAT NEXT?

The computers of each new generation have been more powerful yet smaller than those of the previous generation. They have also been less costly. What will the future bring? In what new directions will computers evolve? What do *you* think?

Certainly, computers as powerful as

ENIAC may soon fit into your shirt pocket and cost no more than a cassette player. Before long computers may be controlling the temperature in your home and telling drivers that it's time to change their engine oil. Already there are computers that use voice synthesizers to speak to you. And there are even computers that respond to spoken commands or to commands given by a touch.

Today, powerful microprocessors are in use everywhere: in office machines, in home appliances, in cars, in robots, and in alarm systems. Yet tomorrow's even more powerful microprocessors will make present-day "advanced" technology seem old-fashioned.

The next step in computer evolution will be the development of the so-called superchip. The superchip, which scientists are currently working on, will take the technology of large-scale integration a step further. Millions, rather than thousands, of integrated circuits will be contained on one compact chip.

Yesterday, computers were used only by scientists and mathematicians. Today, they are used in large corporations, small businesses, factories, schools, libraries, and millions of private homes. Lawyers, doctors, secretaries, farmers, and countless others all find the computer to be an invaluable tool.

The evolution of the computer goes on. How will tomorrow's computer affect *your* life? Time will tell.

The Computer's Place in History

About 3000 B.C.—Abacus used by the Chinese.

1642—Pascal invents first mechanical calculating machine.

1694—Leibnitz's calculating machine.

1801—Jacquard invents punched-card loom.

1830's—Babbage conceives of first programmable computer.

1836—Telegraph invented.

1846—Sewing machine invented.

1860—Internal-combustion engine invented.

1867—Typewriter invented.

1876—Telephone invented.

1890—Hollerith's tabulating machine—first use of electricity for computing.

1895—Radio invented.

1930—Bush invents first analog computer.

1944—Aiken's Mark I—first digital computer.

1946—Mauchly and Eckert complete ENIAC, first completely electronic digital computer.

1948—Transistor invented.

1949—EDSAC, first stored-program computer, completed.

1951—UNIVAC—first commercial computer.

1964—Introduction of integrated circuits.

1965—First minicomputer.

1969—U.S. astronauts land on the moon.

1970's—Large-scale integrated circuits developed.

1977—Apple microcomputer introduced by Wozniak and Jobs.

1980—CPU on a single chip.

1980's—Superchip development.

REVIEW & APPLICATION

SUMMARY

- Computers have evolved over hundreds of years. The modern computer is the product of many people's ideas blended over time. This process of development is still going on.
- Punched cards and electricity helped technology advance from mechanical to electronic calculating machines.
- Improvements in electronic circuitry made possible increasingly powerful computers. First-generation, vacuum-tube computers gave way to second-generation, transistor-powered computers. Third-generation computers used tiny silicon chips engraved with integrated circuits. Then fourth-generation computers were built using large-scale integrated circuits—thousands of ICs squeezed onto single chips. Soon, one superchip will hold millions of ICs.
- Computers will become even more powerful, smaller, and easier to use. If the current trend continues, computers will play an increasingly important role in our lives.

DISCUSSION QUESTION

There's an old saying: "Necessity is the mother of invention." It means that when the need for a tool becomes great enough, someone will invent it. Do you think that saying applies to the development of computers? Why or why not?

VOCABULARY

Match each item in the left column with the correct item on the right.

a. UNIVAC	1. Originated idea of storing programs in computer memory
b. abacus	2. Invented in 1948
c. Vannevar Bush	3. First commercial computer
d. John von Neumann	4. Designed to use punched-card input
e. transistor	5. Oldest mechanical calculating aid
f. Analytical Engine	6. Built first analog computer

REVIEW QUESTIONS

1. In what way was Leibnitz's calculating machine an improvement over Pascal's?
2. What were Ada Lovelace's contributions to the development of computer technology?
3. Who invented the punched-card tabulating machine that was used in the 1890 census?
4. Name and describe the device that opened the door to the third generation of computers.

P R O J E C T S

C In the next chapter you will begin to write programs, and you will need to know how to change the text that appears on your screen. First type: 100 PRINT "THUS IS A TEST" (You'll learn what this means later.) Press RETURN or ENTER. Then . . .

APPLE IIe

Use these keys to move the cursor to the 1 in 100, pressing the ESC key before each one:

A—right, B—left, C—down, D—up. Press the → key to move the cursor along the line. When the cursor is on top of the U, type I. Now use the → key to move the cursor along the rest of the line. Then press RETURN. The line is changed. Now press ESC and use the A, B, C, and D keys to bring the cursor to the beginning of the line again. Use the → key to move the cursor to the first S. Press ESC and use the A key to move the cursor to between A and TEST. Use the → key to move the cursor over the rest of the line. Now press RETURN. To see the change, type LIST 100 and press RETURN.

COMMODORE 64

(Note: Several keys have two functions, depending on whether you hold down the SHIFT key when you press them. For example: the DEL key on the very top right of the keyboard means "delete". However, if you hold the SHIFT key down while you press this key, it is the INST—or insert—key. The arrow keys on the bottom right work the same way.) Use the arrow keys to move the cursor to the U. Now type I. Press RETURN. The line is now changed. Next, use the arrow keys to move the cursor to the space between A and TEST. Press the DEL key five times. Press RETURN. The line is changed. Want the old one back? Move the cursor over the first T in TEST. Press the INST key five times. Now type IS A. Be sure to press RETURN.

IBM PCjr

Use the arrow keys to move the cursor to the U. Type I. Press ENTER. The line is now changed. Next, use the arrow keys to move the cursor to the space between THIS and IS. Press the DEL key five times. Press ENTER. Want the old line back? Move the cursor to the first T in TEST. Press the INS key. Type IS A(space). Press ENTER. The line is back.

TRS-80 Model III

Type EDIT 100 and press ENTER. Use the space bar to move the cursor until it reveals the H. Then type I. This tells the computer you are about to insert something. Now type I again. Press ENTER. To delete the U, type EDIT 100 again, and press ENTER. Press the space bar until it reveals the I. Now type 1D (this means delete 1 character). Press ENTER. Type LIST 100 and press ENTER to see the change. For more practice, try deleting IS A, and then inserting it again.

CHAPTER TEST

Complete this test on a piece of paper numbered from 1 to 16.

ORDERING OF EVENTS

1. List the order in which the following devices were developed.

a. integrated circuit	f. UNIVAC
b. transistor	g. ENIAC
c. large-scale IC	h. abacus
d. Pascaline	i. Differential Analyzer
e. Stepped Reckoner	

MULTIPLE CHOICE

2. Von Leibnitz set out to build a machine that would help:
   a. scientists
   b. merchants
   c. craftspeople
   d. all of the above
3. To store information, the Differential Analyzer used:
   a. chips
   b. boxes
   c. vacuum tubes
   d. punched cards
4. The Mark I was the first:
   a. analog computer
   b. digital computer
   c. calculator
   d. transistor
5. One of the first machines to meet the military's growing need for computer power during World War II was:
   a. UNIVAC
   b. Mark I
   c. EDSAC
   d. ENIAC

FILL-IN

6. The Pascaline used gears, but the Stepped Reckoner used ______.
7. Ada, a programming language developed for military use, is named after ______.
8. Thanks to Herman Hollerith's tabulating machine, the 1890 ______ was completed in less than three years.
9. Punched cards are still used in data processing today, but they are being replaced by ______.
10. ENIAC was built for ______, which used it for almost 10 years.
11. Stored-program computers are ______ and more flexible than earlier computers were.
12. The EDSAC was the first computer in which ______ could be stored.
13. UNIVAC was the first ______ computer.
14. The vacuum-tube machines of the 1950's were the ______ generation of computers.
15. Computers built with transistors cost ______ those built with vacuum tubes.
16. The modern computer is ______ times faster than first-generation computers.

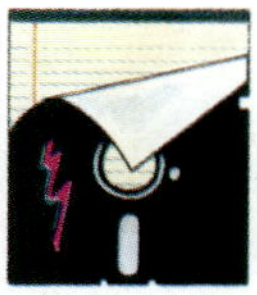

ISSUE: SOFTWARE PIRACY

Bill asks his friend, Joel, for advice about which computer to get.

"Buy the model that I bought," Joel says. "That way if you like one of my programs, you can copy it."

Bill agrees with Joel that copying software is a great way to save money. In fact, Bill has an idea for making money from copying software. He and Joel go to the computer store and split the cost of some new games. They make several copies of each program and sell them to their classmates for half of the store's price.

What Bill and Joel are doing is illegal. It is called **software piracy**.

Most software programs sold in stores are copyrighted. This means that the programs are protected by a federal law called the Copyright Act. This law states that a copyrighted work cannot be copied for selling, renting, or lending without permission from the person or company that owns the copyright. The copyright law protects many kinds of work including books, cartoons, and computer software. After you load a copyrighted software program, one of the first things to appear on the screen is the copyright notice. To find out if a program is copyrighted, look for the word *copyright*, the symbol ©, a date, and the name of the copyright owner.

Let's look at what would happen if the copyright law did not exist. Imagine that you write a song. You find a band to perform it. Then you ask a talent agent to listen to it. Without the copyright law, the agent could steal your song and have another band perform it. The copyright law insures that you have the exclusive right to sell the product (song) that you have created.

Similarly, the copyright law protects software companies. Software companies spend a lot of time and money developing programs. They must be able to sell enough copies of those programs to pay for all of the development costs. People who use pirated software help put software companies out of business. They also drive up the price that honest people pay for the original product.

How can you ever make a duplicate copy of a program? The copyright law allows you to make one copy of each program that you buy in case the original becomes damaged or is lost. Some software companies include a backup copy with the original disk. Others offer to send you a backup copy if your original disk is damaged. These policies are intended to discourage people from making illegal copies of software.

Some software companies use another method to prevent piracy. They add a copy-protect code, to their programs. The code makes it difficult for people to copy the information on the disk.

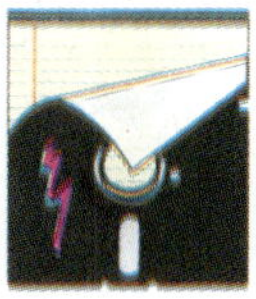

UNIT REVIEW

CONCEPTS

- How much does a computer really know?
- List the benefits and limitations of computer use.
- Do you think people's response to the computer is any different from people's response to the telephone when it was first invented? Why or why not?

CAREERS

- How can people find jobs in the computer industry?
- What do the careers described in this unit have in common? How do they differ?

ISSUES

- What is the purpose of copyright laws?
- Why is a copyright law applied to computer software?
- What do you think should be done to prevent software piracy?

APPLICATIONS

- If you were interested in buying a home computer, what information would you need in order to make a wise buying decision? Where would you find this information?
- What questions should a person ask before deciding which input devices to buy?
- The Lee family is investigating buying a computer. The XZAP model seems to meet their needs. Before buying an XZAP, should they investigate what software is available? Explain your answer.

TO FIND OUT

- Gather information on local computer clubs. Find out where and when they meet. Are they machine-specific? What topics are discussed at the meetings?
- Make a list of computer retailers in your community. Include their addresses and phone numbers. What brands of computers does each retailer carry?

!1
@2
#3
$4
%5
W
E
R
T
S
D
F
G
X
C
V
→
Esc
Ct

UNIT TWO

The POWER OF PROGRAMS

If you were going to build a bookcase, you'd follow a step-by-step plan. First, you'd decide exactly what sort of bookcase you wanted: its length, width, and number of shelves. Once your design was set, you'd gather your tools and supplies and get started. When you finished, you'd check your work carefully and make any needed changes.

Programming a computer—giving it a set of instructions to follow—has a lot in common with building that bookcase. To write a program, you begin by deciding exactly what task you want to accomplish. Then you work on developing and refining your program. You don't use carpentry tools, of course. Instead, you use a programming tool: the computer.

In this unit, you'll learn about programming: its purpose, power, and importance. You'll also learn about computer *languages*, especially the easy-to-learn language called *BASIC*.

CHAPTER

3 4 5 6 7

INTRODUCTION TO PROGRAMMING

Do you want to play a computer game? Use a computer to write a story? Turn your computer into a piano or a drawing pad? You can do all these things. But . . .

For a computer to do something—anything—it must have a set of instructions. Without instructions the computer is as useless as a phonograph without a record. You can buy instructions for the computer in the form of computer software, such as a game or a word-processing program, or you can create your own instructions.

Creating instructions for the computer is called writing a computer program, or **programming**. In this chapter you will begin to learn how to write some simple programs. Writing even simple programs can help you to understand better how a computer and computer software work.

Programming can also be a very exciting hobby. Many students go on to create complicated programs as a hobby. Some students even turn their hobbies into jobs.

Whether or not you go on to develop a hobby or a career as a programmer, you should enjoy being in charge of the computer as you learn about programming.

WHAT IS A COMPUTER LANGUAGE?

Instructing a computer is done with a **computer language**. A computer language is a set of words, symbols, and commands that a computer can "understand." Think of this example: If you study French you learn words and rules of grammar that another speaker of French can understand. If you study a computer language, you learn words and rules of grammar called **syntax** rules that a computer can understand. Most French words are not familiar to you when you first see them. But many computer languages use words that are mostly English words, such as PRINT, RUN, and NEW. These words have special meanings in a computer language.

Computer languages are not spoken to the computer (except in some experimental systems with limited vocabularies). Instead, you type the computer language on the keyboard. The computer then translates what you typed into electrical impulses that represent 0's and 1's—the form in which the computer can understand and carry out your instructions. To translate your instructions, the computer needs a **language processor** that is either built into the computer itself or loaded into the computer from a disk. The language processor acts somewhat like a human interpreter who listens to someone speaking French and then tells you what the words mean in English. It does the translating.

There are many different computer languages. You may have heard of BASIC, Pascal, Logo, FORTRAN, COBOL, and others. For your computer to understand one of these languages, it needs a translator for that language.

Why are there different computer languages? The reason for this is that different languages work well for different kinds of tasks. You will read about this in more detail in Chapter 7.

In this book you'll be learning something about the computer language called **BASIC**. BASIC is considered to be an all-purpose language because many different kinds of tasks can be done using it. BASIC is also quite easy to learn. These facts make BASIC a popular first computer language to study.

Key Points

• A computer language is a set of words, symbols, and commands that a computer can "understand."

• A language processor enables a computer to translate what you've typed into electrical impulses.

• BASIC is a multipurpose computer language that is available on most microcomputers.

Review Questions

1. What does a computer need in order to "understand" a computer language?
2. In what form does the computer understand your instructions?

THE PRINT STATEMENT

PRINTING WITH QUOTATION MARKS

You load a game into the computer. The game's title appears on the display screen. Next, you see messages instructing you on how to play the game. You play the game. If you do well you see a message like "FABULOUS JOB, PAT! YOU SCORED 429,665 POINTS!" In BASIC you tell the computer to print messages on the screen by using a PRINT statement.

A PRINT statement tells the computer to put letters, numbers, or symbols on the screen.

A PRINT statement consists of the **keyword** PRINT—the word in the statement that tells the computer what to do—followed by whatever you want to be printed. In BASIC this is what you type, or enter, to tell the computer to print "GOOD WORK!" on the screen:

```
PRINT "GOOD WORK!"
```

When you press RETURN the computer will carry out your instruction. This is what you'll see:

```
PRINT "GOOD WORK!"
GOOD WORK!
```

The line that you typed appears first. When you press RETURN the computer's response appears under what you typed.

Let's look again at what you typed:

```
PRINT "GOOD WORK!"
```

Notice that the messages you want the computer to type have to go inside quotation marks("). The quotation marks tell the computer to print what is between them. When the computer carries out the statement, it doesn't print the quotation marks; it prints what is inside them.

DOING ARITHMETIC WITH PRINT

Here is another use of PRINT:

```
PRINT 5+5
```

This PRINT statement will instruct the computer to do arithmetic for you:

```
PRINT 5+5
10
```

When you use the PRINT statement without quotation marks and with numbers and arithmetic symbols, the computer calculates the answer and prints it on the screen.

```
PRINT 6-1
5
PRINT 7+8
15
```

You can see that for addition and subtraction the computer uses the arithmetic symbols + and −. The multiplication and division symbols used in BASIC are different from the usual arithmetic symbols, however.

BASIC Arithmetic Symbols

+ means "add"
− means "subtract"
* means "multiply"
/ means "divide"

You can also enter single numbers. When you don't instruct the computer to do an arithmetic operation, it will just print the number itself.

```
PRINT 7
7
```

THE MEANING OF QUOTATION MARKS

What happens when you use quotation marks with numbers and symbols?

```
PRINT "10*10"
10*10
PRINT 10*10
100
```

The computer prints whatever you put within the quotation marks, so it prints "10*10" instead of doing the arithmetic. To have the computer do the arithmetic, leave out the quotation marks.

You might be wondering about the spaces in the statements that you have seen. The BASIC language is not very concerned about spaces. It usually makes it easier to read what you have typed if you put a space after a keyword like PRINT. But it isn't necessary. Just be sure that you put spaces where you want them inside your quotation marks. The computer will print exactly what you have typed there. Notice how the computer echoes the spacing in the following PRINT statements:

```
PRINT "GOODWORK!"
GOODWORK!
PRINT "GOOD WORK!"
GOOD WORK!
```

Key Points

• A PRINT statement containing quotation marks tells the computer to print what is between the quotation marks.
• A PRINT statement typed without quotation marks and with numbers and arithmetic symbols (+, −, *, /) tells the computer to do the arithmetic and print the result on the screen.

Review Questions

1. What will the computer print if you enter these statements?

```
PRINT "HAPPY NEW YEAR"
PRINT 6*7
PRINT "48/8"
```

2. What, if anything, is wrong with these statements?

```
PRINT HAPPY THANKSGIVING!
PRINT "6+6"
PRINT 5x5
```

3. What do you type to tell the computer to put "OK" on the screen?

COMPUTER PROGRAMS

PROGRAM LINES AND LINE NUMBERS

So far, you have learned how to use the computer in **immediate mode**. In immediate mode you can instruct the computer to do one task at a time—to print a few words or the answer to one arithmetic problem. Usually, you want it to do more complex tasks. You might want the computer to print review questions, check your answers, and print your score. To do this kind of complex task, you use the computer in **program mode**. In program mode the computer can be instructed to carry out a whole series of steps in a specific order.

To carry out complex tasks, you write a computer program, which consists of a series of program lines. Each line consists of a line number followed by one or more of the kinds of statements that you've just read about.

Here is an example of a simple two-line program:

```
10 PRINT "ADD 2 AND 2."
20 PRINT 2+2
```

This program has two lines, with one statement per line. Each line is a separate instruction to the computer. The line numbers tell the computer in what order to do the instructions. The line numbers here are 10 and 20. The computer will carry out line 10 first and line 20 second.

THE RUN COMMAND

Has the computer carried out these instructions yet? No, it hasn't. In immediate mode the computer carries out your instructions as soon as you enter them. However, in program mode a program statement is stored in the computer's RAM and is carried out *only* when you enter a system command: RUN.

RUN is a system command that causes the computer to carry out the instructions in a program.

Let's see what happens in this program when RUN is entered:

```
10 PRINT "ADD 2 AND 2."
20 PRINT 2+2
RUN
ADD 2 AND 2.
4
```

The computer "runs," or carries out, all the program instructions in the order of the line numbers, one at a time.

Unlike program lines, system commands have no line numbers in front of them, so they go to the computer in immediate mode. They are not stored in RAM, and they are executed as soon as you enter them. If you wanted to run a program a second time, you would have to type RUN again. But you would not have to type the program lines again, since they are stored in RAM.

```
10 PRINT "I AM A"
20 PRINT "COMPUTER WHIZ."
RUN
I AM A
COMPUTER WHIZ.
RUN
I AM A
COMPUTER WHIZ.
```

Each time this program is run, the lines "I AM A" and "COMPUTER WHIZ." will appear on the screen.

You can put two or more different PRINT statements on one line. You simply separate them with a semicolon(;). For example, if you enter

```
PRINT "THE ANSWER IS "; 2+2
```

the computer will respond by printing the message that is in between the quotation marks on the screen and then printing the sum of 2+2 next to it. It will print:

```
THE ANSWER IS 4
```

THE LIST COMMAND

After you have entered a program—or even when you're typing it—you can have the computer display the program lines that are in the memory. To do this, type the word LIST and press RETURN.

LIST is a system command that causes the computer to display all the

program lines currently in the memory.

This is how LIST works

```
10 PRINT "WILL A DISK DRIVE?"
20 PRINT "CAN A COMPUTER BYTE?"
LIST
10 PRINT "WILL A DISK DRIVE?"
20 PRINT "CAN A COMPUTER BYTE?"
```

When you type LIST the computer displays the program. A program can be listed as long as it is in RAM. You could also list the program after running it. LIST is useful when you want to make corrections or changes in your program.

You can enter program lines in any order, but the computer will process them in numerical order. If you enter line 10 first, line 30 second, and line 20 third, the computer will run the lines in the order 10, 20, 30. When you list the program, you will see them arranged in the correct order.

```
10 PRINT "THE SUM OF 2+2 IS:"
30 PRINT "IS THAT RIGHT?"
20 PRINT 2+2
LIST
10 PRINT "THE SUM OF 2 + 2 IS:"
20 PRINT 2 + 2
30 PRINT "IS THAT RIGHT?"
RUN
THE SUM OF 2 + 2 IS:
4
IS THAT RIGHT?
```

Notice that the program lines are numbered by tens. Numbering the lines by tens, or even hundreds, makes it easier to insert new lines in between the old ones if you want to make changes in the program.

THE REM STATEMENT

It is usually a good idea to put "notes" in the program that tell what it does or, if it is a very complex program, what various parts of it do. But how can you do this without affecting the running of the program? You can use a REM statement. REM stands for "remark."

Look at this program and its output.

What effect does the REM statement have on the program?

```
10 REM ADD TWO NUMBERS
20 PRINT "5+5 = "; 5+5
30 PRINT "IS THAT RIGHT?"
RUN
5+5 = 10
IS THAT RIGHT?
```

The computer ignored what was typed on the line after the keyword REM. Whenever a computer encounters a REM statement, it simply skips the statement and goes on to the next program line. REM statements are used to label or explain a program or parts of a program, or to add comments to a program. The REM statement will appear every time the program is listed, but it will not affect the running of the program.

The REM statement is used for making comments in a program. A REM statement is listed but not carried out.

THE END STATEMENT

When you have completed a program, you should type an END statement to tell the computer where the end of the program is.

An END statement instructs the computer to stop running a BASIC program.

At this point all the programs that have been described will work without an END statement. In Chapter 6 you'll find types of programs that won't work without END. Also, some mainframe computers require END statements for all programs. It's a good idea to get into the habit of typing an END statement.

```
10 REM ONLY ONE LINE PRINTS.
20 PRINT "SHORT AND SWEET"
30 END
RUN
SHORT AND SWEET
```

THE NEW COMMAND

As long as the computer's power is on, the program that you typed remains in the computer's memory. You can see the program when you list it. If you want to begin a new program, you must clear the memory first. You do this with the command NEW.

The NEW command clears the computer's memory.

If you try to list or run the program after typing NEW, you'll find that it is not in RAM anymore. See how NEW works:

```
LIST
10 REM ONLY ONE LINE PRINTS.
20 PRINT "SHORT AND SWEET"
30 END
NEW
LIST
RUN
```

It is a good idea to type NEW before you begin a new program. Otherwise, you may find that lines from old programs show up in your new program.

Key Points

- In immediate mode you can instruct the computer to carry out one task at a time. In program mode the computer can be instructed to carry out a whole series of steps in a specific order.
- A program is made up of a series of program lines. Each line consists of a line number that is followed by one or more statements.
- RUN is a system command that causes the computer to carry out the instructions in a program.
- LIST is a system command that causes the computer to display all the current program lines on the screen.
- The computer lists and runs the lines of a program in numerical order, even if they are not entered in order.
- REM statements are used for making comments in a program.
- An END statement instructs the computer to stop running a BASIC program.
- The NEW command clears the computer's memory.

Review Questions

1. Look at this program and then answer the questions that follow:

```
10 PRINT "2*8 = "; 2*8
30 PRINT "2*9 = "; 2*9
20 PRINT "2*10 = "; 2*10
```

   a. What will the computer display when you run the program?

b. What order will the lines be in when you list the program?
c. What effect will adding the line "5 REM MULTIPLY BY 2" have on the program when you list and run it?
d. What will the command NEW do? What will you see when you list the program? When you run it?

EDITING COMPUTER PROGRAMS

CORRECTING ERRORS

If, when baking a loaf of bread, you mix in five cups of flour instead of one cup, the bread you produce will be inedible. When writing a computer program, however, you always have a chance to correct your errors. As you may remember, mistakes in programs are called bugs and part of being a good programmer is being able to find and fix all the bugs in your program. The program isn't done until all the bugs have been corrected.

As you type programs on the keyboard, chances are that you will make mistakes. The most common mistakes are typing mistakes. You might type "PIRNT" instead of "PRINT," for example. This kind of mistake is called a **syntax error**. Syntax errors include mistyping a keyword, leaving out quotation marks, or other misuses of the computer language.

When you make a mistake like this, you can correct it by moving the cursor back and retyping. If you have already pressed RETURN or don't find the error until the program is run, you can correct the error by retyping the line.

```
10 PIRNT 7*7
20 PRINT 4*4
30 END
RUN
? SYNTAX ERROR IN 10
```

When this program is run, the computer would not understand the word "PIRNT." Because this is not a BASIC keyword the computer printed an **error message**. An error message is put on the screen by the computer to tell you that something is wrong and it cannot continue the program. Different computers have different error messages. The error message "SYNTAX ERROR IN 10" tells you that you made a syntax error. It even tells you the line in which the error was made—line 10.

Here's how to correct the bug. Simply retype line 10 and run the program.

```
10 PIRNT 7*7
20 PRINT 4*4
30 END
RUN
? SYNTAX ERROR IN 10
10 PRINT 7*7
RUN
49
16
```

When a new line 10 is typed, the old line 10 is automatically erased from memory and replaced with the new line. If the program is listed, only one line 10 will appear on the screen—the new one.

The following program contains syntax errors—a quotation mark is missing in line 30 and the keyword in line 40 is misspelled. Notice, too, that there is a misspelling in line 10. These errors were found and corrected before the program was run. Notice that the listing does not show the old lines.

```
10 REM ADDING TWO NUBMERS
20 PRINT "6+6 = "; 7+6
30 PRINT 7+7 = "; 7+7
40 EDN
10 REM ADDING TWO NUMBERS
30 PRINT "7+7 ="; 7+7
40 END
LIST
10 REM ADDING TWO NUMBERS
20 PRINT "6+6 = "; 7+6
30 PRINT "7+7 = "; 7+7
40 END
RUN
6+6 = 13
7+7 = 14
```

Since the computer ignores a REM statement, the misspelling in the REM statement would have had no effect on the running of the program. But it's a good idea to correct it anyway.

Correcting the three lines had no effect on the other line in the program. Now the program runs the way you want it to. Or does it? Look at the output. The first answer is incorrect because there is a mistake in line 20. This kind of error is called a **logic error**. Logic errors often don't prevent a program from running, but they do usually cause a program to give the wrong answer. Logic errors include entering incorrect data, using the wrong keyword, and numbering program lines in the wrong order.

When you write programs, don't just run the program and look for error messages from the computer. Make sure that what you see on the screen is what is supposed to be there. The computer will do whatever you tell it to do, even if it makes no sense!

ADDING AND REMOVING LINES

It is common in debugging a program to discover that you have left out a step. Look at this program:

```
10 PRINT "ROSES ARE RED."
20 PRINT "SUGAR IS SWEET."
30 PRINT "AND SO ARE YOU."
40 END
```

The line "VIOLETS ARE BLUE." was left out of the poem and needs to be added. The statement must be added between lines 10 and 20. Let's call it line 15.

```
15 PRINT "VIOLETS ARE BLUE."
LIST
10 PRINT "ROSES ARE RED."
15 PRINT "VIOLETS ARE BLUE."
20 PRINT "SUGAR IS SWEET."
30 PRINT "AND SO ARE YOU."
40 END
```

When you list the program, the program lines will appear in the correct order.

Look at the following example. You'll see that it might look better with more space between the title and the names of the two colors.

```
NEW
10 PRINT "MY FAVORITE COLORS:"
20 PRINT "RED"
30 PRINT "BLUE"
40 END
RUN
MY FAVORITE COLORS:
RED
BLUE
```

Space can be added by adding a line to the program. To print a blank line, just type PRINT.

```
10 PRINT "MY FAVORITE COLORS:"
15 PRINT
20 PRINT "RED"
30 PRINT "BLUE"
40 END
RUN
MY FAVORITE COLORS:

RED
BLUE
```

Changes in a program to improve the appearance of something on the screen are very common.

Sometimes when you are editing a program, you will find a line that you don't need. To remove a line, just type the line number and press RETURN.

```
10 PRINT "WORDS FROM CENORTU"
20 PRINT
30 PRINT "COUNTER"
40 PRINT "OUTRAGE"
50 PRINT "TROUNCE"
60 END
40
LIST
10 PRINT "WORDS FROM CENORTU"
20 PRINT
30 PRINT "COUNTER"
50 PRINT "TROUNCE"
60 END
```

Typing 40 and pressing RETURN removed that line from memory.

Key Points

- To make a change in a line after you have entered it, retype it.
- To add a line between two other lines, give the new line a number that falls between the other two line numbers.
- To print a blank line, type PRINT.
- To remove a line, type the line number and press RETURN.

Review Questions

1. How would you change this line after you had entered it?

```
10 ROM ADDING TWO NUMBERS
```

2. How would you add a line between lines 5 and 10?
3. How would you remove line 75?

VARIABLES

THE LET STATEMENT

If you were going to write a program to print department store bills, you could write a separate program for each customer. One program might look like this:

```
10 PRINT "CUSTOMER: MS. JONES"
20 PRINT "AMOUNT OWED: $20.00"
30 END
```

But this is not very efficient. A much better method would be to write one program that could be used for all your customers. In this program you would change, or *vary*, the name of the customer and the amount that each customer owes. In this way you are making use of the computer's unique ability to do the same operation over and over with different data each time.

Any item in a program that can vary, like the name of a customer, is stored in a special location in the computer's memory. This location is called a **variable**.

A	B	C
40	20	18

Think of these boxes as variables, or locations. These variables have data stored in them. In this case the data are numbers.

One variable has the number 40 stored in it, one has 20, and one has 18. The data stored can be changed at any time. In order to indicate which variable is being referred to, it must be labeled—or given a variable name. In BASIC variables are usually named with a letter, a letter followed by a number, or two letters. Q, D2, and RP are all valid variable names, but 2D is not a valid name because it does not begin with a letter. It is a good idea to use meaningful variable names, such as PR for "price." Look at the three boxes again.

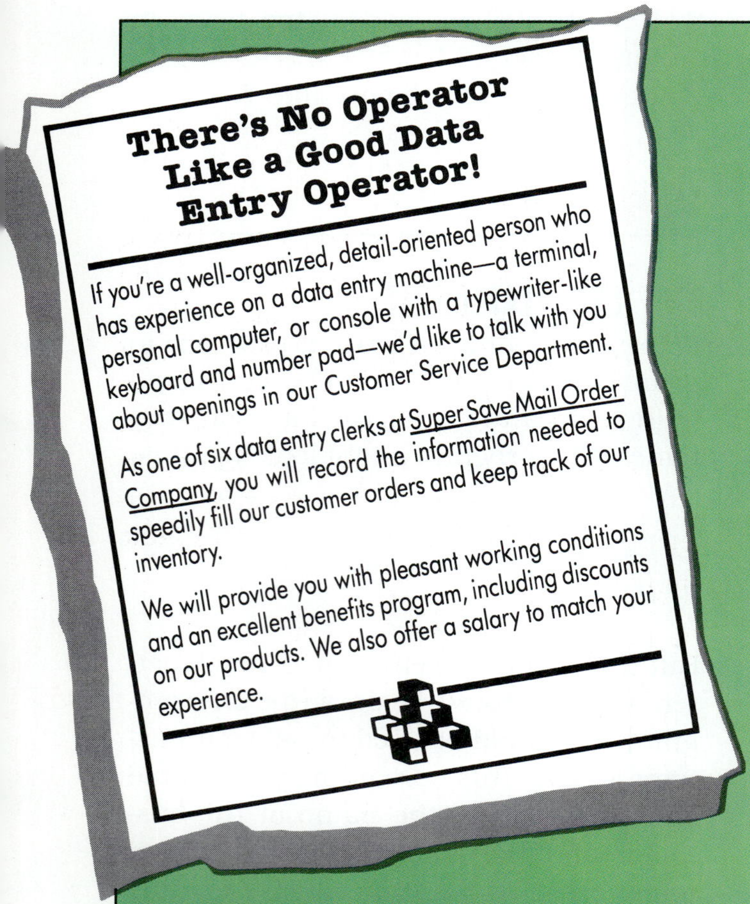

THAT'S MY JOB

Richard Kelso, a data entry operator for about four years, says: "I have had jobs entering all kinds of data at banks, manufacturing firms, and insurance agencies. You name the place—I've worked there.

"Sometimes the work seems a little repetitious. That's why I like being able to move around from company to company. I've never had a problem finding work, and I enjoy the challenge of building my speed in entering different kinds of data on different machines.

"I get a sense of satisfaction from working quickly and accurately. That's what makes me good at my job."

MORE INFORMATION

Data entry operators generally operate one or more types of data entry machines.... Job candidates should have a high school diploma and be able to accurately type 40–55 words per minute.... Jobs are often available in large companies, where data entry operators work under close supervision as part of a team.

The current content of the variable A is the number 40; the content of B is 20; and the content of C is 18.

A shorter way of saying this is:

A = 40 B = 20 C = 18

When you want to set up a variable in a computer program and put some data in it, you use the LET statement.

A LET statement is used to instruct the computer to store data in a variable.

Here is how a LET statement works:

```
10 LET A=100
20 PRINT A
30 END
RUN
100
```

The LET statement instructed the computer to store a value of 100 in variable A. This was checked with a PRINT statement. The PRINT statement told the computer to print whatever value was stored in A. It printed 100. Now add two lines to the program, list it, and run it.

```
25 LET A=A+10
27 PRINT A
LIST
10 LET A=100
20 PRINT A
25 LET A=A+10
27 PRINT A
30 END
RUN
100
110
```

The computer assigned the value 100 to A and printed it. Then it added 10 to the value of A and assigned the sum—110—as the new value of A, which it then printed.

You can do math with variables also. Here's an example where the values in two variables are stored in a third variable. Then the value in that third variable is printed.

```
10 LET A=5
20 LET B=25
30 LET C= A+B
40 PRINT C
50 END
RUN
30
```

You can do math without storing the result in another variable.

```
5 REM ADD THREE NUMBERS.
10 LET J=15
20 LET M=10
30 LET N=20
40 PRINT J+M+N
50 END
RUN
45
```

Here, three variables—J, M, and N—are set up, and a number is stored in each. Then the PRINT statement causes the computer to add the numbers stored in each variable and print the sum.

Remember, the data in a variable can change. The computer will look at the current value in the variable and do its arithmetic with that number. Here's an example of a variable being changed in the middle of the program and two different results being printed:

```
10 LET A=5
20 PRINT 2*A
30 LET A=3
40 PRINT 2*A
50 END
RUN
10
6
```

The first time the computer multiplied 2 times A, A was 5; the next time it multiplied 2 times A, A was 3.

STRING VARIABLES

So far, you have looked only at variables that store data which are numbers. Variables that hold numbers are called **numeric variables**. Data can also be letters. A variable that stores letters is called a **string variable** because it contains a string of letters (which may or may not be words). A string variable can also contain symbols or numbers.

A string variable, like a numeric variable, is named with a letter or a combination of letters and numbers. But the name is followed by a dollar sign. The dollar sign looks a little like an "S" and stands for "string." L$, B2$, and ZZ$ are string variables. You would pronounce these names "L-string," "B-two-string," and "ZZ-string."

Again, you use a LET statement to set up string variables. Here is an example:

```
10 LET A$="MS. JONES"
20 PRINT A$
30 END
RUN
MS. JONES
```

Notice two things about this program. First, when you set up a string variable, you must use quotation marks around the letters, symbols, or numbers that are part of the data to be stored in the variable. The quotation marks are not part of the data. Second, you can print a string variable with a PRINT statement, just as you would print words or numbers.

Key Points

- A variable is a location in the computer's memory in which you can store data temporarily.
- The LET statement instructs the computer to put data into a variable.
- A numeric variable is a variable that can store numbers.
- A string variable is a variable that can store letters, numbers, or symbols.
- You can print a string or numeric variable or do arithmetic with numeric variables by using a PRINT statement that includes the names of the variables.

Review Questions

1. Give an example of a name for a numeric variable and a name for a string variable.
2. How would you store the number 100 in a numeric variable? How would you store "HELLO!" in a string variable?

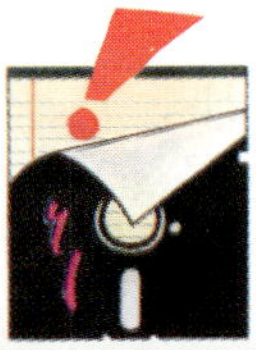

REVIEW & APPLICATION

SUMMARY

• A program is made up of numbered program lines, each containing one or more instructions. A computer carries out the instructions in the numerical order of the line numbers.

• You can make a change in a program line by retyping it. You can remove the line by typing its number and pressing the RETURN key. You can add a line to a program by giving the new line a number between the numbers of the lines above and below it.

• In BASIC a PRINT statement tells the computer to display information on the screen. The information may be letters, numbers, or symbols that you have typed between quotation marks, or it may be the results of an arithmetic problem.

• The system command RUN tells a computer to carry out the instructions in a program. A LIST command tells the computer to list the program lines in its memory. A NEW command clears the computer's memory.

• A REM statement, which is used to include comments in a program, does not affect the running of the program. An END statement tells the computer that it has reached the end of a program.

• You can use variables to store data in a computer's memory. Numeric variables are for storing numbers, and string variables are for storing numbers, letters, or symbols. A LET statement tells the computer to store data in a variable.

VOCABULARY

Match each item in the left column with the correct item on the right.

a. program	1. Translates BASIC into 1's and 0's
b. language processor	2. Rules of grammar for a computer language
c. syntax	3. A place in RAM for storing data
d. variable	4. A set of instructions for a computer

REVIEW QUESTIONS

1. How do computer languages save time and effort for programmers?
2. What is the difference between a logic error and a syntax error?
3. What is the difference between program mode and immediate mode?

DISCUSSION QUESTION

Do you think that most "computer errors" are actually the result of mistakes that were made by people?

PROJECTS

Try each of the following statements on the computer. Before entering each one, see if you can predict what the result will be. Notice what happens if you make a typing mistake. What message does the computer print? Does the computer give you an error message for every mistake? What about arithmetic mistakes or spelling mistakes inside quotation marks?

```
PRINT "GOOD WORK!"
PRINT 7
PRINT 8+3
PRINT 89+33+9
PRINT 400*10
PRINT 660/80
PRINT "5*8"
```

Enter the program below. Remember to type NEW and to put a line number before each statement. If you make a mistake, retype the line.

```
10 PRINT "ADD 2 AND 2"
20 PRINT 2+2
30 END
```

Now type these commands in order: `1.RUN; 2.LIST; 3.RUN; 4. NEW; 5. LIST; 6. RUN.`

Enter the program again. This time, add a line 5 with a REM statement in it. Then run and list the program.

Add line 15 to the program.

```
15 PRINT "AND PRINT THE
   ANSWER"
```

List and run the program. Delete line 15 from the program. List and run it.

Type NEW. Then enter the program to set up and print a variable.

```
10 LET A=8
20 PRINT A
30 END
```

Run the program. Now change line 10 to set A equal to different numbers. Each time, run the program again.

Type NEW. Enter the program and run it. Then change line 10 to assign a different name to NA$ and run it again.

```
10 LET NA$="RONALD ROBOT"
20 PRINT "MY NAME IS: ";NA$
30 END
```

Change the program to include a number variable. Then add a line to say "MY AGE IS: " and print the numeric variable.

Further Practice

Go back to the sample screens in the chapter and reproduce them on your computer.

Make a list of all the BASIC keywords in this chapter and tell what they do.

Enrichment

Enter this on your computer: PRINT 9999*99999999. Does the answer look strange? Do some research about scientific notation.

CHAPTER TEST

Write your answers on a sheet of paper numbered 1 through 14.

MULTIPLE CHOICE

1. BASIC is a:
   a. program
   b. computer language
   c. string variable
   d. computer
2. When you type computer language on a keyboard, the computer translates what you typed into electrical impulses that represent:
   a. BASIC
   b. FORTRAN
   c. the English alphabet
   d. 0's and 1's
3. If you are working in immediate mode, entering the BASIC statement PRINT "CATS" will cause the computer to:
   a. print the word "CATS" on paper.
   b. display the word "CATS" on the screen with no quotation marks.
   c. display the word "CATS" on the screen with quotation marks.
   d. do nothing.
4. When you enter a program line, it is:
   a. stored on a disk.
   b. stored in the computer's RAM.
   c. carried out immediately by the computer.
   d. none of the above.
5. The computer processes program lines:
   a. in numerical order.
   b. only when you enter a RUN command.
   c. only if they contain no syntax errors.
   d. all of the above.
6. A variable is a:
   a. location in memory.
   b. program line.
   c. syntax error.
   d. type of output.

FILL-IN

7. To translate your instructions, a computer needs a __________ processor.
8. In BASIC, you use a __________ statement to instruct a computer to display the answer to a calculation.
9. In __________ mode, the computer can be instructed to carry out a series of instructions in a specific order.
10. A computer program consists of a series of program __________.
11. System commands go to the computer in __________ mode.
12. __________ is a command that tells the computer to display the program lines in its memory.
13. With a __________ statement, you can include notes in a program without affecting how the program runs.
14. An __________ statement tells the computer to stop running a BASIC program.

CHAPTER

4 5 6 7 8

MORE BASIC

Now that you have started programming, you may be thinking about some programs that you would like to write. In this chapter you will learn some new BASIC keywords that will make it possible for you to write more complex and interesting programs. You'll also begin to understand how games and other computer software work.

WORKING WITH VARIABLES

"HI! WHAT'S YOUR NAME?" asks the computer. You type your name—Pat—on the keyboard and press RETURN. Then the computer says, "PAT, LET'S PLAY A GAME."

This is an example of an **interactive program**. It allows you to communicate, or interact, with the computer. Let's look at a statement that enables you to write a program that will interact with you—or with anyone else who uses it.

THE INPUT STATEMENT

Remember that a variable is a location in memory in which you can store data. You have learned how to put data into a variable with the LET statement. Each time you want to change the value in the variable, you have to edit the program to change the LET statement.

It is possible to change the value of A each time a program is run without editing. To do this, an INPUT statement is used. An INPUT statement acts like a LET statement in that it sets up a variable. But the value that it stores in the variable depends on what you type on the keyboard as the program is run.

Here is how an INPUT statement containing numeric data works:

```
10 PRINT "TYPE ANY NUMBER."
20 INPUT A
30 PRINT "YOUR NUMBER IS ";
A
40 END
RUN
TYPE ANY NUMBER.
? 15
YOUR NUMBER IS 15
```

At the point that the computer has reached the INPUT statement, it prints a prompt such as a question mark on the screen and waits for the user to type a number and press RETURN. (It will wait until you type something or until you actually stop the program from running, perhaps by turning the computer off.)

If you enter 15, this is what is now stored in A in the computer's memory:

A

15

Let's run the program again and see what's in memory this time.

```
RUN
TYPE ANY NUMBER.
?100
YOUR NUMBER IS 100
```

A

100

The INPUT statement causes the computer to stop each time the program is run and wait for the user to give it a value to store in a variable.

Here is another program. What will you see if you run the program and type 5

when the computer pauses for input? If you run it again and type 6? If you run it a third time and type 150?

```
10 PRINT "TYPE A NUMBER."
20 INPUT X
30 PRINT "TWICE THAT IS "; 2*X
40 END
```

You will see 10, then 12, then 300. Each time you run the program, the value in X will change depending on what you type.

INPUT WITH STRING VARIABLES

Just as you can use the LET statement to set up a string variable, you can use the INPUT statement with string variables.

```
10 PRINT "WHAT IS YOUR NAME?"
20 INPUT A$
30 PRINT "HELLO, "; A$
40 END
RUN
WHAT IS YOUR NAME?
? JENNIFER
HELLO, JENNIFER
```

This time, the computer waits for you to type a string of characters instead of a number. Those characters can be anything that you can type on the keyboard—letters, symbols, or numbers.

Next time the program is run, what will happen if the user types "ANTHONY", "JOHN JONES, JR.", or "123#$%^456"? Each time the program is run, the computer will print "HELLO," and the current value of A$: HELLO, ANTHONY; HELLO, JOHN JONES, JR.; or HELLO, 123#$%^456.

Key Points

- The INPUT statement causes the computer to stop each time the program is run and wait for the user to enter a value to be stored in a variable.
- Each time a program is run, a different value can be stored in a variable with an INPUT statement.
- An INPUT statement can be used to set up both numeric and string variables.

Review Questions

1. Write a statement that causes the computer to pause and wait for a person's name to be typed.
2. What will this program print if the user types 5 for the first input and "DOG" for the second input?

```
10 PRINT "TYPE A NUMBER."
20 INPUT N
30 PRINT "TYPE AN ANIMAL."
40 INPUT S$
50 PRINT "I'LL GIVE THE "; S$
60 PRINT N; " PEANUTS."
70 END
```

PLANNING YOUR PROGRAMS

FLOWCHARTS

As you write longer programs, it's important to plan them in advance. You'll make fewer mistakes and you'll find it's easier to write the programs.

When you write programs it's also very important to get the steps in the right order. You have to set up a variable *before* you use it in a PRINT statement. You have to ask for input *before* you print it.

Some computer programmers use **flowcharts** to plan a program and to get the steps in the right order. A flowchart is a kind of picture or diagram of a program, showing the major steps in the program in order.

Here is what a flowchart might look like if you were programming yourself—not the computer—to cross the street:

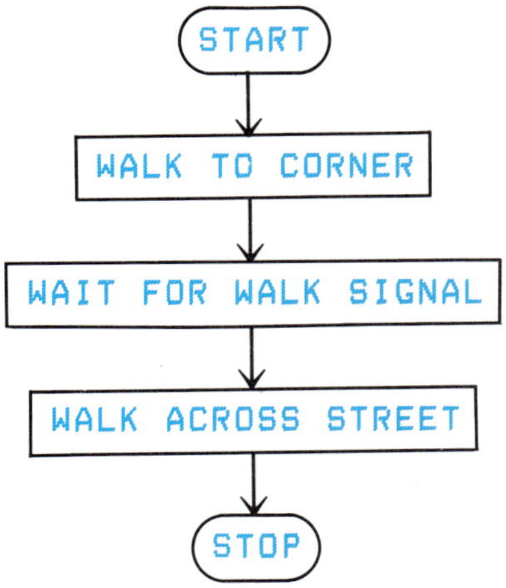

Each shape on the flowchart shows a step in the activity. The START and STOP shapes show the beginning and the end of the activity. The arrows show the order of steps—the "flow" of the program. It shows that you have to wait for the walk signal before you can cross the street, for example.

Here is what a flowchart for a simple program might look like:

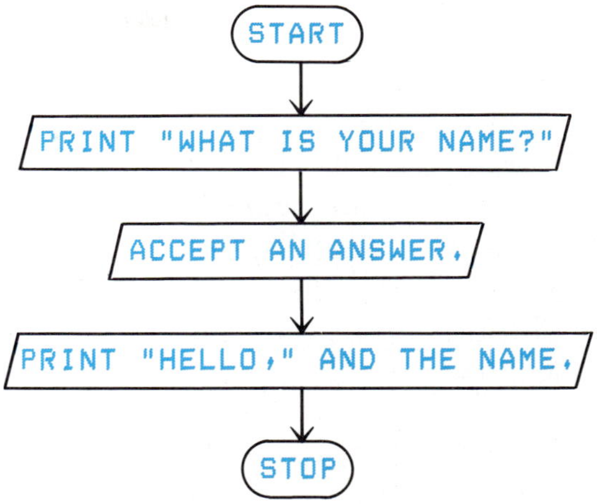

Once you have designed a flowchart, you have a guide to writing your program. You can translate each of the steps in the flowchart into one or more program statements. Here's the program that you would write using this flowchart:

```
10 PRINT "WHAT IS YOUR NAME?"
20 INPUT N$
30 PRINT "HELLO, "; N$
40 END
```

Usually, you wouldn't write a flowchart for such a simple program. But it is useful at first to do a flowchart for even very simple programs. It's a good idea to get into the habit of writing logical—and complete—plans for your programs.

FLOWCHART SYMBOLS

Several different kinds of shapes, or symbols, are used in flowcharts. The different shapes stand for different kinds of actions. These three symbols are found in most flowcharts:

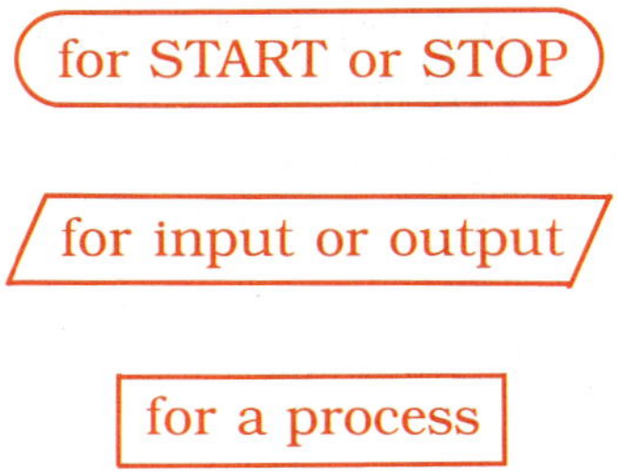

The oval START/STOP shape shows where the program begins and ends. The input/output shape—it's a parallelogram—indicates that something is input or output. Input is information that comes from outside the program, like the information typed by a user in response to an INPUT statement. Output is information that comes out of the computer's CPU. It might be displayed on the screen with a PRINT statement, stored on a disk, or typed on a printer.

The rectangular process symbol is used to indicate the internal processing that the computer makes. This includes putting a variable in memory with a LET statement.

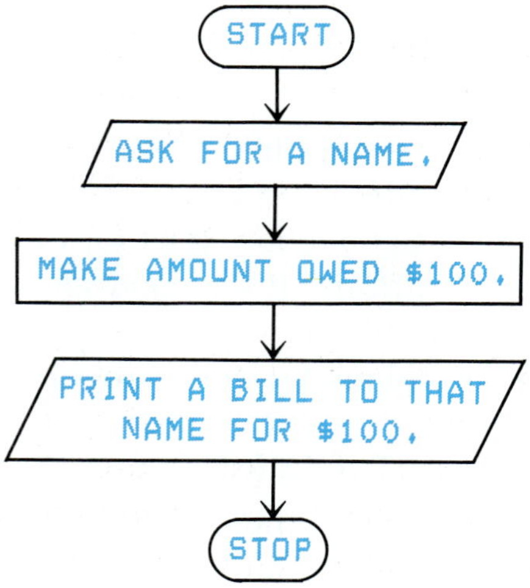

Each step of this flowchart can be written as one BASIC statement. For example, you would take step three, "MAKE AMOUNT OWED $100", and turn it into the statement LET A = 100.

Key Points

- A flowchart is a diagram or picture of a program that shows the major steps in the program in order. A flowchart helps you plan your program before you write it so that you remember all the steps and do them in the correct order.
- In a flowchart you use different shapes for different actions. Three of these are the START/STOP shape (oval), the input/output shape (parallelogram), and the process shape (rectangle).

Review Questions

1. What does this shape represent on a flowchart?

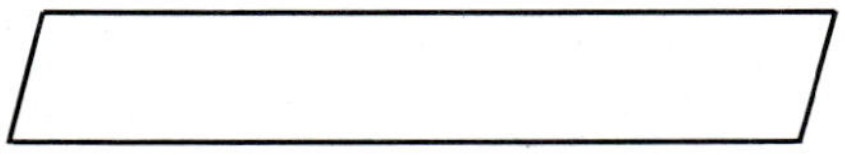

2. Write a flowchart for a program that asks for a number and prints it on the screen.

DECISION MAKING IN A PROGRAM

Imagine that you're playing a geography game on your computer. The message on the screen says, "WHAT'S THE CAPITAL OF NEBRASKA?" You enter "LINCOLN". Now the computer must tell you that your answer was right or that it was wrong. How does the computer make a choice of what action to take? One way is with an IF...THEN statement.

THE IF...THEN STATEMENT

An IF...THEN statement causes the computer to look at an expression, such as B=6 or B$="BILLY BUDD". The action that the computer takes next depends on whether the expression is true or false. The different actions are referred to as different **branches** of a program.

In an IF...THEN statement, the expression right after the IF is a condition. The branch the computer takes depends on whether the condition is true or false.

Here's how an IF...THEN statement looks in a program:

```
10 PRINT "WHAT IS 5+5?"
20 INPUT A
30 IF A=10 THEN PRINT "RIGHT!"
40 END
```

Line 30 contains the IF...THEN statement. Notice that the words IF and THEN appear in the line. The computer is told in that line to look at the value in A. *If* it is 10 the computer will go on to the rest of the line and *then* print 'RIGHT!" Let's see what happens when the program is run and 10 is typed.

```
RUN
WHAT IS 5+5?
? 10
RIGHT!
```

After the answer was entered, the computer checked the value in A. It was 10. The computer went on to do the rest of the IF...THEN statement. It printed the message "RIGHT!"

What would have happened if the user hadn't typed 10?

```
RUN
WHAT IS 5+5?
? 5
```

When A is 5, the computer does not print "RIGHT!" It only prints "RIGHT!" *if* the value in the variable equals 10. So the computer went to the next line in the program. The computer is said to "fall through" to the next line. In this case the next line was an END statement, and so the program ended.

BRANCHES IN FLOWCHARTS

In flowcharts, diamond-shaped boxes, called decision boxes, are used for IF...THEN statements. Different points on the diamond stand for different decisions that the computer can make. Here is the flowchart for the program you've just looked at:

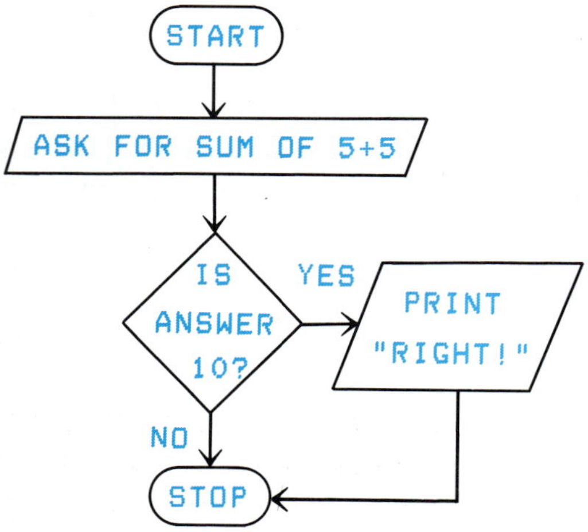

Look at the two arrows coming out of the decision box. If the answer to the question in the decision box is yes, the program flow goes one way. If the answer is no, it goes another way. In one direction it prints "RIGHT!" before the program ends. In the other direction the program just ends.

Who is answering the question in the decision box? Is it the user? No, it isn't. The computer decides if the answer to the question in the decision box is yes or no, true or false.

COMPARISONS

When checking the value in a numeric variable, four types of comparisons can be made:

= means "equal to"
> means "greater than"
< means "less than"
<> means "not equal to"

Here's how IF...THEN statements are used to make these comparisons:

```
IF A=100 THEN PRINT "OK"
```
(prints "OK" when A is equal to 100)
```
IF A>100 THEN PRINT "OK"
```
(prints "OK" when A is greater than 100—such as 101)
```
IF A<100 THEN PRINT "OK"
```
(prints "OK" when A is less than 100—such as 95)
```
IF A<>100 THEN PRINT "OK"
```
(prints "OK" when A is not 100)

MORE ELABORATE BRANCHES

The programs that you have been looking at print something on one branch of the program and simply end on the other branch. Here is a flowchart of a program that won't end immediately on either branch:

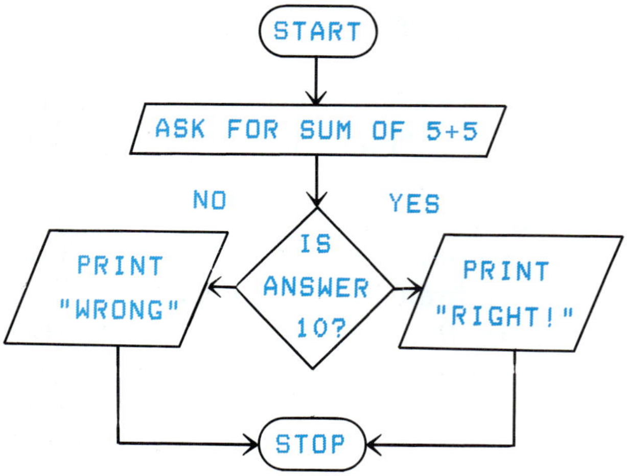

Any number that the user types will either be 10 or a number other than 10. The computer has a branch with a message for any number that the user types. This is what the program written from this flowchart looks like:

```
10 PRINT "HOW MUCH IS 5+5?"
20 INPUT N
30 IF N=10 THEN PRINT "RIGHT!"
40 IF N<>10 THEN PRINT "WRONG"
50 END
RUN
HOW MUCH IS 5+5?
?6
WRONG
```

Here the user typed a number that didn't equal 10, so the computer printed the response called for in line 40. This is the left-hand branch of the flowchart.

Look back at the other program (page 113) in this section on decision making. Can you add a line to this program so whatever the user types, the computer prints a response?

Here is a program that prints different messages depending on whether the answer is correct, too large, or too small.

```
10 PRINT "HOW MUCH IS 5+5?"
20 INPUT N
30 IF N=10 THEN PRINT "RIGHT!"
40 IF N<10 THEN PRINT "TOO LOW"
45 IF N>10 THEN PRINT "TOO HIGH"
50 END
RUN
HOW MUCH IS 5+5?
?6
TOO LOW
```

How would you have drawn the flowchart for this program? The flowchart needs two different decision boxes. One judges whether the answer is correct. The other judges whether a wrong answer is too high or too low.

Follow the branches of the flowchart with your finger for an input of 10, an input of 5, and an input of 50. Can you find the path through the program for each input?

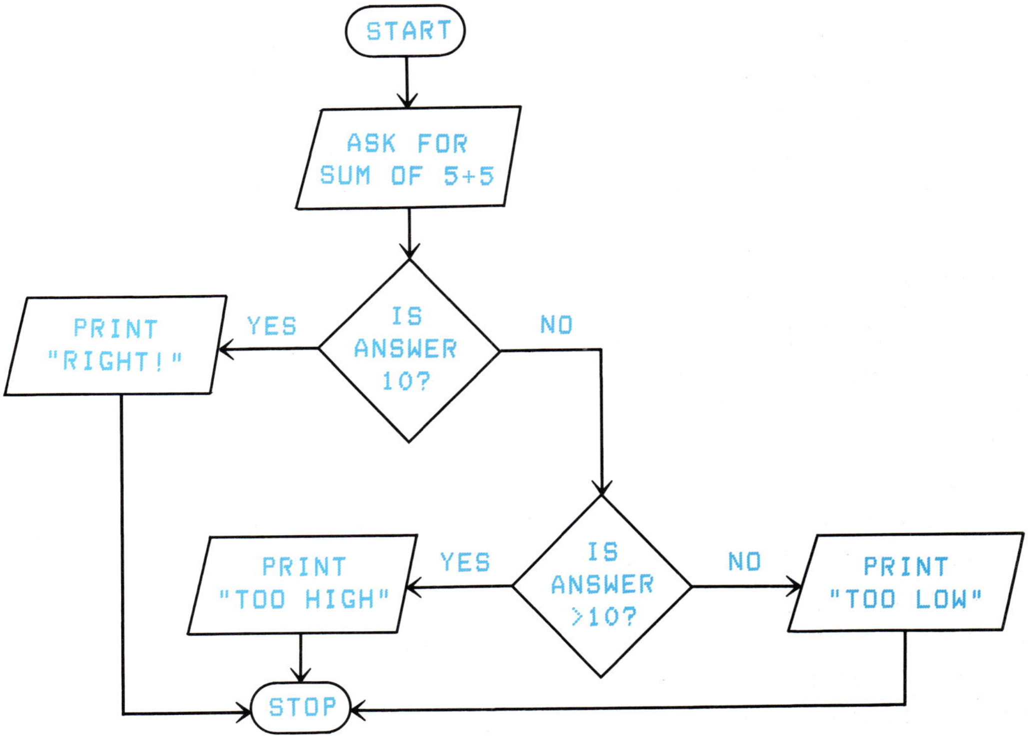

IF...THEN WITH STRING VARIABLES

Now that you know how to use the IF...THEN statement with numeric variables, let's see how you can use it with string variables. When you use the IF...THEN statement with string variables, you'll be using the = and < > signs for comparison. The computer will simply be deciding whether or not one string of characters is equal to another.

This is what a statement will look like:

IF A$ = "TRIGGER" THEN PRINT "RIGHT"

Here's how that statement would look in a program:

```
10 PRINT "NAME ROY ROGERS'S HORSE."
20 INPUT Z$
30 IF Z$="TRIGGER" THEN PRINT "RIGHT"
40 IF Z$<>"TRIGGER" THEN PRINT "WRONG"
50 END
RUN
NAME ROY ROGERS'S HORSE.
?LASSIE
WRONG
```

The IF...THEN statement compares the string in the variable Z$, character by character, with the string in the program line. The computer will decide that the two strings are equal only if every character is the same. If the user types "TRIG" or "_TRIGGER" or "Trigger", the computer won't consider that equal to "TRIGGER".

Key Points

• With an IF...THEN statement, the computer looks at an expression and takes different actions depending on whether the expression is true or false. The IF...THEN statement can be used with both string and numeric variables.

• The diamond-shaped box in a flowchart indicates a decision that is to be made. When the computer reaches a decision point in a program, it decides whether the answer to a question is yes or no, and it then follows the branch for that answer.

• The symbol = means "equal to," > means "greater than," < means "less than," and < > means "not equal to."

Review Questions

1. Write a statement that will instruct the computer to print "PANCAKE" if R is 9.
2. Write a statement that will instruct the computer to print "KING TUT" if A$ is "MARY JANE".
3. Look at this program:

```
10 PRINT "TYPE A NUMBER>8"
20 INPUT A
30 IF A>8 THEN PRINT "GOOD"
40 IF A<8 THEN PRINT "SORRY"
50 END
```

   What will the computer print if the user types 7? 28? 8?
4. Write a flowchart for a program to ask someone's name and print "HI" if that name is "SUSAN". Then write the program.

JUMPS IN A PROGRAM

THE GOTO STATEMENT

What do you think happens when the computer reaches line 20?

```
10 PRINT "THE QUICK BROWN FOX"
20 GOTO 40
30 PRINT "SUDDENLY"
40 PRINT "JUMPS OVER THE DOG."
50 END
```

Did you guess that the computer would jump to line 40? The GOTO statement in line 20 tells the computer to go to line 40. The computer will skip over any statements between line 20 and line 40. Then it will go on from line 40. This is what the program will print when you run it:

```
RUN
THE QUICK BROWN FOX
JUMPS OVER THE DOG.
```

The computer skipped the line between lines 20 and 40. Therefore, it did not print the word "SUDDENLY".

The GOTO statement causes the computer to skip to the line number called for in the statement. GOTO is not conditional.

When you write a GOTO statement, you must tell the computer what line number to go to. For example, GOTO 40 means "go to line 40," and GOTO 2000 means "go to line 2000." Of course, you must have a line 40 or a line 2000 in the program so that the computer has some place to go. Otherwise, it will give you an error message when you try to run it.

LOOPS

Here is a GOTO statement that sends the computer back to an earlier line in the program. What do you think will happen when this program is run?

```
10 PRINT "BANANAS"
20 GOTO 10
30 END
```

The computer would print "BANANAS" forever! The only way to stop this program is to reset the computer or turn it off.

The program will keep running and printing because of line 20. Line 10 prints a word. Line 20 sends the computer back to line 10 to print the word again. When the computer finishes printing, it goes on to line 20. Line 20 sends it back again. The computer will never get past line 20 to reach the end.

When the computer goes back to, or repeats, a part of the program, this is called a **loop**. When the loop never ends, it is called an **endless loop**.

```
10 PRINT "HELLO"
20 GOTO 10
30 END
```

There are many situations in which you might want to repeat one section of a program—or even the whole program itself. But usually you don't want to repeat it forever. You can control a loop with an IF...THEN statement.

Here, lines 15 and 17 have been added to the program:

```
10 PRINT "HELLO"
15 INPUT Z$
17 IF Z$="GOOD-BYE" THEN GOTO 30
20 GOTO 10
30 END
```

Line 15 asks for input. Line 17 checks that input with an IF...THEN statement. If the condition in line 17 is met, the computer skips to line 30 and the program ends.

Let's run the program twice. The first time, the user types "GOOD-BYE". The program ends.

```
RUN
HELLO
?GOOD-BYE
```

The second time, the user types several responses, and "HELLO" is repeated.

```
RUN
HELLO
?HOW ARE YOU?
HELLO
?HELLO TO YOU
HELLO
?GOOD-BYE
```

You have seen the IF...THEN statement used with PRINT and GOTO statements. You can use the IF...THEN statement with any BASIC statement. These are all possible uses of IF...THEN:

- `IF A=5 THEN LET C=A`
- `IF A$="OK" THEN LET C=10`
- `IF A=10 THEN GOTO 1000`
- `IF B$="OK" THEN END`

Here is a program that asks for the answer to a problem over and over until the user gets it right. When the answer is correct, the program will end.

```
10 PRINT "WHAT IS 2+2?"
20 INPUT A
30 IF A=4 THEN GOTO 60
40 PRINT "NO, TRY AGAIN."
50 GOTO 10
60 PRINT "GOOD"
70 END
RUN
WHAT IS 2+2?
?3

NO, TRY AGAIN.
WHAT IS 2+2?
?4

GOOD
```

What happened when the user typed 3 for the input? The value of A was not equal to 4, so the computer continued to line 40. At line 50 it was sent back to line 10, and it asked the question again.

What happened when the user typed 4? The expression A = 4 in line 30 was true, so the computer skipped to line 60.

There are several ways to program a loop. Look at this program:

```
10 PRINT "WHAT IS 2+2?"
20 INPUT A
30 IF A<>4 THEN GOTO 60
40 PRINT "GOOD"
50 END
60 PRINT "NO, TRY AGAIN."
70 GOTO 10
```

This program produces the same result as the previous one. Here, when the answer is 4, the expression A < >4 in line 30 is false, and the computer continues to line 40 and then to line 50, where the program instructs the computer to stop the run. When the answer is a number other than 4, the expression in line 30 is true, and the computer goes to line 60 and then to line 70. Line 70 sends the computer back to line 10.

Key Points

- The GOTO statement causes the computer to skip to the line number called for in the statement.
- A GOTO statement can send the computer forward or backward in a program.
- Loops in programs cause the computer to repeat all or part of the program. When used with an IF...THEN statement, the loop repeats until a particular condition is met.

Review Questions

1. Write a statement for line 10 that will cause the computer to skip to line 100. Then write a statement for line 30 that will make the computer skip to line 15.
2. Write a statement for line 20 that will cause the computer to skip to line 50 whenever T is 9.
3. Write a statement for line 80 so that the computer will skip to line 10 whenever E$ is not "ADA LOVELACE".
4. Write two program lines that create an endless loop. The computer should print "SAY UNCLE." in each loop.
5. Add an INPUT statement and an IF...THEN statement to end the loop when the user types "UNCLE".

MORE LOOPS

THE FOR...NEXT LOOP

Sometimes you want to repeat part of a program only a certain number of times. Perhaps you want to give the user only three tries to add 2 and 2, or perhaps you want to send a bill each month for twelve months. Using a FOR...NEXT loop is one method by which you can set the number of times that a loop will run.

Look at the first two lines in this program. They form a FOR...NEXT loop.

```
10 FOR X=1 TO 3
20 NEXT X
30 END
```

Line 10 starts the loop. Line 20 ends it. Any lines that you put between lines 10 and 20 will be part of the loop.

Let's put line 15 in the loop and run the program.

```
10 FOR X=1 TO 3
15 PRINT "A CLOVER HAS 3 LEAVES."
20 NEXT X
30 END
RUN
A CLOVER HAS 3 LEAVES.
A CLOVER HAS 3 LEAVES.
A CLOVER HAS 3 LEAVES.
```

The computer printed "A CLOVER HAS 3 LEAVES." three times. Notice that line 10 said "1 TO 3". The computer counted from 1 to 3 and printed the sentence each time. What would happen if line 10 were "FOR X = 1 TO 100"?

How does the computer count the right number of loops? Line 10 indicates that the variable X will increase from 1 to 3. The end of the loop, "NEXT X," tells the computer to increase the value of X by 1 each time it reaches that line. When X becomes greater than 3, the loop will end and the program will continue from there.

Let's see what happens in the variable X. Line 10 says that X starts at 1.

X

| 1 |

The computer prints "A CLOVER HAS 3 LEAVES." Line 20 says "NEXT X". X increases by 1.

X

| 2 |

The computer goes back to line 10. It prints "A CLOVER HAS 3 LEAVES." It comes to line 20. Line 20 says "NEXT X". X increases by 1.

X

| 3 |

The computer goes to line 10. It prints "A CLOVER HAS 3 LEAVES." It comes to line 20. X increases by 1.

X

| 4 |

Now X is 4. The loop ends and the computer moves to the next line.

In a FOR...NEXT loop, the FOR statement sets up a variable and indicates its starting and ending values. The NEXT statement tells the computer to increase the variable and return to the beginning of the loop if the variable's value is not beyond the ending value.

This program will show what is in the variable on each loop, because line 20 tells the computer to print the value in E. The program has been run once.

```
10 FOR E=1 TO 5
20 PRINT E
30 NEXT E
40 END
RUN
1
2
3
4
5
```

What will the loop at the top of the next page cause the computer to print?

```
10 FOR J=1 TO 50
20 PRINT "A LOOP"
30 NEXT J
40 PRINT "ENOUGH LOOPS"
```

The computer will print "A LOOP" 50 times. At this point the FOR...NEXT loop will be completed, and the computer will continue to line 40. Then it will print "ENOUGH LOOPS".

The FOR line of the loop can start the variable at any number and cause it to end at any number.

```
FOR K=10 TO 20...NEXT K
```
(counts from 10 to 20)

```
FOR P=5 TO 500...NEXT P
```
(counts from 5 to 500)

```
FOR J=2 TO 10...NEXT J
```
(counts from 2 to 10)

How many loops are there in "FOR J = 2 TO 10...NEXT J"? There are nine complete loops—a loop when J is 2, when J is 3, 4, 5, 6, 7, 8, 9, and 10.

TIME-DELAY LOOPS

Here is a loop that doesn't print anything or do anything else on the screen:

```
10 FOR X=1 TO 2500
20 NEXT X
```

The only thing this loop does is to take some time to be completed. It takes the computer time to carry out every statement. The computer only appears to do something instantaneously because it is so very fast. It will take the computer perhaps a second or two to go through this loop 2500 times. This kind of delay can be useful in a program where you want to leave a pause between screen displays.

THE STEP FUNCTION

The computer doesn't have to count loops by 1. It can count them by 2's or 3's or 4's or any other increment. The STEP function in the FOR...NEXT loop tells the computer what number to count by.

```
10 FOR X=1 TO 9 STEP 2
20 PRINT X
30 NEXT X
40 END
RUN
1
3
5
7
9
```

Each time the computer reached line 20, it printed the value in X. Each time the computer reached line 30—the NEXT line—it added 2 to the value in X.

The STEP function tells the computer how much to add to the variable when it reaches the NEXT statement.

You can step forward or backward with the STEP function.

```
10 FOR X=10 TO 1 STEP -1
20 PRINT X
30 NEXT X
40 PRINT "LIFTOFF!!!"
50 END
RUN
10
9
8
7
6
5
4
3
2
1
LIFTOFF!!!
```

Notice that X started at 10 and went down to 1 by steps of minus 1. Just remember to put the starting number first.

EXITING FROM A LOOP

Remember that you can interrupt an endless loop with an IF...THEN statement. You can also limit the number of times that a FOR...NEXT loop runs. Here is a loop that runs 3 times, or until the user enters a correct answer.

```
5 FOR T=1 TO 3
10 PRINT "WHAT IS 2+2?"
20 INPUT A
30 IF A=4 THEN LET T=3
35 NEXT T
40 END
RUN
WHAT IS 2+2?
?3
WHAT IS 2+2?
?2
WHAT IS 2+2?
?1
```

In this run the program ran through the loop 3 times.

```
RUN
WHAT IS 2+2?
?4
```

This time, the user typed 4 on the first loop. The variable T was set to 3 by the IF...THEN statement—"IF A = 4 THEN LET T = 3". When the NEXT statement was reached, 1 was added to T, T became equal to 4, and the loop ended.

Key Points

- In a FOR...NEXT loop, the FOR statement sets up a variable and indicates its starting and ending values. The NEXT statement tells the computer to increase the variable and return to the beginning of the loop if the variable's value is not beyond the ending value.
- Using a FOR...NEXT loop that does not include another statement simply causes a time delay in the program.
- The STEP function tells the computer how much to add to the variable when it reaches the NEXT statement. Without a STEP function, the computer will increase the variable by 1.

Review Questions

1. Write three program lines that form a loop that will print "THREE STATEMENTS" 3 times.
2. How many times will this loop print "FOUR"?

```
10 FOR D=6 TO 22 STEP 4
20 PRINT "FOUR"
30 NEXT D
```

REVIEW & APPLICATION

SUMMARY

- Creating a flowchart before you write a long program can help you to write your instructions in the correct order.
- Flowcharts use different shapes to represent different actions to be taken. They use arrows between the shapes to show the order in which the steps will be done.
- Using INPUT statements, you can create an interactive program with numeric or string variables that change each time the program is run.
- With IF...THEN statements you can write programs that cause computers to make decisions.
- When checking a number against the value in a numeric variable, the computer can determine whether the number is equal to, greater than, less than, or not equal to the value. When comparing a string of characters with the data in a string variable, the computer can decide if they are equal or not equal.
- With a GOTO statement you can direct the computer to a specific line in the program. To tell the computer to repeat part of a program, you create a loop. You can use an IF...THEN statement to prevent the loop from repeating endlessly.
- A FOR...NEXT loop causes the computer to repeat part of the program a specific number of times. FOR...NEXT loops can be used to leave pauses in programs.

VOCABULARY

Match each item in the left column with the correct item on the right.

a. flowchart	1. Repetition of program lines
b. branches	2. Diagram of a program
c. interactive program	3. A statement that tells the computer to display a prompt
d. loop	4. A statement that gives the computer a choice
e. IF...THEN	5. Two or more actions a computer can take
f. INPUT	6. Allows user to communicate with computer

REVIEW QUESTIONS

1. What are two different statements that you can use to set up a variable? How do they differ from each other?
2. What would be the output of the following program?

```
10 FOR X=500 TO 5 STEP -5
20 PRINT X
30 NEXT X
40 END
```

DISCUSSION QUESTION

Do you think the usefulness of computers in business would be as great as it is if it wasn't possible to write interactive programs? Why or why not? Would computers be as useful in education?

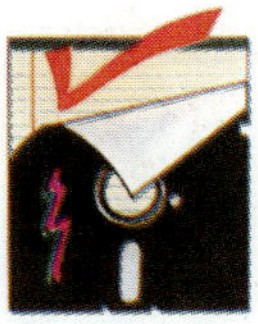

P R O J E C T S

C Enter this program.

```
10 PRINT "TYPE A NUMBER"
20 INPUT A
30 PRINT A
40 END
```

Run the program several times using different inputs. What happens when you enter a word?

C Type NEW, enter, and run the program. Try different inputs. What happens if you type a number?

```
10 PRINT "WHAT'S YOUR NAME?"
20 INPUT N$
30 PRINT "HELLO ";N$
40 END
```

C Type NEW. Then enter a program that uses a FOR...NEXT loop and instructs the computer to print LOOP ten times.

C Enter and run this program:

```
10 FOR X=1 TO 4
20 PRINT "TEST"
30 NEXT X
40 END
```

Now change line 20 to

```
20 PRINT "TEST";
```

How are the two outputs different?

C What do you think the output from this program will be? Type NEW and enter and run it.

```
10 GOTO 40
20 PRINT "DIFFICULT,"
30 GOTO 140
40 PRINT "COMPUTERS ";
50 GOTO 100
60 FOR X=1 TO 3
70 PRINT "VERY ";
80 NEXT X
90 GOTO 180
100 PRINT "CAN BE ";
110 GOTO 20
120 PRINT "THEY CAN ";
130 GOTO 160
140 PRINT "BUT"
150 GOTO 120
160 PRINT "ALSO BE "
170 GOTO 60
180 PRINT "MUCH FUN."
190 END
```

Further Practice

C Go through the sample screens in this chapter and reproduce them on your computer.

D Remember that list you made of BASIC keywords? Well, now you know a lot more keywords. Add them to the list.

D Write a flowchart for a program that asks for a name and prints HELLO if the name is Cindy.

Enrichment

D Different machines have different rules for naming variables. Find out what they are for the school's computer(s).

CHAPTER TEST

Write your answers on a sheet of paper numbered 1 through 13.

MATCHING

1. Match the program statement on the left with the computer action on the right.

a. INPUT	1. goes to a line
b. IF...THEN	2. makes a decision
c. GOTO	3. repeats a loop
d. FOR...NEXT	4. displays a prompt

MULTIPLE CHOICE

2. Which of the following symbols can be used to tell a computer to compare a number with the value in a numeric variable?
   - a. =
   - b. >
   - c. <>
   - d. <
   - e. all of the above
   - f. none of the above
3. A flowchart:
   - a. helps you avoid syntax errors
   - b. helps you write the steps of a program in the correct order
   - c. shows you how each statement should be worded
   - d. all of the above
4. A rectangle in a program flowchart represents:
   - a. input or output
   - b. output only
   - c. processing
   - d. a decision
5. An endless loop:
   - a. can be stopped by the user's input
   - b. can be used to create a brief time delay in a program
   - c. causes the program to stop
   - d. causes the computer to repeat a part of the program until the computer is turned off or reset
6. A STEP function in a FOR...NEXT loop tells the computer:
   - a. to repeat the loop forever
   - b. what value is in a variable
   - c. to go to the end of the program
   - d. how much to add to the variable

FILL-IN

7. When a program contains an INPUT statement, the ____________ determines the value in the variable.
8. A flowchart is a diagram that shows the major steps of a ____________ in order.
9. The ____________ in a flowchart show the order in which the steps occur.
10. The ____________ in a flowchart represent different kinds of actions.
11. The ____________ of a program are the directions a computer can take.
12. In a flowchart, a ____________ represents an IF...THEN statement.
13. If a program includes the statement "GOTO 80", the program must also include a ____________.

CHAPTER

5 6 7 8 9

TOP-DOWN PROGRAMMING

PROGRAM STRUCTURE

FLOWCHARTS

You've been writing flowcharts before you write your programs. This helps ensure that you get all the steps into your program and get them in the right order. Remember that in writing a flowchart you plan the logical flow of your program. Once the flowchart is written, you can translate it into a program by writing one or more statements for each step in the flowchart.

However, when you begin to plan more complex programs, you'll find that the flowcharts also become more complex. When you have a great many steps and a great many branches, you simply can't find a place for all of them on the flowchart. This makes it very hard to check the flowchart you've written to be sure that you haven't left anything out. To handle more complex programs, you need another way of planning them.

MODULAR DESIGN

In engineering, education, programming, and other fields, a **module** is a self-contained unit that performs one specific task which is needed to accomplish a larger task. For example, the word *module* is used in the space program to refer to a part of a spaceship that performs a specific task. A lunar landing module lands on the moon. A power module provides power to the ship in space. A waste-disposal module gets rid of garbage. All of these modules are necessary for getting spaceships to the moon and back.

In a computer program, a module is a self-contained part of the program that performs a specific programming task. For example, a program might have an input module and a print module. A program that is divided into modules in the planning and programming stages has a **modular design**.

A modular program is said to have a **top-down structure** because when you plan it, you start at the "top" with the most general module and work your way "down" to include all the modules that make up that module. This allows you to break a complex program into parts to make programming more efficient and easier.

Let's see what top-down modular design looks like for an activity, like playing a baseball game.

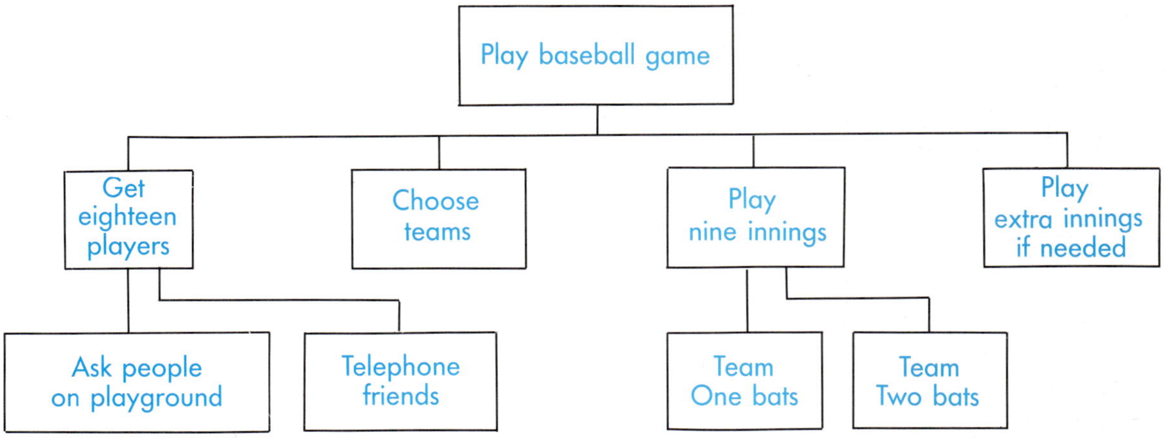

The top module, "Play baseball game," is the main task. The four modules under that module show four tasks that must be done in order to accomplish the main task. You can see that these modules look like items you might put on a flowchart.

Every module at every level of the design is part of the modules above it. Each is a task that is a part of the larger task. For example, to play baseball you must have eighteen players. And to get eighteen players you must call or ask friends to play. "Ask people on playground" involves looking for people the right age, because you don't want players under the age of nine. To ask someone to play, you have to approach that person. You have to ask a question. You have to listen to the response. You may have to offer the person a position to play.

How far you break the modules down is determined by how much information you need in order to understand the task that you want to accomplish. At some point the steps that make up a module will be obvious. For example, it would not make sense to break "Ask a question" down into "Open your mouth," "Engage your vocal cords," and so on. You don't have to break that module down further.

PROGRAM MODULES

Suppose that you are going to use a computer to give a quiz. Here is a modular design for the program. You start with the main module and the three modules that make it up. The three tasks that you have to do to give the quiz are ask the questions, check the answers, and grade the quiz. If this were a flowchart, you would know that this is the order in which you would carry out the tasks. You would ask all the questions, check all the answers, and then give a grade. However, in a modular design you can't necessarily tell the order of steps from the modules. You might ask a question and check it, then ask another question and check it, and so on. It doesn't matter. You have the modules that are needed to do the task in any order.

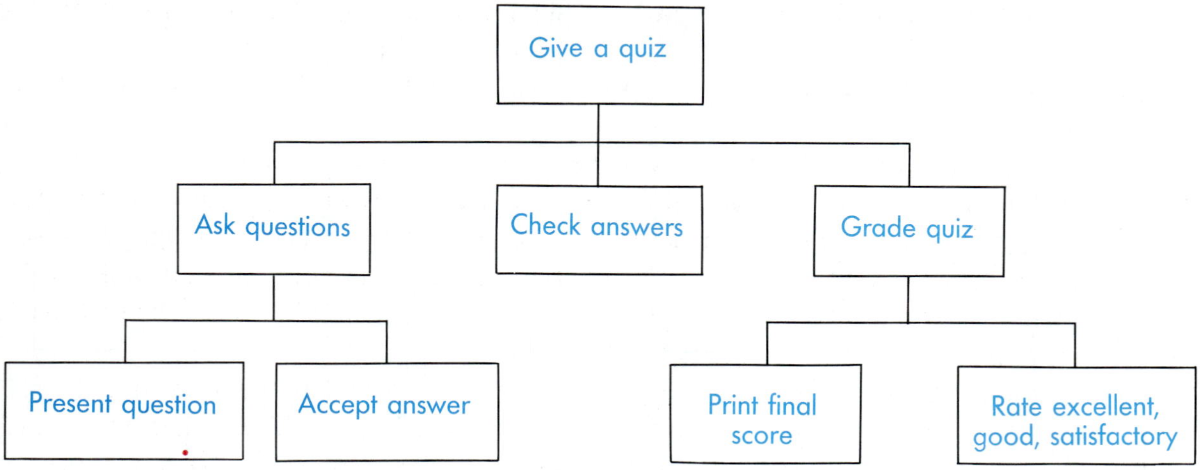

Look at the module "Ask questions" and the two modules that are part of it. Does this look familiar? It should, because you have made flowcharts for this kind of task. This is the point in top-down design at which you can use a flowchart. You can make a flowchart of an individual module and the modules that make it up. The flowchart for the "Ask questions" module would look like this:

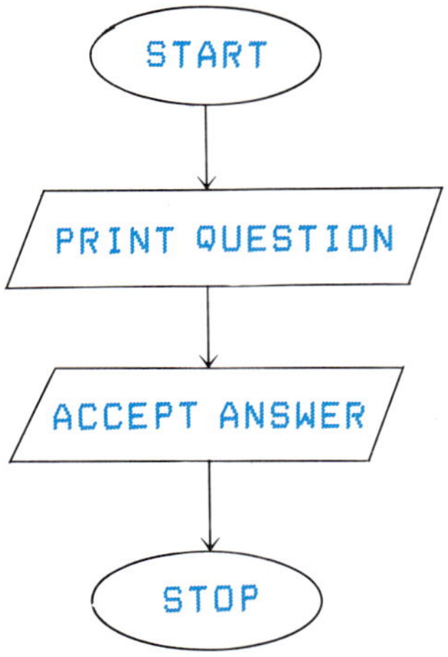

Flowcharts can be used when planning the parts of a program that correspond to specific modules in your modular design.

Key Points

- Flowcharts help you to get the steps of your program in order. However, flowcharts for complex programs can become complicated to understand.
- Top-down structure, or modular design, helps you to plan, write, and debug programs more easily.
- A program module is a self-contained part of the program that performs a specific task. In a top-down structure, it is part of the module above it. In turn, it is made up of modules that are lower down in the structure.
- Flowcharts can be used to help you understand the steps involved in carrying out an individual module.

Review Questions

1. Why is modular programming also called top-down programming?
2. How do you decide that you have broken down the modules far enough?

MODULES IN BASIC

SUBROUTINES

You have learned how to create a modular design for a complex task and how to make the individual modules in the design into flowcharts. It would be fairly easy to write BASIC programs based on each flowchart, but if you did this, you would have a lot of small, individual programs. They wouldn't work together to perform the main task. How can you solve this problem?

The answer is simple. You don't use each flowchart to write a program. Instead, you use each one to create a **subroutine**. A subroutine in a program is like a module in your design. It is self-contained, it accomplishes a task, and it can be made up of other subroutines as well.

Here is a program with a short subroutine. Lines 10 to 40 are the main program. Lines 100 and 110 make up the subroutine.

```
10 PRINT "WHAT'S YOUR FAVORITE FOOD?"
20 GOSUB 100
30 PRINT "I LIKE ";F$;", TOO."
40 STOP
100 INPUT F$
110 RETURN
```

(Lines 10–40: main program; lines 100–110: subroutine)

Look what happens when the program runs. Notice the order in which the lines are carried out.

```
RUN
WHAT'S YOUR FAVORITE FOOD?
?YOGURT
I LIKE YOGURT, TOO.
```

Although line 100 comes toward the end of the program, it is executed right after line 10. This is because line 20

```
20 GOSUB 100
```

sends the computer to the subroutine that starts at line 100. The subroutine starts by accepting an input. Line 110 returns the computer back to the statement after the GOSUB statement in the main program. Since the computer left the main program at line 20, it now continues with line 30. Therefore, the computer carries out the instructions in this order: 10, 20, 100, 110, 30, 40. It stops at line 40 because of the STOP statement in that line.

The GOSUB statement sends the computer to a subroutine. A GOSUB statement includes the line number where the subroutine starts.

The RETURN statement tells the computer that the subroutine has ended and it should return to the main program. A RETURN statement always goes at the end of the subroutine.

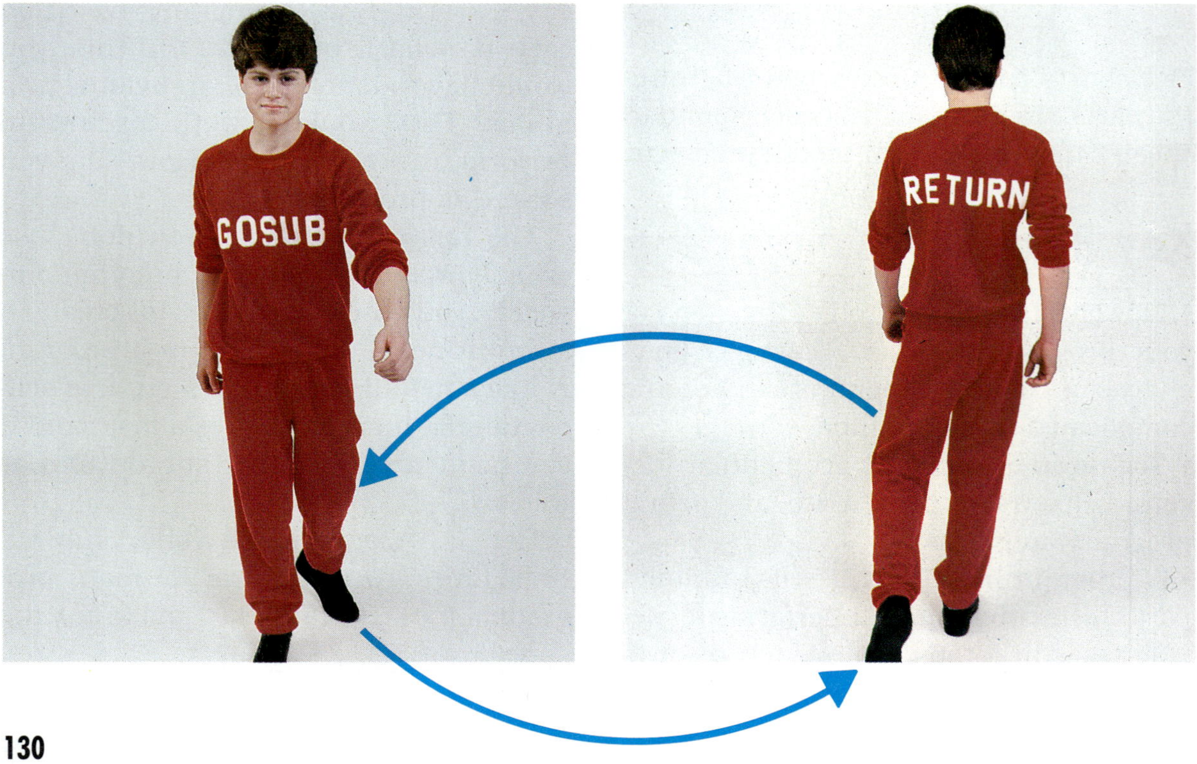

The STOP statement may be used instead of END at the end of a main program when a subroutine follows.

Here is a program that calls the same subroutine twice. Twice in this program the words "TYPE A NUMBER" and the input question mark appeared on the screen. This is because the subroutine that starts at line 200 was called twice, once from line 30 and once from line 70. Each time, line 220 sent the computer back to the correct place in the main program. The RETURN statement sends the computer back to the statement after the GOSUB statement *that called the subroutine.*

Subroutines can be very useful for performing the same task many times in a program. Using subroutines makes programming easier, since it saves your having to type the same lines over and over. A program can contain many subroutines.

```
10 REM GUESS A SQUARE ROOT                      ⎫
20 PRINT "WHAT'S THE SQUARE ROOT OF 25?"        ⎪
30 GOSUB 200                                    ⎪
40 IF A<>5 THEN PRINT "WRONG"                   ⎪
50 IF A=5 THEN PRINT "RIGHT"                    ⎬ main
60 PRINT "WHAT'S THE SQUARE ROOT OF 49?"        ⎪ program
70 GOSUB 200                                    ⎪
80 IF A<>7 THEN PRINT "WRONG"                   ⎪
90 IF A=7 THEN PRINT "RIGHT"                    ⎪
100 STOP                                        ⎭
200 PRINT "TYPE A NUMBER."                      ⎫
210 INPUT A                                     ⎬ subroutine
220 RETURN                                      ⎭
RUN
WHAT'S THE SQUARE ROOT OF 25?
TYPE A NUMBER.
?6
WRONG
WHAT'S THE SQUARE ROOT OF 49?
TYPE A NUMBER.
?7
RIGHT
```

PROGRAMMING USING A MODULAR DESIGN

STEPS TO FOLLOW

When you design and write a program in a top-down fashion, there are certain steps that you should follow. You already know the first step. This section will explain and illustrate the others.

1. Plan the program from the top down. Create a modular design starting with the main task in the top module. The modules that follow should show the steps that need to be performed in order to accomplish the main task.

2. Indicate which of the modules will be subroutines and what their beginning line numbers will be.

3. Following the modular design, write your program from the top down as well. Program the main modules, then the next lower modules, and so on.

4. Test and debug the program as you proceed. *Do not* wait until the program is complete to run and test it. Test each module as you program it.

5. To help you do steps 3 and 4, write **throw-away code** for the lower modules as you are writing the upper ones. Throw-away code consists of program lines in BASIC that fill in parts of a program so that you can test other parts. As you complete the program, you replace the throw-away code with the real program statements.

6. Explain what each subroutine does, both in the program by using REM statements and in written documentation.

Let's see how these steps are carried out in an actual program.

PROGRAMMING THE TOP MODULE

Here is the program that we began planning earlier in the chapter. The modules have been numbered to indicate which ones will be subroutines and what their beginning line numbers will be. Since the second module, "Check answers," isn't broken down any further, it is given a line number.

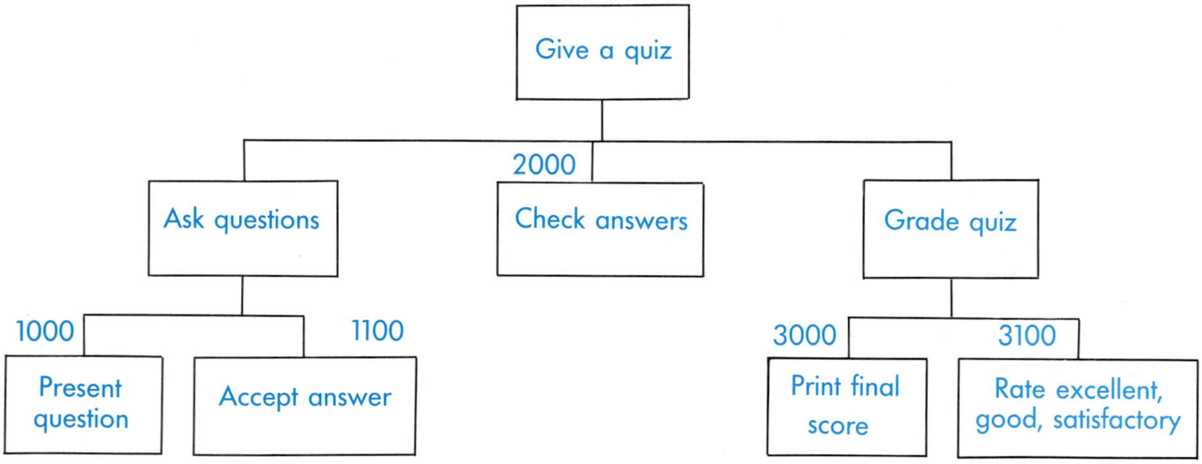

Notice that the subroutines under the first module are numbered 1000 and 1100. The next module is numbered 2000, and the next two subroutines are numbered 3000 and 3100. Numbering each module as a group makes it easier to keep track of which module your program lines belong to.

The next step is to write the program from the top down. This means writing the top module, "Give a quiz," first. Since this module consists of three lower modules, the programming code will consist of GOSUB statements that call these subroutines.

REM statements will be included in the

program to explain the purpose of the tasks that the subroutines perform. The completed program will show the flow of what is done first, what is done second, what is repeated in a loop, and so on.

The quiz will ask three questions about the state of Illinois:

1. What is the capital of Illinois?
2. What is the largest city in Illinois?
3. What lake is in northern Illinois?

Since the form of each of these questions is similar and each answer is a word or words, a loop can be used to present the questions and accept the answers. A series of three IF...THEN statements can be used to change the question and answer each time the loop runs.

Notice that extra REM statements—including some with lines of asterisks (*)—have been added to make the listing easier to read. Notice, too, the REM statements just before each GOSUB. They explain what the subroutines will do and are very similar to the labels in the modules of the design.

```
10 REM THREE QUIZ QUESTIONS
20 REM ASK QUESTIONS, CHECK ANSWERS,
30 REM AND GRADE QUIZ
40 REM Q=MAIN LOOP, S=SCORE (NUMBER RIGHT), Q$=QUESTION, A$=ANSWER,
   SA$=STUDENT ANSWER
50 REM *** BEGINNING OF MAIN PROGRAM ***
60 LET S=0
70 FOR Q=1 TO 3
80 REM SUBROUTINE--ASK QUESTION
90 GOSUB 1000
100 REM ACCEPT ANSWER
110 GOSUB 1100
120 REM SUBROUTINE--CHECK ANSWER
130 GOSUB 2000
140 NEXT Q
150 REM SUBROUTINE--GRADE QUIZ
160 GOSUB 3000
170 REM RATE SCORE
180 GOSUB 3100
190 END
200 REM *** END OF MAIN PROGRAM ***
```

When programming, it is a good idea to explain in a REM statement at the beginning of the program the type of information that will be stored in the variables you will be using. Line 60 sets the variable S (for "Score") to 0. This line is said to **initialize** the variable. Why is this necessary? Imagine that you run the completed program and get all three questions right. S will equal 3, so the computer will print your score as being 3. Then your friend runs the program. If you haven't turned the computer off, it will start the run with a value of 3 stored in the variable S. Let's say your friend gets all three questions right, too. S will equal 6, and the computer will print your friend's score as being 6!

TESTING THE TOP MODULE

As mentioned in the steps for designing and writing a top-down program, the top module should be tested before any others are written. However, if this program is run now, you will get an error message at the first GOSUB statement because line 1000 has not been written yet. You need to write throw-away code to take the place of the unwritten subroutines.

For each subroutine the code should print a message telling you that you have reached the subroutine. It should also contain a RETURN statement. The RETURN statement is probably the only part of the subroutine that will remain when the real code is written. This is what the subroutines 1000, 1100, 2000, 3000, and 3100 might look like in throw-away code:

```
1000  PRINT "QUESTION "; Q
1099  RETURN
1100  PRINT "ANSWER "; Q
1199  RETURN
2000  PRINT "CHECK "; Q
2030  PRINT "SCORE "; Q
2099  RETURN
3000  PRINT "SCORE = "; S
3099  RETURN
3100  PRINT "EVALUATE SCORE"
3199  RETURN
```

Notice that the variable Q from the FOR ...NEXT loop is used to count the questions and answers. Now look at what the output is when the program is run.

```
RUN
QUESTION 1
ANSWER 1
CHECK 1
SCORE 1
QUESTION 2
ANSWER 2
CHECK 2
SCORE 2
QUESTION 3
ANSWER 3
CHECK 3
SCORE 3
SCORE=0
EVALUATE SCORE
```

The material on the screen doesn't look anything like the final version of the program. But it tells you that your top module is working perfectly. The questions, answers, and scores are coming up in the correct order. They are followed by the final score and evaluation of the score.

Once a module has been tested and corrected, you know that any bugs that appear later will be found somewhere else in the program. This helps in locating errors.

PROGRAMMING LOWER MODULES

Next, add the questions and answers to the loop so that they can be used in the lower modules.

```
71  IF Q=1 THEN LET Q$ = "WHAT IS THE CAPITAL OF ILLINOIS?"
72  IF Q=2 THEN LET Q$ = "WHAT IS THE LARGEST CITY IN ILLINOIS?"
73  IF Q=3 THEN LET Q$ = "WHAT LAKE IS IN NORTHERN ILLINOIS?"
74  IF Q=1 THEN LET A$ = "SPRINGFIELD"
75  IF Q=2 THEN LET A$ = "CHICAGO"
76  IF Q=3 THEN LET A$ = "LAKE MICHIGAN"
```

Notice that each time the computer goes through the Q loop, the value of Q$ and A$ will change.

Note that lines 71 to 76 have *not* yet been tested. If they contain any spelling errors or any errors in BASIC, the errors will not show up until the questions are actually printed on the screen and the answers are checked.

Next, let's write the program code for the first two subroutines, "Ask question" and "Accept answer." The throw-away code will be replaced with real program statements. The only code that will remain will be the RETURN statements in lines 1099 and 1199.

```
1000 PRINT
1010 PRINT "QUESTION "; Q
1020 PRINT
1030 PRINT Q$

1100 PRINT
1110 PRINT "TYPE YOUR ANSWER."
1120 INPUT SA$
```

Now let's run the program to test these new modules. This time, part of what appears on the screen will be what the final result should be. Part will still be throw-away results.

```
RUN
QUESTION 1
WHAT IS THE CAPITAL OF ILLINOIS?
TYPE YOUR ANSWER.
?ANY ANSWER
CHECK 1
SCORE 1
```

(QUESTION 1 through TYPE YOUR ANSWER.: final result; ?ANY ANSWER: throw-away response; CHECK 1 / SCORE 1: throw-away result)

```
QUESTION 2
WHAT IS THE LARGEST CITY IN ILLINOIS?
TYPE YOUR ANSWER.
?ANY ANSWER AGAIN
CHECK 2
SCORE 2
QUESTION 3
WHAT LAKE IS IN NORTHERN ILLINOIS?
TYPE YOUR ANSWER.
?ANY ANSWER ONCE MORE
CHECK 3
SCORE 3
SCORE=0
EVALUATE SCORE
```

Notice that it doesn't matter what input is typed because the answer-check module hasn't been written yet. But you can see that the correct questions were asked each time the loop was run. You also know that the questions were typed correctly and that the subroutine that puts them on the screen is working.

Here is the program code for the subroutine "*Check answer*":

```
2000  IF SA$<>A$ THEN PRINT "INCORRECT"
2010  IF SA$<>A$ THEN GOTO 2099
2020  PRINT "CORRECT"
2030  LET S=S+1
2099  RETURN
```

If a correct answer is entered, the computer skips lines 2000 and 2010, and executes the PRINT statement in line 2020. Line 2030 tells the computer to add 1 to the current value of S. (Remember that S was set to 0 in line 60.) If you get all the answers correct, S will be 3 when you complete the program.

Now let's run the program to test the new module. Notice that the correct message prints for each given response. The score is also correct.

```
RUN

QUESTION 1

WHAT IS THE CAPITAL OF ILLINOIS?

TYPE YOUR ANSWER.
?CHICAGO
INCORRECT


QUESTION 2

WHAT IS THE LARGEST CITY IN ILLINOIS?

TYPE YOUR ANSWER.
?CHICAGO
CORRECT


QUESTION 3

WHAT LAKE IS IN NORTHERN ILLINOIS?

TYPE YOUR ANSWER.
?LAKE MICHIGAN
CORRECT

SCORE=2
EVALUATE SCORE
```

At this point you should run the program several times, answering different questions incorrectly each time. This way, you can check that the computer prints the correct message for a given response. If it doesn't, the subroutine "*Check answer*" must be checked. If it is correct, then the lines in the main module that specify the questions and answers must be checked again.

Now let's add the program code for the two final subroutines—"Print score" and "Rate score."

```
3000 PRINT "YOUR SCORE IS "; S
3100 IF S=3 THEN PRINT "SUPER!"
3110 IF S=2 THEN PRINT "GOOD."
3120 IF S<2 THEN PRINT " PRACTICE."
```

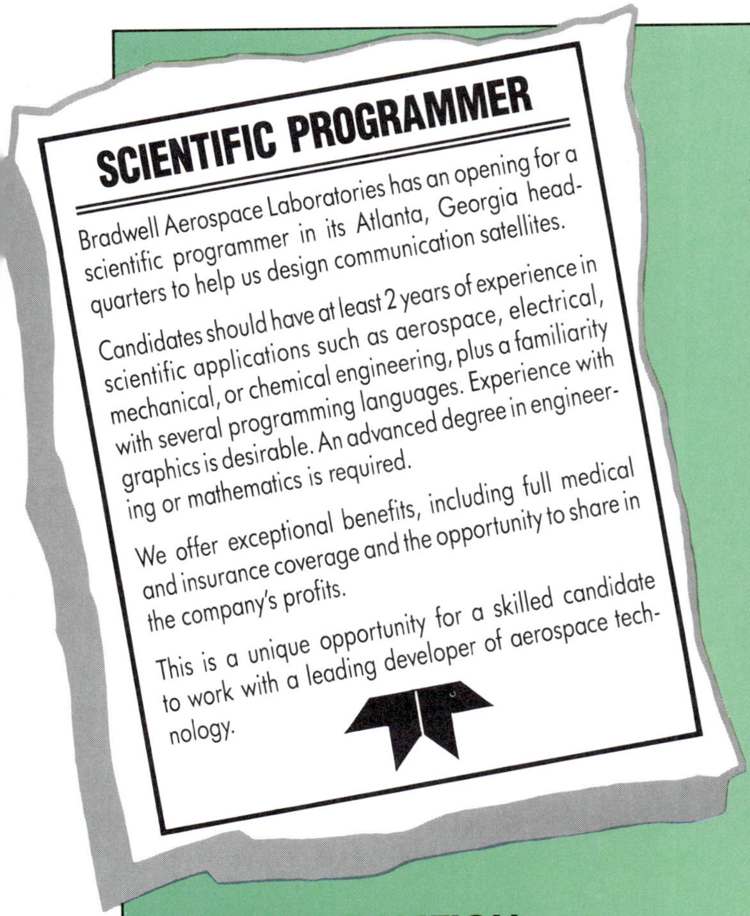
SCIENTIFIC PROGRAMMER

Bradwell Aerospace Laboratories has an opening for a scientific programmer in its Atlanta, Georgia headquarters to help us design communication satellites.

Candidates should have at least 2 years of experience in scientific applications such as aerospace, electrical, mechanical, or chemical engineering, plus a familiarity with several programming languages. Experience with graphics is desirable. An advanced degree in engineering or mathematics is required.

We offer exceptional benefits, including full medical and insurance coverage and the opportunity to share in the company's profits.

This is a unique opportunity for a skilled candidate to work with a leading developer of aerospace technology.

THAT'S MY JOB

Russell Taragan, a scientific programmer at Regional Hospital, says:

"This career allows me to pursue my interest in science. It also makes me feel like I'm doing something that helps other people, since scientific programming is important in the medical field.

"The hours are long, especially when you get involved in a complicated project and when there are deadlines to meet. On the other hand, the pay is good, and there are many areas where I can apply my skills in the future.

"The people that would do best in this field are ones with a deep interest in science or math."

MORE INFORMATION

Scientific programmers are responsible for designing, writing, testing, and debugging programs in aerospace and medical fields.... They also write program documentation and provide technical guidance to program users.... Scientific programming is a stable field of employment, supported both by government and industry.

```
LIST
10 REM THREE QUIZ QUESTIONS
20 REM ASK QUESTIONS, CHECK ANSWERS,
30 REM AND GRADE QUIZ
40 REM Q=MAIN LOOP, S=SCORE (NUMBER RIGHT), Q$=QUESTION, A$=ANSWER,
   SA$=STUDENT ANSWER
50 REM ***BEGINNING OF MAIN PROGRAM***
60 LET S=0
70 FOR Q=1 TO 3
71 IF Q=1 THEN LET Q$ = "WHAT IS THE CAPITAL OF ILLINOIS?"
72 IF Q=2 THEN LET Q$ = "WHAT IS THE LARGEST CITY IN ILLINOIS?"
73 IF Q=3 THEN LET Q$ = "WHAT LAKE IS IN NORTHERN ILLINOIS?"
74 IF Q=1 THEN LET A$ = "SPRINGFIELD"
75 IF Q=2 THEN LET A$ = "CHICAGO"
76 IF Q=3 THEN LET A$ = "LAKE MICHIGAN"
80 REM SUBROUTINE--ASK QUESTION
90 GOSUB 1000
100 REM ACCEPT ANSWER
110 GOSUB 1100
120 REM SUBROUTINE--CHECK ANSWER
130 GOSUB 2000
140 NEXT Q
150 REM SUBROUTINE--GRADE QUIZ
160 GOSUB 3000
170 REM RATE SCORE
180 GOSUB 3100
190 STOP
200 REM ***END OF MAIN PROGRAM***
1000 PRINT
1010 PRINT "QUESTION "; Q
1020 PRINT
1030 PRINT Q$
1099 RETURN
1100 PRINT
1110 PRINT "TYPE YOUR ANSWER."
1120 INPUT SA$
1199 RETURN
2000 IF SA$<>A$ THEN PRINT "INCORRECT"
2010 IF SA$<>A$ THEN GOTO 2099
2020 PRINT "CORRECT"
2030 LET S=S+1
2099 RETURN
3000 PRINT "YOUR SCORE IS "; S
3099 RETURN
3100 IF S=3 THEN PRINT "SUPER!"
3110 IF S=2 THEN PRINT "GOOD."
3120 IF S=1 THEN PRINT "PRACTICE!"
3199 RETURN
```

```
RUN

QUESTION 1

WHAT IS THE CAPITAL OF ILLINOIS?

TYPE YOUR ANSWER.
?SPRINGFIELD
CORRECT


QUESTION 2

WHAT IS THE LARGEST CITY IN ILLINOIS?

TYPE YOUR ANSWER.
?PEORIA
INCORRECT


QUESTION 3

WHAT LAKE IS IN NORTHERN ILLINOIS?

TYPE YOUR ANSWER.
?LAKE HURON
INCORRECT

YOUR SCORE IS 1
PRACTICE!
```

Again, the program should be run several times to be sure that the correct evaluation message comes up each time.

All the throw-away code has now been replaced. The program has been tested in such a way that when the last module was written, very little remained to be tested. If no testing had been done until after the entire program had been written, think how different the testing process would have been. It would have taken a long time to locate any errors in logic or any typing errors.

DOCUMENTING THE PROGRAM

This program you have just written contains REM statements that explain what the variables are used for and what the subroutines do. You should also write this information on paper, both for your own use later and for anyone else who may later work with your program.

Key Points

- Plan, write, and test your programs from the top down. Test each module before going on to write other modules.
- Use throw-away code for lower modules when you write and test higher ones.
- Explain variables and subroutines in REM statements and in documentation.

Review Questions

1. Look back at the top module of the quiz program on page 133. Which subroutines are in the loop? Why are some subroutines not in the loop?
2. How would you change the program to ask another question about Illinois?

OTHER LANGUAGES

STRUCTURED LANGUAGES

You've already learned something about the BASIC language. You will probably go on someday to learn other programming languages as well. Different languages are designed for different purposes. BASIC is an all-purpose language, meaning that you can do almost anything in BASIC. But some things will be rather hard to do in BASIC. For example, although you have seen how to write programs with a top-down structure in BASIC, other languages make it easier to write such structured—or modular—programs.

Logo is a structured language that is often taught in schools and is available for many microcomputers. You may be familiar with Logo because many schools use it to do "turtle graphics." A **turtle** is a cursor on the screen. It's called a turtle because it is often shaped like one. You can tell the turtle to move left, right, up, down, or turn a certain number of degrees. You can see the turtle move on the screen. The turtle can also draw on the screen. If you tell it to put its pen down, it traces a line as it moves, or it can pick up the pen and not draw a line. (There are also mechanical turtles that move on the floor.)

Logo is a language that can help you to write structured programs. For example, in Logo you can tell the turtle to carry out a set of commands that draws a rectangle on the screen. Then you can call that set of commands "box." Each time you tell the turtle to "DO BOX," it will draw the rectangle. "Box" has become a module of a program. You can create a whole series of routines that draw different shapes or parts of pictures. Then you can combine them all in one statement and call the whole thing "house." Then you can make "house" part of another routine, and so on. Your whole program can consist of a series of statements defining different routines and then a few statements calling these routines in the correct order.

Logo doesn't just do turtle graphics, it is a complete language. But whether you use the language to draw a house or compute complex mathematical functions, the modular structure of the language is the same.

Pascal is also a structured language. Pascal has some features that make structured programming easier. For example, it allows you to indent the statements in a loop so that you can see the beginning and the end of each loop. Pascal also has certain requirements that make you plan your program carefully. For example, it requires you to define all your variables before you begin.

One characteristic of Pascal is that it is often a **compiled language**. A compiled language is one that must be translated by a **compiler** into code that the computer can understand before the program can be run.

The original program is called the **source code**. The compiled, translated program is called the **object code**. Object code is in machine language—commands that the computer can use directly. On the other hand, an **interpreted language** is translated line by line by an **interpreter** as the program runs.

When you run a program in a compiled language, you must wait for the whole program to be translated before the run actually starts. However, once the run starts a compiled language runs much faster than an interpreted one, since each line of the interpreted program must be translated before it can be run. There are compiled and interpreted versions of BASIC, but it is very likely that the version you're using is interpreted.

It takes time to compile a program. Each time you make a change in the program or add a new module, you must let the computer compile the whole program before you can run it.

LANGUAGES FOR OTHER TASKS

Some languages are very well suited to tasks that are hard to do in BASIC. For example, **FORTRAN** is a language that is very similar to BASIC, but it is better for scientific applications. (BASIC is actually a simpler version of FORTRAN.) FORTRAN contains commands that make it easier to do engineering problems and use mathematics for solving scientific problems. It allows the programmer to program mathematical formulas more easily than does BASIC. FORTRAN is available for some microcomputers.

COBOL is a language that was developed mainly for large computers and may be available on a few microcomputers. It is designed for business uses and is particularly good for report writing. It makes it easy to set up very complicated reports with rows and columns, and to print these on the screen or a printer.

ASSEMBLY LANGUAGE

The languages described so far are called **high-level** languages because they are far removed from the low-level machine language binary commands that the computer can understand directly. Many students who begin with BASIC go on to learn to write assembly-language programs. **Assembly language** is not a high-level language. It is much closer to the machine language of the computer.

In assembly language you work with what you might think of as building blocks to create your program. Because you can use these blocks in many ways, you can create commands that don't exist in BASIC. You can also control the computer directly and control external peripherals like home security systems through the computer. A program that is written in assembly language also runs much faster than a program that is written in BASIC because it does not need to be interpreted like BASIC.

Assembly language can also be used to write programs that will run on several different computers. Any computer with the same computer chip will use the same assembly language.

Unfortunately, assembly language is very difficult to use. It takes much longer to write a program in assembly language than it does in any high-level language. Assembly language is not a structured language, so it is very difficult for someone else to understand your programs. It is easy to make mistakes in the programs and hard to find them, and it takes a long time to change the programs.

Key Points

• Different languages are good for different purposes.
• A program that is written in a compiled language must be translated by a compiler from source code into object code before it can be run.
• Interpreted languages are translated by an interpreter, one line at a time, as the program is run.
• Assembly language allows you to command the computer directly.

Review Questions

1. What are some examples of high-level languages?
2. Distinguish between source code and object code.
3. Can BASIC be used to write structured programs?

How Do Languages Get Their Names?

Some languages are named after people.

• As you may remember, Ada is a programming language named for Augusta Ada Byron, the Countess of Lovelace.
• Pascal is named for the seventeenth century French mathematician Blaise Pascal, who built the first calculator, the Pascaline.

Some language names are initials.

• PL/1 (Programming Language 1)
• APL (A Programming Language)

Many language names are acronyms. An acronym takes the first letter of each of the several words of a name to make a word, as in UNICEF, the United Nations International Children's Emergency Fund. Computer languages that are acronyms don't always take just the first letter, however.

• BASIC (Beginners' All-purpose Symbolic Instruction Code)
• FORTRAN (FORmula TRANslator)
• LISP (LISt Processor)
• PILOT (Programmed Inquiry) Learning Or Teaching)
• COBOL (COmmon Business Oriented Language)

Augusta Ada Byron, Countess of Lovelace, is considered to be the first programmer.

REVIEW & APPLICATION

SUMMARY

• For a program that is too complex to be shown clearly in a flowchart, you need a modular, or top-down, design. A modular design starts with the most general description of a task and breaks it down into more and more specific tasks.

• In BASIC a GOSUB statement sends the computer to a subroutine, which may be a module of a program. A complex program may consist almost entirely of GOSUB statements.

• A RETURN statement tells the computer to stop running a subroutine and go back to the point where it left the main program.

• When programming from a modular, or top-down, design, program the top module first, then the next lower modules, and so on.

• Test each module as soon as you have programmed it. This allows you to find errors faster than if you waited until the entire program was written.

• Use throw-away code to stand for the real program lines in subroutines until you have written them.

• Use REM statements as well as documentation to explain how your program and each of its subroutines work.

• Programming languages serve different purposes. They differ in what kinds of commands they use, in how easy it is to use them, and in how structured they are.

VOCABULARY

Match each item in the left column with the correct item on the right.

a. subroutine	1. Set the value of a variable
b. compiler	2. A structured programming language
c. initialize	3. A compiled, translated program
d. object code	4. Translates language into computer code
e. Logo	5. Self-contained program part

REVIEW QUESTIONS

1. Why do you need a modular design, rather than just a flowchart, to plan a complex program?
2. What is the function of a RETURN statement in BASIC?
3. In what order should you write the parts of a modular program?
4. How does an interpreted language differ from a compiled language?
5. How is a high-level computer language different from a low-level language?

DISCUSSION QUESTION

Do you think it makes sense for several people to work together in writing a complex program? What problems and advantages might teamwork offer?

PROJECTS

Complete and run the program. Line 20 should accept input for the string variable A$ and line 30 should print the input.

```
10 PRINT "TYPE A WORD"
20
30
40 PRINT "GO AGAIN, Y/N": INPUT Q$
50 IF Q$="Y" THEN GOTO 10
60 END
```

Run the program to make sure that it works properly. Notice line 40. You can put two statements on a line if you separate them with a colon (:). You have to be careful, though, with IF...THEN statements. For example, given the line:

```
50 IF X=4 THEN LET D=1: GOTO 130
```

The computer will only read the GOTO statement if X equals 4. If X does not equal 4, the computer will skip the rest of the line.

Change line 30 to

```
30 PRINT RIGHT$(A$,4)
```

Run the program. Enter BACKYARD as your input. The computer should print YARD. Enter different words. When you think you understand what line 30 does, stop the run.

Now change line 30 to

```
30 PRINT LEFT$(A$,4)
```

Enter BACKYARD again.

RIGHT$ (right string) (X$,n) takes the rightmost n characters in X$. (X$ stands for the name of the string, and n for the number of characters.) LEFT$ (left string) (X$,n) takes the leftmost n characters in X$.

Change line 30 so that it prints the right ten characters of A$. Do the same with LEFT$.

Change line 30 to

```
30 PRINT MID$(A$,5,4)
```

Run the program and enter BACKYARD. Now change line 30 to

```
30 PRINT MID$(A$,2,3)
```

Run the program with several different inputs. MID$(X$,n1,n2) takes n2 characters from X$, starting with character #n1.

Further Practice

Enter the quiz program from the chapter into your computer and run it.

Take out that list you've been making of BASIC keywords and their functions. Add to it the keywords that you learned in the chapter.

Enrichment

Modify the quiz program from the chapter so that it tells you what percentage of answers you got correct.

CHAPTER TEST

Write your answers on a sheet of paper numbered 1 through 12.

MULTIPLE CHOICE

1. In writing a program with subroutines, you should explain what each subroutine does:
   a. by using REM statements
   b. by writing documentation
   c. by using REM statements and documentation
   d. by creating a flowchart

2. A GOSUB statement must include:
   a. an END statement
   b. a line number
   c. quotation marks
   d. a RETURN statement

3. Following a modular design, you would write a program:
   a. from the top down
   b. one module at a time
   c. using throw-away code
   d. all of the above

4. Programs that are written in assembly language:
   a. are easy to write
   b. run faster than those written in BASIC
   c. can run on only one computer
   d. must be interpreted

MATCHING

5. Match the language with the correct description.

a. Pascal	1. for business reports
b. FORTRAN	2. uses a "turtle"
c. COBOL	3. useful in science
d. Logo	4. allows indented loops

6. Match each item on the left with the correct function on the right.

a. compiler	1. stops program
b. RETURN	2. translates source code
c. GOSUB	3. ends subroutine
d. END	4. starts subroutine

FILL-IN

7. A modular program has a __________ structure.
8. When writing a modular program, you use flowcharts to plan __________.
9. A program line that sets a variable to 0 or some other value is said to __________ that variable.
10. Throw-away code is eventually replaced with __________.
11. A program that is written in an interpreted language must be __________ line by line as it runs.
12. Source code is another name for the original, uncompiled __________.

ISSUE: COMPUTER TRESPASSING

One day at school, Jane copied the password for the school's computer from her teacher's grade book. Later, Jane used her home computer, a modem, and a telephone to "call up" the school's computer. She typed the password to access the student records. Then she located the records for her class and changed her history grade from a "D" to an "A."

What Jane did was against the law. She did not have permission to use the school's computer system. Breaking into a computer system (using it when you don't have permission) is a crime. It is called **computer trespassing**.

People break into computer systems for many reasons. They might do it to find out private records, to change or destroy information, to steal money or goods, or simply to show they know how to do it.

Computer trespassing is a serious problem. Important information—ranging from medical records to top secret military information—is often stored in computer systems. If someone changes, destroys, or steals the information, he or she might cause great damage. For example, a trespasser in a hospital computer system might endanger a patient's health by changing his or her medical records. In the case of a government computer system, a computer trespasser might threaten national security by stealing military information. A trespasser in a bank's computer system might steal millions of dollars.

How can we prevent computer trespassing? One way to protect information stored in computer systems is to use passwords or number codes. The words or codes are programmed into the computer system. The system will admit only those people who enter the correct code. An alarm alerts a security guard if someone enters an incorrect code more than once.

Some computer systems use cryptography (secret writing) to protect information. Such systems store information in the computer in coded or scrambled form. If you don't know how to unscramble the information, it is meaningless.

Federal and state laws also protect information stored in computer systems. One federal law, the Counterfeit Access Device and Computer Fraud and Abuse Act of 1984, prohibits people from using a computer system without permission. It also prohibits the use of a computer system: (1) to steal money or goods worth $5,000 or more; (2) to use, change, destroy, or reveal restricted information in government files; (3) to obtain financial information and credit records that are protected by other federal laws.

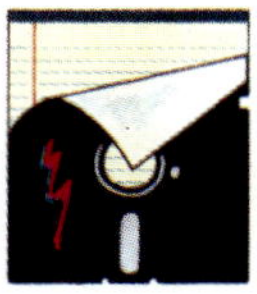

UNIT REVIEW

CONCEPTS

- "Should I learn to program?" is a frequently asked question. What arguments would you use to convince people to learn some programming?
- Why is it easier to detect errors in a high-level language than it is to detect errors in machine language?

CAREERS

- Which of the careers described in the first two units most interests you? Why?
- Why do most professional programmers know and use several different programming languages?

ISSUES

- Describe the effects on society of unauthorized access to computer systems.
- How can companies and other organizations protect themselves against computer trespassers?
- Do you think that the media has glorified software pirates, computer trespassers, and other criminals of the computer age? Explain your answer.

APPLICATIONS

- If you could develop computer programs, what types might you write? Why? What types would you buy instead? Why?
- Name five tasks that are appropriate for a computer program. Name five tasks that are inappropriate for a computer program.

TO FIND OUT

- Research college entrance requirements. Find out if colleges require incoming students to know how to program. If so, must students know specific computer languages? Prepare a report on your findings.

UNIT THREE

USING APPLICATION SOFTWARE

Imagine that merely by saying a magic word you can become a skilled worker in any occupation you chose. *Abracadabra*—you're a writer writing books and magazine articles. *Presto-chango*—now you're a financial wizard working on Wall Street. *Alakazam*—you're an automotive designer drawing plans for the sleek new Turbo-350ZX Wondercar.

Too bad it's not that easy, isn't it? Here's some good news, though: It's up to you to develop the skill, but once you do, the computer can help you apply it. As if by magic, this electronic tool can help you write, draw, do financial calculations, or perform numerous other tasks at home or on the job.

In this unit, you'll learn about four kinds of applications software. These programs, and others like them, will enable you to use a computer to do many different tasks quickly, efficiently, and creatively.

CHAPTER

6 7 8 9 10

WORD PROCESSING

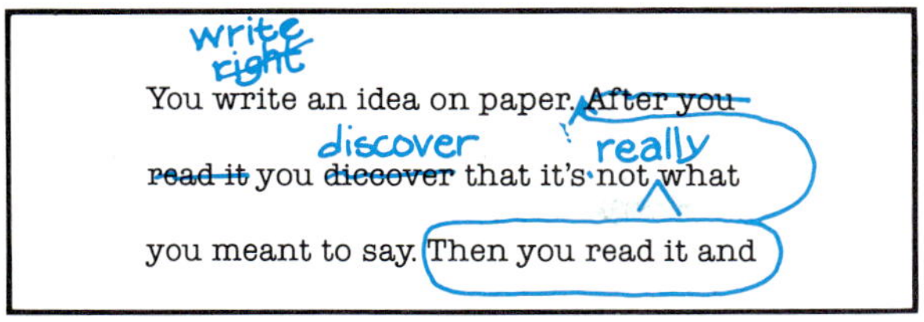

Wait. Let's start over. Have you ever had trouble writing something? You write an idea on paper. Then you read it and you discover that it's not really what you meant to say. You try crossing out some of the words and adding new ones. But that makes your paper look messy, so you throw it away and start again.

The same thing happens the second time. Finally, you get it right. Then you notice a misspelled word. Do you have to start again?

You don't if you're using a computer and a **word-processing program**. A word-processing program allows you to correct misspelled words quickly and easily. You can also erase, add, and move words or paragraphs from one place to another by pressing a few keys. And your work stays neat, clean, and readable.

WHAT EQUIPMENT IS REQUIRED?

To run word-processing software, you must, of course, have a computer. If the computer does not come with a display screen, you will need a separate screen. Most word-processing software comes on disks, so a disk drive is required. It's also good to have a couple of blank disks, in case you want to save something that you have written. And if you want to put what you've written on paper, you'll need a printer.

HOW DOES WORD-PROCESSING SOFTWARE WORK?

Word-processing software works like any other computer program—you simply load the program into your computer. Then you type on the computer keyboard just as you would type on a typewriter.

As you type, the words appear on the screen. The words that you type are also stored in the computer's memory, so you can save your writing on a disk and work on it later, just as you can save a computer program on a disk and run or change it later. If you have a printer, you can print your writing on paper in much the same way that you print the output from the computer on paper. In fact, you can print as many copies of your work as you like without having to retype it.

HOW TO USE A WORD-PROCESSING PROGRAM

You're probably thinking, "Word-processing software sounds great, but how do I use it?" There are many answers to that question, because there are many different word-processing programs available. How you operate a program depends on which program you are using. Before you use a word-processing program, you should read the documentation carefully in order to determine exactly what that particular program does and exactly what you have to do to run it. Let's talk about word processors in general, though. Most word-processing programs perform the same basic functions.

Suppose that you have just bought a word-processing program. What do you do first? After loading the program you will probably see a copyright notice and the title of the program on the screen. After that a menu usually appears. Here is a sample word-processing menu:

```
*  *  *  *  MENU  *  *  *  *
<CREATE>
<EDIT>
<FORMAT>
<PRINT>
<SAVE>
<EXIT>
DIRECTIONS: Use the arrow keys
to move the cursor to your
choice. Then press RETURN.
```

This menu provides an overview of some of the functions that word processors perform. In this chapter you'll learn what all of these functions mean and how you can use them in a typical word-processing program.

```
*  *  *  *  MENU  *  *  *  *
<CREATE>
<EDIT>
<FORMAT>
<PRINT>
<SAVE>
<EXIT>
DIRECTIONS: Use the arrow keys
to move the cursor to your
choice. Then press RETURN.
```

CREATING A DOCUMENT

Let's start by creating a **document**, or **file**. In a word-processing program, a document refers to anything that you write. A document could be a school report, a letter to a friend, or a list of things that you have to do.

How does the computer know the difference between your school report and the letter that you write to your friend? The word-processing program uses a **filename** to keep track of each document. A filename is a short title that you give to your document. Some word-processing programs have rules for selecting filenames. For example, some programs don't allow filenames that contain blank spaces. Others limit the length of the filename to eight characters.

In any case, you should choose a filename that's easy for you to remember. That will make it easier for you to find your file if you want to save it and come back to it later. If you were writing a report on computer trivia, for example, your document's filename could be "TRIVIA."

Once your document has a filename, you can start typing it into the computer. You type on the computer keyboard just as you would on a typewriter. There is one difference, though.

When you use a word-processing program, you don't have to worry about running out of space at the end of a line. When you reach the end of a line, the cursor automatically moves to the beginning of the next line. If a word is too long to fit on a line, the word-processing program moves the entire word to the next line. This word-processing feature is called **word wrap**. Let's see how word wrap works.

```
Computers can help us under_
```

You're typing this line, and you've paused in the middle of the word *understand.* The cursor is at the right edge of the screen. What will happen when you type the *s*?

```
Computers can help us
unders_
```

The whole word (or what there is of it) will be moved down to the next line. The only time you have to hit the RETURN key is at the end of a paragraph.

```
* * * * MENU * * * *
<CREATE>
<EDIT>
<FORMAT>
<PRINT>
<SAVE>
<EXIT>
DIRECTIONS: Use the arrow keys
to move the cursor to your
choice. Then press RETURN.
```

EDITING A DOCUMENT

Now you're ready to start writing. Here's the first sentence of your computer trivia report:

```
Computers can help us
understand the language of
the anceinnt_
```

You made a mistake already. You spelled *ancient* wrong. How do you correct it? With most word-processing programs, you can type over a mistake exactly as you would if the mistake had occurred in a program that you were writing. One way to do this is to **delete,** or take out, the last few letters by using the DEL key.

```
Computers can help us
understand the language of
the anc_
```

Then you can retype the word correctly. Another way to fix the error immediately would be to move the cursor over the *e* and type an *i*. This would bring the cursor over the *i*, where you would type an *e*.

```
Computers can help us
understand the language of
the anciennt
```

Then you could move the cursor back after the *t* and continue typing.

```
Computers can help us
understand the language of
the anciennt Egyptians. The
Egyptians used an alphabet
made up of symbols called
hieroglyphics. Now there's a
word-processing program that
lets scholars spell out
hieroglyphics on the
computer._
```

But wait. The word *ancient* is still misspelled. To delete everything after the error would mean a lot of retyping. Fortunately, there's another way to make the correction.

You can simply position the cursor over the extra *n* and then hit either one key or a combination of two keys to delete the letter. The word-processing program will automatically move the rest of the text over to fill in the gap.

```
the ancient Egyptians. The
```

The important thing to keep in mind with all of these editing techniques is that you have to move the cursor to the

The TRS-80 does not have a delete key. The back space key must be used to delete letters.

error. You may be looking at a screen that is full of text, but you can only change the part beneath the cursor.

Defining Text. What if you need to delete more than a few letters? Most word-processing programs provide a faster way to delete a **block** of text. A block is a section of your document that you want to handle as a unit. A block of text can be anything from a word to an entire document.

If you want to delete a block of text, you define it first by marking its beginning and its end. To define a block on most word processors, you place the cursor at the beginning of the text and press one or more keys. Then you move the cursor to the end of the text and press one or more keys. Here is an example of a defined block of text:

```
Late in 1974, Les Solomon
was preparing an article for
Popular Electronics about the
first widely available home
computer. Made by a company
called MITS, the computer
had no name. Solomon asked
his daughter, who was
watching "Star Trek," a
television show about the
crew of the starship
ENTERPRISE, what the
computer on the ENTERPRISE
was called. She told him
that it had no name either.
Then she said, "Why don't
you call your computer
Altair? That's the name of
the planet the ENTERPRISE is
going to in this episode."
The Altair computer went on
to become the biggest
selling computer of its
time.
```

Once you define a block of text, you can delete it by simply pressing one or two buttons.

```
Late in 1974, Les Solomon
was preparing an article for
Popular Electronics about the
first widely available home
computer. Made by a company
called MITS, the computer
had no name. Solomon asked
his daughter, who was
watching "Star Trek," what
the computer on the
ENTERPRISE was called. She
told him that it had no name
either. Then she said, "Why
don't you call your computer
Altair? That's the name of
the planet the ENTERPRISE is
going to in this episode."
The Altair computer went on
to become the biggest-
selling computer of its
time.
```

Retrieving Text. When you delete a block of text, where does it go? Some word-processing programs keep the text that you delete in a special part of the computer's memory called a **buffer**. If the deleted text is in the buffer, you can retrieve it if you change your mind and decide to use it. Your material is only stored in the buffer until you delete something else, though. Then the new material replaces the old material in the buffer, and the original text is erased from the computer's memory.

Moving Text. After you define a block of text, you can do more than simply delete it. Let's say that you want to switch the first sentence and the second sentence in the following paragraph from your computer trivia report:

The typewriter was first introduced in the 1870's by E. Remington and Sons.

```
More than six thousand
students in Albuquerque, New
Mexico, blamed a computer
for their failing grades.
Can computers make mistakes?
The students' names were
programmed into the computer
by mistake when the machine
was printing out failing
grades. It really wasn't the
computer's fault, though.
The programmer was
responsible for giving the
computer the wrong list of
students.
```

First you define the beginning and the end of the block that you want to move. In this case you define the sentence, "Can computers make mistakes?" Next, you move the cursor to indicate where you want the text to go—in this case, to the beginning of the paragraph. Then you press one key or a combination of keys, and the sentence is moved. This is how the beginning of your new paragraph looks:

```
Can computers make mistakes?
More than six thousand
students in Albuquerque, New
Mexico, blamed a computer
for their failing grades.
The students' names were
programmed into the
```

Copying Text. Here are some words from a song about word processing. The first paragraph is the chorus. It is repeated after each verse of the song.

```
Word process your work; step
  up to high tech
With a hey-nonny-nonny and a
  split nanosec.
When you use a computer to
  prepare compositions,
You don't rub out deletions
  or ink in additions.
So word process your work;
  step up to high tech
With a hey-nonny-nonny and a
  split nanosec.
Erasers and pencils and pens
  you can scrap,
While the end of the line
  brings a gift called word
  wrap.
So word process your work;
  step up to high tech
With a hey-nonny-nonny and a
  split nanosec.*
```

*Song by S. Pearl

If you were typing this song on a typewriter, you would have to type the chorus over and over again. With a word-processing program, you only have to type it once. Most programs let you duplicate text without destroying the original. You can copy a block of text, leave it in its original location, and repeat it in one or more other places as well.

To copy a block of text, you follow the procedure you used to move text. First you define it. Then you move the cursor to a location where you want the text to appear. You press one or more keys, and the defined text appears in the new location as well as in the old one. You follow the same procedure for repeating the defined text in other locations.

Inserting Text. You may want to make additions to your text after you finish it. Suppose that you are writing the following for your computer trivia report:

```
You've heard of recycled
bottles and cans. Have you
heard about recycled
computers? Di-Core is a
company that takes apart old
computers in search of
re-usable parts and precious
metals.
```

After you finish the report, you discover that you have left out some information. You didn't say where Di-Core is located. How do you add the information?

Most word-processing programs have a

Computerized word processing has replaced typewriting in many modern offices because of its efficiency and flexibility.

feature that allows you to make insertions anywhere in the text. You can insert characters, words, sentences, or blank spaces by pressing a few keys.

First, you move the cursor to the place where you want to add words—in this case, between the words *company* and *that* in your report. Next, you press one key or a combination of two keys. Then you type the additional words—in this case, "in Brooklyn Park, Minnesota,". The rest of the text automatically moves over to make room for the new text that you added.

```
You've heard of recycled
bottles and cans. Have you
heard about recycled
computers? Di-Core is a
company in Brooklyn Park,
Minnesota, that takes apart
old computers in search of
re-usable parts and precious
metals.
```

Once your correction is made, you have to press another button or combination of buttons to instruct the computer to stop inserting and to allow you to type normally again.

Searching for text. Have you ever been told that you use a certain word too much in your writing? Sometimes it's difficult for writers to keep track of how many times they use the same word in a particular document, especially if it's a long document.

Most word-processing programs allow you to locate a word or a short phrase each time it occurs in your text. To do this, you press one or more keys and then type the word or phrase that you are looking for. Then the word-processing program shows you, one by one, all the occurrences of the word or phrase in your document. Suppose, for example, that you write this section of your report:

```
Luncheonettes have been a
part of traditional Japanese
culture for a long time. Now
Japanese luncheonettes have
taken a step into the
future. Some luncheonettes
in Tokyo have word
processors and printers
available for the customers
of the luncheonettes to use.
```

After rereading the section, you realize that you have used the word *luncheonettes* a few too many times. That's not a problem. All you have to do is instruct the computer to search for the word *luncheonettes.* The cursor will move to the first place where the word appears—right at the beginning of the section. You can delete it, change it, or leave it alone. Then you strike a key, and the cursor automatically moves to the next place where *luncheonettes* appears.

```
Snack bars have been a
```

The computer finds the words by comparing sequences of letters. Along with the word itself, the machine will find every other word that contains the same sequence of characters. For example, if a word processor is searching for *word*, it will also stop when it finds *words, worded,* and *wording.* With some word-processing programs, you can prevent this from happening by typing a space before and after the word that you want to find.

Replacing text. Have you ever finished a report and then realized that you misspelled a word, misused a word, or had a factual error that you repeated many times? You probably had to find each occurrence of the word or fact, erase it, and write in the correct replacement. Chances are that your efforts resulted in a messy paper.

You can avoid this problem with most word-processing programs. They quickly find and neatly replace errors. To do this, you have to press a special function key or the control key and another key, type the characters you want the computer to find and the characters you want to replace them with. Some word-processing programs show you each occurrence of the word or phrase and give you the option of changing it or leaving it as it is. Others make all of the changes automatically.

WP Operators, Work for a Bank

The Burton Bank has immediate openings for Word Processing Operators. High school diploma and good typing skills (45–60 wpm) required. One year of experience on a word-processing system preferred, but will train qualified candidates on the job. Operators should be good spellers, have a knowledge of grammar, and be attentive to detail.

Our word-processing operators prepare proposals, reports, and letters for all departments of Burton Bank. Opportunities for advancement to supervisory positions. Hours: 8:30 A.M. to 4:30 P.M. or 5:00 P.M. to midnight. Occasional overtime required. Excellent medical and dental benefits; good starting salary.

THAT'S MY JOB

David Hollis, a word processing operator, has this to say:

"Word processing is better than just typing—you can make changes much more easily, and you don't need to use messy correcting fluid or tape. It's challenging because you working with an interesting piece of equipment.

"I enjoy doing complicated jobs such as editing and moving paragraphs from one page to another. I rarely get tired of watching the machine doing most of the work.

"What I do get tired of is sitting. And sometimes the screen bothers my eyes. Then I take a break. When I sit back down, I'm ready for a new document."

MORE INFORMATION

Secretarial jobs are one of forty occupations that will have the largest growth in the next ten years.... Secretaries with WP skills will be in highest demand.... Employment is available in a wide range of businesses and government agencies.... WP jobs can lead to more responsible positions.

Key Points

- Word processing is a computerized method of writing, editing, and printing text.
- A document is anything that you write with a word-processing program. You must give each document a different filename.
- Word-processing programs automatically move the cursor from the end of one line to the beginning of the next line. This feature is called word wrap.
- A block of text is a section of a document that you want to handle as a unit. You define a block of text by marking its beginning and its end. Once you define a block of text, you can delete it, move it, or copy it.
- Word-processing software also allows you to insert text into the middle of something that you've already written.

Review Questions

1. What are the two ways in which you can delete text with a word-processing program?
2. What is the difference between moving a block of text and copying it?

* * * * MENU * * * *

<CREATE>
<EDIT>
<FORMAT>
<PRINT>
<SAVE>
<EXIT>
DIRECTIONS: Use the arrow keys to move the cursor to your choice. Then press RETURN.

FORMATTING A DOCUMENT

Before you print your document, you can choose how you want it to look on paper. This is called **formatting**. Some word-processing programs ask you to do this before you start writing. Others wait until you are ready to print your document and then give you a list of choices. The instructions that you use to tell the computer how to print your document are called **formatting commands**.

What are some of the choices that you have for formatting text? Most word-processing programs allow you to adjust the **line spacing** on your document. That means that you can select the amount of empty space between printed lines. You can print your document using either single-spaced or double spaced text.

Single-spaced text looks like
the type that you are reading now.

Double-spaced text looks like

the type that you are reading now.

Some programs allow you to print your document using triple-spaced text as well. You can also choose how much of a margin you want between your writing and the edges of the paper.

Some word-processing programs have a formatting command that prints **justified** lines. Justified lines form straight margins on both sides of this paper. For example, the text in this book is justified, but the text in this paragraph is not justified.

Another formatting command allows you to decide where you want to place tab stops in your text. **Tab stops** are specific locations on a line of text. They allow you to indent the beginning of paragraphs and create columns of information.

Other formatting commands take care of underlining words, centering words between the left and right margins, and numbering pages. Some word-processing programs also give you several print styles to choose from. For example, you could select regular type or italic type. Italics are often used for printing foreign words, such as *computadora* and *ordinateur* (the Spanish and French words for "computer").

Some word-processing programs show the results of your formatting decisions on the screen so that you can see how your printed document will look. This is called **on-screen formatting**. Other programs have **off-screen formatting**. These programs store the formatting commands in memory but don't show the results until you print the document.

Key Points

- Formatting commands are instructions that you use to tell the computer how to arrange your writing on paper.
- Line spacing is the amount of empty space between printed lines. Depending on your word-processing program, you can choose single-spaced, double-spaced, or triple-spaced lines.
- You may also be able to choose the styles of type in which your document will be printed.
- On-screen formatting shows how a printed document will look. Off-screen formatting doesn't show the results of the formatting decisions until the document is printed.

Review Questions

1. What does it mean when someone says that a document is justified?
2. What are two things that you can do with a tab stop?

```
*   *   *   *   MENU   *   *   *   *
<CREATE>
<EDIT>
<FORMAT>
<PRINT>
<SAVE>
<EXIT>
DIRECTIONS: Use the arrow keys
to move the cursor to your
choice. Then press RETURN.
```

PRINTING A DOCUMENT

Your word processor and printer work together to carry out formatting commands. Some printers are capable of performing more formatting functions than others. For example, your word-processing program may allow you to print italic type, but if your printer can't produce italic type, the command is useless. The reverse is also true. A printer can't produce italic type if it's hooked up to a word-processing program that won't allow it.

There are many different kinds of printers. The two most common types for word processing are **dot-matrix printers** and **letter-quality printers**.

A dot-matrix printer forms characters

by using pins to strike an ink ribbon against a piece of paper. The resulting text is made up of tiny dots. The print quality depends on how many pins are used. The more expensive printers use more pins for better print. Dot-matrix printers also print graphics, since the computer can arrange the pins in any pattern, not just to form letters.

A letter-quality printer types solid characters that look similar to the print produced by an electronic typewriter. It prints in much the same way that a typewriter does, using metal letters to strike an ink ribbon against a piece of paper. Sometimes the letters are arranged around a wheellike device. This is called a **daisy wheel**. You can get different type styles by changing the daisy wheel. Because letter-quality printers use fixed letters, they can't print graphics.

Letter-quality printers usually work more slowly than dot-matrix printers. A letter-quality printer averages between 12 and 45 characters per second. A typical letter-quality printer takes about forty-five seconds to print a full page of text. On the other hand, a dot-matrix printer averages between 80 and 200 characters per second. A typical dot-matrix printer produces a page of text in about twenty seconds—that's less than half the time that a letter-quality printer takes.

A dot-matrix printer strikes a ribbon with tiny pins, creating characters made up of dots. A daisy-wheel printer uses solid characters on spokes.

```
*  *  *  *  MENU  *  *  *  *
<CREATE>
<EDIT>
<FORMAT>
<PRINT>
<SAVE>
<EXIT>
DIRECTIONS: Use the arrow keys
to move the cursor to your
choice. Then press RETURN.
```

SAVING A DOCUMENT

Although your writing is stored in the computer's memory, it remains there only as long as the power is on and the word-processing program is running. If you want to save your document so that you can edit it later, you must transfer it to a disk. Once the computer transfers your writing from its memory onto a disk, you have a permanent record of it.

It's usually a good idea to save a document every so often while you're working on it. This way, if anything disastrous happens your document is safe because it is on the disk. You may think that this is unnecessary, but when your dog walks by your desk and accidentally pulls out the plug of your computer, erasing the report you've been working on for the last three hours, you'll wish that you'd saved it.

SPECIAL WORD-PROCESSING FEATURES

Most word-processing programs allow you to create, edit, format, print, and save documents. Some of them also allow you to perform more complex functions. The following are two examples of the sophisticated features that some programs have.

SPELLING CHECKERS

Some word-processing programs come with a **spelling checker**. A spelling checker works with a word-processing program to find misspelled words in your document. It does this by matching each word in your document with a list of words that have been programmed into its memory. This list is usually called a **dictionary**, but the name is misleading. Spelling checkers have no way of knowing what a word means. Their "dictionaries" are simply lists of properly spelled words.

When a spelling checker finds a word that does not match any of the words in its dictionary, it displays that word. Then you decide whether to change it or, if it is spelled correctly, add it to the spelling checker's dictionary. This is often necessary, since the dictionary does not contain every word you will want to use. Unusual words, technical terms, and proper names will usually need to be added to the dictionary.

While a spelling checker can help you with your writing, it is not a substitute for good language skills. Because it only matches combinations of letters, a spelling checker cannot determine whether you are using words correctly. For example, if you use *too* in a sentence that requires *two*, a spelling checker will not detect the error because *too* is spelled correctly.

If you are typing the sentence "I wish I were at the beach" and you make a mistake and type "I fish I were at the beach," the spelling checker will not detect the error, since *fish* is properly spelled.

MERGE

Ann just purchased a lawn mower. She plans to use it to trim her neighbors' lawns for extra cash during the summer. To attract customers, Ann plans to deliver a copy of a letter that contains her name, phone number, and rates to all of her neighbors.

Ann could easily duplicate the letter on a photocopying machine, but she wants to personalize it for each neighbor. To personalize the letters, Ann uses a word-processing program that allows her to **merge** files. Merging means instructing the computer to combine information from two or more files into one printed document. In this case the computer will combine a file containing Ann's letter with a file containing the names and addresses of her neighbors. As a result, each printed letter will bear the name and the address of a different neighbor. The first part of the letter—Mr. Morales's name and address—came from one file. The rest of the letter came from another file. But Mr. Morales will not be able to tell.

Mr. Morales
1213 Paddock Drive
Kansas City, MO 64108

Dear Mr. Morales:

How would you like to hire a
responsible student to mow
your lawn this summer? My
name is Ann Wolf. I am
fourteen years old and am
experienced in lawn care. I
have a new lawn mower that's
hungry. Please let me feed
it on your lawn. I only
charge $10 per lawn.
Call me to arrange an
appointment. My phone number
is 769-5031.

Thanks,
Ann

By merging files, letters and other documents can be personalized. The names from one file are merged with the body of a letter in another file.

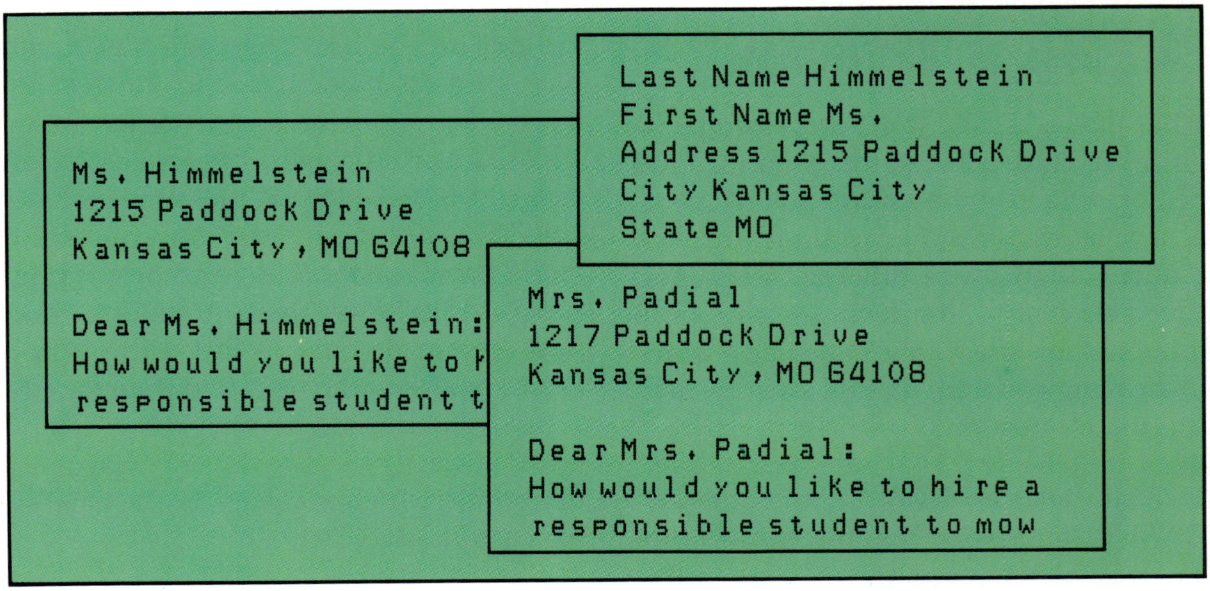

Key Points

• Dot-matrix and letter-quality printers are the two most common types of printers used for word processing. Dot-matrix printers produce graphics and text that are made of tiny dots. Letter-quality printers produce text that is made of solid characters, but they do not print graphics.

• A spelling checker works with a word-processing program to locate misspelled words in a document.

• Merge is a function that allows word-processing programs to combine information from two or more files into one printed document.

Review Questions

1. What's the difference between a dot-matrix printer and a letter-quality printer?
2. How does a spelling checker locate misspelled words in a document?

SELECTING A WORD-PROCESSING PROGRAM

What makes a good word-processing program? That depends entirely on how the person who is buying it intends to use it. A novelist would want certain features. A student might want different ones. And the owner of a store might want still others. Someone who is choosing a word-processing program should start by asking three questions:

1. What tasks do I want to accomplish?
2. What tasks can this word-processing program accomplish?
3. How easily can this word-processing program accomplish these tasks?

The first question is the most important one. Potential buyers must know what kind of writing they plan to do with a word-processing program before they can choose the program that's best for them. For example, someone who plans to use the program for simple writing tasks like letters and school reports doesn't need sophisticated functions like the ability to merge two different files. A simple, basic program will do. On the other hand, someone who plans to use the word-processing program to produce a community newsletter should look for a more sophisticated program with many features, such as one that allows the user to select a variety of type styles.

Once a potential buyer has made a list of necessary features, it should be a simple matter to find a program that offers just those features. It should be, but it often isn't. Many software packages will have all the features except one or will come with one or two extra features that are not on the list. Then the buyer will have to decide whether it is worth it to pay extra for features that aren't really necessary or if it's better to give up a feature or two in order to save some money. Last but not least, the buyer should check how easily the word-processing program performs these functions. The best way to do that is to load the program, type in some text, and then try editing it. Some programs are easier to operate than others. Buyers have to determine which software is the easiest for them to work with.

REVIEW & APPLICATION

SUMMARY

- A word-processing program allows you to correct errors and make other changes in text faster and more easily than you can with a typewriter.
- Once you have saved your writing on a disk, you can print as many copies of it as you want without retyping it.
- At the end of a line, a feature called word wrap moves the cursor to the beginning of the next line automatically.
- To correct an error, you can move the cursor to the character you want to change and simply type the correct character over it.
- You can define blocks of text and delete them, move them, or copy them by pressing a few keys.
- You can insert new text in the middle of what you have already written. The program automatically adjusts the rest of the text.
- A word-processing program can show each place in the text where a given word or phrase appears, and change the word or phrase for you automatically.
- With a word-processing program you can design how you want your document to look on paper. The program will automatically format it according to your instructions.
- A word-processing program may allow you to merge information from two or more files into one printed document.

VOCABULARY

Match the terms in the left-hand column with the definitions on the right.

a. filename	1. having straight left and right margins
b. block	2. a section of text that is treated as a unit
c. format	3. combine data from two files into one document
d. justified	4. the title of a document
e. merge	5. how a document will look on paper

REVIEW QUESTIONS

1. What points might you have to consider in choosing a filename for your document?
2. What must you do when you reach the end of a paragraph when using a word-processing program?
3. How can you define a block of text with a word-processing program?
4. Why should you save your document on a disk from time to time as you continue to work on it?

DISCUSSION QUESTION

Can you think of some instances when using a word-processing program would *not* be easier than using a typewriter? If so, what are they?

P R O J E C T S

This program is a spelling checker with a very limited dictionary.

```
10 DIM W$(50)
20 PRINT:PRINT "ENTER TEXT:"
30 INPUT A$:LET C=0
40 LET W=1:FOR X=1 TO LEN(A$)
50 IF MID$(A$,X,1)=" "THEN
    LET W$(W)=MID$(A$,C+1,X-C
    -1):LET C=X:LET W=W+1
60 NEXT X
70 LET W$(W)=RIGHT$(A$,X-C-1)
80 FOR X=1 TO W:LET Z=0:RESTORE
90 FOR Y=1 TO 40:READ D$
100 IF D$=W$(X) THEN LET
     Y=40:LET Z=1
110 NEXT Y
120 IF Z=1 THEN GOTO 180
130 PRINT W$(X)
140 PRINT "1) CHANGE 2) KEEP"
150 INPUT Q
160 IF Q=2 THEN GOTO 180
170 PRINT "CHANGE TO
     WHAT";:INPUT W$(X)
180 NEXT X
190 FOR P=1 TO W:PRINT W$(P) ; " ";
200 NEXT P:END
210 DATA A,THE,AN,TO,AT,OF,
     FOR,AND,WITH
220 DATA YOU,I,HE,SHE,IT,
     THEY,US,WE,THEM
230 DATA GO,WENT,SEE,SAW,
     WILL,IS,AM,ARE
240 DATA WAS,WERE,CAN,HOME,
     SCHOOL,WORK
250 DATA TABLE,CHAIR,BOOK,
     HOUSE,STORE
260 DATA FRIEND,COMPUTER,
     TEACHER
```

Line 40 contains a LEN function. This returns the number of characters in (or LENgth of) the string variable. If you entered twenty-five characters for the INPUT statement in line 30, then the X loop would run from 1 to 25.

Look at the P loop in lines 190 and 200. When P = 1, the computer prints W$(1) (W-string sub-1). When P = 2, W$(2) is printed. W$ is called an **array**. An array is a list—in this case a list called W$. The first item on the list is W$(1), the second item is W$(2), and so on. In this case, W$(1) is the first word of your text, W$(2) is the second, and so forth. (These values are assigned in line 50.)

If your array has more than ten items, you need to use a DIM, or dimension, statement as in line 10. DIM tells the computer the maximum number of items in the array.

This program's dictionary is the list of words contained in the DATA statements in lines 210 to 240. The Y loop in lines 90 to 110 contains a READ statement. Each time the loop is run, the READ statement tells the computer to assign the next item in the DATA statements to D$. The first time through the loop, D$ = "A". The twelfth time through the loop, D$ = "HE". The RESTORE statement in line 80 tells the computer to start over with the first item—the word *A*—in the first DATA statement.

CHAPTER TEST

Write your answers on a sheet of paper numbered 1 through 10.

MATCHING

1. Match each term with its definition.

a. dot-matrix printer	1. moves cursor to next line
b. menu	2. forms text from dots
c. buffer	3. lists program choices
d. word wrap	4. section of memory

MULTIPLE CHOICE

2. A word-processing program allows you to:
   a. make a change on a page without having to retype it.
   b. print as many copies of a document as you want without retyping it.
   c. move a paragraph from one place to another in a document.
   d. all of the above
3. To print graphics, you would use:
   a. a letter-quality printer
   b. a buffer
   c. a daisy wheel
   d. a dot-matrix printer
4. You would use the merge feature of a word-processing program to:
   a. combine two paragraphs into one.
   b. print a document.
   c. combine data from two files into a report.
   d. all of the above.
5. The most efficient way to move a block of text within a document is to:
   a. define it, move the cursor to the new location, and press one or more keys.
   b. define it, copy it to the new location, go back to the old location, define it again, and delete it.
   c. use the merge feature.
   d. none of the above.

FILL-IN

6. As you type with a word-processing program, your words appear on a ______________.
7. When you use a particular word-processing program, you should read its ______________ carefully to determine exactly what it does and exactly what you must do to run it.
8. Your ______________ commands tell the computer how your document should look when it is printed.
9. ______________ allow you to indent the beginnings of paragraphs and create columns of information.
10. A daisy wheel may be used with a ______________ printer.

CHAPTER

7 8 9 10 11

DATA-BASE MANAGEMENT SYSTEMS

Have you ever collected baseball cards? Catalogued the stamps in your collection, including the date you bought each one and the price you paid for it? Kept a list of the names and addresses of your friends and relatives, noting their birthdays? If you have collected information of any kind and kept some sort of record or file, then you have created a *data base*.

You probably refer to the data base occasionally to refresh your memory. You check your baseball card on Nolan Ryan to find out the number of strikeouts he pitched in 1984. You evaluate the cost of stamps at Ferguson's Philatery using your own price records. When March rolls around, you look up your entry on Aunt Mabel to make sure that you don't miss her birthday. You scan your lists or flip through your cards until you find the information that you seek.

If you have ten cards, this is pretty easy. If you have thirty, it may take awhile. If you have over two hundred, you may forget what you're looking for before you find it.

Imagine getting the information you need by simply entering a command or two on your computer keyboard. Many people do this. They use **data-base management systems**—special software developed for record keeping—to create electronic files. Then the computer does all the work of sorting through the files to retrieve specific information. Sound intriguing? This chapter will give you an idea of how and why you might put a data-base management system to work for you. You will also learn how to evaluate and select the data-base management software program that will best serve your specific needs.

USING DATA BASES

Before explaining exactly what a data-base management system is and how it works, let's go back to the concept of a data base. *Data*, as you know, are facts or figures. A **data base** is a source of facts and figures—it is a collection of related information.

You already are familiar with many data bases. Some, such as a baseball card collection, are ones you developed yourself. But the data bases you use most often have probably been created by others. Can you name some of these? A telephone directory is a data base. So is a dictionary . . . and a television program guide. These collections all differ from one another in both content and format. But each is a data base simply because it is a source of information.

CHARACTERISTICS OF A GOOD DATA BASE

A useful data base has four important characteristics.

1. It is complete. The more complete a data base is, the more likely it is to have the information that you need. For example, you'll find Dave Winfield's batting average only if you have his baseball card. You'll be able to check your friend Jan's telephone number only if you've listed it in your address book.

2. It is well organized. You might organize facts alphabetically, chronologically, or by topic. How you organize your data base depends on both its content and its intended use.

The more structured your data base is, the easier it is to find information. Thus if you've sorted your stamps by country and added index tabs to your album, you'll have little difficulty finding the pages with stamps of Burundi. If within the Burundi section you've arranged the stamps chronologically, you'll quickly find the set of animal stamps issued by that country in 1964.

Another equally good way to organize your stamps would be topically—with sections on animals, flowers, people, transportation, and so on. Within each section the stamps could be organized alphabetically by country. Then you can turn to the section of animal stamps issued by the kingdom of Burundi and easily find the set that you have in mind.

3. It is up-to-date. Your data base can be accurate and complete only if it is up-to-date. Generally, you'll need to revise and/or expand a data base to reflect changes in the information it includes. To make sure that Uncle Fred speedily receives your postcard, you must be sure to send it to the *new* address recorded in your address book. To boast a complete collection of American League baseball cards, you must continually add cards with statistics about new players.

4. It can be used efficiently. When a data base is complete, well organized, and up-to-date, there is a good chance that it can be used efficiently. You should be able to get the information that you need when you want it.

Collectors of everything from stamps to baseball cards are using computer data bases to store and retrieve information about their hobbies.

This computer operator at a large insurance company helps maintain a huge data base containing information on thousands of policy holders.

COMPUTERIZING A DATA BASE

As you have seen, you can set up a useful data base manually—and you do, whenever you create any kind of list or record to organize information. But what happens when your collection of data gets really big? You start out with notes on a single index card. Gradually you accumulate a pile of index cards. You set up an organizational system and file the cards in a box. Before long there's a second box, and then a third. Soon you need an index to your index cards in order to find information!

That's where a computer and a data-base management system come in handy. A computer, as you know, is an ideal tool for collecting and manipulating data. A data-base management system, or **DBMS**, is a special program designed to enable you to manage data on a computer in a useful way. With a data-base management system, you can transfer the contents of your cards, notebooks, and file cabinets onto disks. Then you can use the computer to retrieve the data, organize it, update it, and even sort through it for specific information. Need an alphabetical list of all the players in your baseball card collection? A list of those players born in 1957? A list of shortstops? Tell the computer what you want. In seconds it pulls the information out of your data base and displays it on the screen.

THE ADVANTAGES OF USING ELECTRONIC FILES

The larger and more complex your collection of data is, the more likely it is that you should set up electronic files. Using electronic files, you can store data more efficiently in much less space. You can retrieve information in much less time with much less trouble.

To get a better idea of the advantages of using electronic files, let's compare what happens when you try to find a book using a familiar data base—a library card catalogue—and a computerized data base—a computerized catalogue. Consider the following situation.

You are interested in finding a book about the history of Australia. Assume that your library has a closed stack system for nonfiction books. You cannot just go up to the shelves and browse. To look at a book, you must fill out a request form, listing the title, author, and call number. A library clerk then brings the book to you. The library is often busy and you must wait your turn. Since you can request only three books at a time, you must select your books carefully.

The card catalogues of this library have been put into a computerized data base.

Using a card catalogue. Since you are not looking up a book by title or author, you go over to the *ART–BUH* drawer in the subject card catalogue. You turn to the section with cards headed "Australia." If you'd bother to count, you'd find nearly 150 cards. You pull the drawer out of the cabinet and take it over to a table where you sit thumbing through the cards. Patiently you go past the cards with the subheadings "Antiquities," "Bibliography," "Biography," "Civilization," "Colonies," "Commerce," and "Constitution." Some time later you come to "Description and History." You mark down six titles, authors, and call numbers; replace the drawer in the cabinet; and turn in your book requests, three at a time.

Using a computer catalogue. You go over to a computer terminal near the information desk. You sit down, read the greeting on the screen, type "F SUBJECT AUSTRALIA, HISTORY," and press RETURN. The computer is alerted that you are interested in books on Australian history. Next you indicate that you want to see a description of the history books. You enter "DISPLAY FULL." The computer responds by flashing on the screen

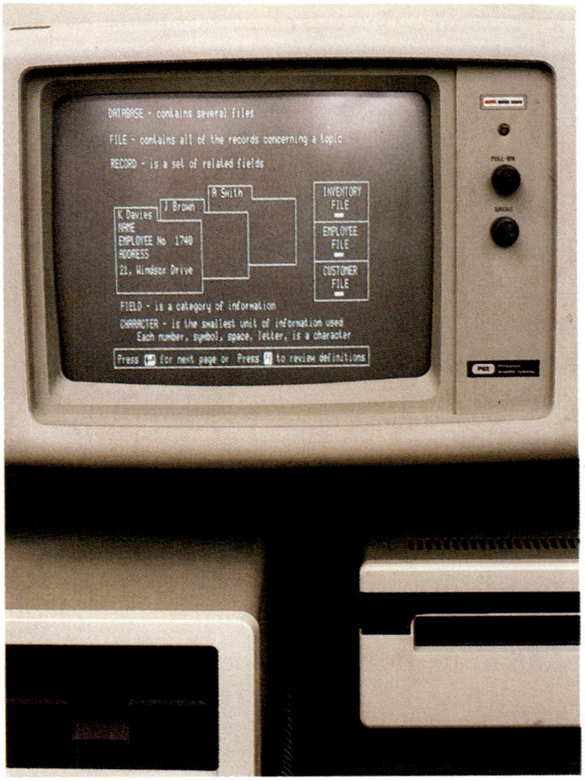

Many data-base management software programs have menus to help you create and update files.

a key number, the title, author, publication information, and description of each of the Australia history books in the library's collection. You direct the computer to print out the titles, authors, and call numbers of the six books of interest to you by entering their key numbers. You have a list of books in hand in a matter of seconds.

By using a computerized catalogue, you have saved yourself the time and effort involved in searching through a drawer full of cards. The library, in turn, has simplified its record keeping and saved storage space—no more title, author, and subject cards (all containing basically the same information); no more filing and reorganizing to update the system; no more bulky cabinets. Savings like these in space, time, and effort have led many libraries, schools, hospitals, businesses, and government agencies to set up electronic files.

Key Points

- A data base is a collection of related information, such as a set of baseball cards or an address file.
- A good data base is complete, well organized, and up-to-date, and you can use it efficiently.
- The larger and more complex a data base becomes, the more likely it is that a computer could help you to manage and use it efficiently.

Review Questions

1. How do you organize a data base?
2. What advantage does an electronic data base have over a large card index?

SETTING UP A DBMS

Now that you know the advantages of electronic files, let's set up a data-base management system in order to learn how one works. Assume that you are in charge of your school's video library. You have access to a microcomputer and are interested in computerizing your ever-expanding catalogue. Since you already have a data base—a title and a subject card catalogue—you have a good idea of the kind of information that people want and how they can best find it. After consulting with the computer lab instructor, you buy a DBMS. You're ready to begin.

LEARNING THE JARGON

Before turning to the computer, you review the documentation that accompanies the program and become familiar with the terminology, or jargon, of a DBMS. You learn three important words: **field**, **record**, and **file**.

Field. A field is a single category of information in your data base. It can be made up of numbers, letters, or a combination of numbers and letters. You look at a catalogue card in your current data base and identify eleven fields, including type of movie, movie title, and call number.

Record. A record is a collection of fields. Each catalogue card with all its entries about a single movie is a record. Since your catalogue currently consists of title and subject cards, you have two records for each movie listed in your data base.

File. A file is a collection of related records. Your subject catalogue is one file; your title catalogue is another. Your DBMS will eliminate duplicate records and combine the two files.

While every data base consists of fields, records, and files, some can handle more data than others. Say that this particular program allows 65 characters in a field, 12 fields in a record, and 300 records in a file. Each letter, number, or space in an entry counts as one character. You note that in setting up your DBMS you'll have to shorten the descriptions of the movies. After making this minor adjustment,

This index card is one record in a file of a data base. Each piece of information—such as the movie title—is a field within the record.

Drama
V025

Lassie Come Home; MGM; 1943; Fred M. Wilcox;
Roddy McDowall, Elizabeth Taylor.

88 minutes; Technicolor; Beta/VHS

First of Lassie series. Financial difficulties force a rural family to sell its beloved collie, but she finds her way home.

you'll have plenty of room for the data that you want to store.

GETTING ORGANIZED ON PAPER

Exactly what categories of data should you store? To make sure that you structure your DBMS in a useful way, it's worthwhile to organize it on paper first. You must carefully consider what fields of information to include.

You examine the eleven fields of information in your data base. Some of them provide information that is helpful in finding a specific movie. Some of them provide information that is helpful in deciding whether or not to choose that movie. Since all of the fields contain useful information and your program allows twelve fields, you decide to include all eleven in your computerized data base. You list the fields as follows:

1. Type of Movie
2. Call Number
3. Movie Title
4. Studio
5. Year of Release
6. Director
7. Leading Actors
8. Running Time
9. Color Process
10. Video Format
11. Description

CREATING A FORMAT

By listing the fields to be included in each record, you have created a **format**—a blank data-entry form. You're now ready to list your fields and create your format on computer.

You load the program into the computer and wait. After you pass through an introductory screen, a menu appears:

```
          *Main Menu*
A = Add/Inspect/Update a Record
C = Create a New File
L = Generate a List
R = Generate a Report
S = Select a Record
X = Exit from System
```

You enter "C" for "Create a New File," and the program directs you to name the new file.

```
Create a New File
Enter the new file name
you wish to create:
```

Your file name should say something about the kind of data you are organizing. You enter the word "Video." The program then asks you to define your fields and tells you how to go about it.

```
Define Your Fields for File:
Video
Field titles--to 15 characters
Field lengths--to 65 characters
Field types--a = alphanumeric
             n = numeric
Field #1
   Title:
```

You begin by defining Field #1. First you must choose a title, or name. This title can be up to 15 characters long. You count the characters of the title for Field #1 on your list (Type of Movie) and find that it is 13 characters long. You enter "Type of Movie" as your first title.

Next you must set the length of Field #1. The longest movie classification in your catalogue is 15 characters (Science Fiction). But you want to make sure that you'll always have room for a double classification (Science Fiction/Comedy). You enter "30" for the field length.

Finally you must specify the type of field, **alphanumeric** or **numeric**. An alphanumeric field consists of letters and numbers or of letters only. *Wizard of Oz* and *101 Dalmatians* are alphanumeric. A numeric field consists of numbers only. *1941* is an example of a numeric entry. You enter "a" for the first field.

You go through a similar procedure for the other ten fields. When you have defined all eleven fields, you can display, or show, your field descriptions on the screen. A screen listing the first six fields might look like this:

```
Fields for File: Video
        Title                Length   Type
1. Type of Movie               30       a
2. Call Number                  5       a
3. Movie Title                 50       a
4. Studio                      30       a
5. Year of Release              4       n
6. Director                    25       a
```

ENTERING DATA

Once you have defined the fields, you have finished creating your data-entry form. It's time to get to work and actually enter all the data from your catalogue.

You exit to the main menu to find out how to call up a blank data entry form. Then you enter "A" for "Add/Inspect/Update a Record," and the program asks you to name the file in which you'd like to enter a record.

```
Add/Inspect/Update a Record
Enter the file name:
```

After you enter "Video," you see the standard format that you have created by listing and defining your fields.

```
File: Video
Record: 1
 1. Type of Movie:
 2. Call Number:
 3. Movie Title:
 4. Studio:
 5. Year of Release:
 6. Director:
 7. Leading Actors:
 8. Running Time:
 9. Color Process:
10. Video Format:
11. Description:
```

You fill in the blank record, field by field. The completed record for the movie *Lassie Come Home* looks like this.

```
File: Video
Record: 1
 1. Type of Movie: Drama
 2. Call Number: V025
 3. Movie Title: Lassie Come Home
 4. Studio: MGM
 5. Year of Release: 1943
 6. Director: Fred M. Wilcox
 7. Leading Actors: R. McDowall,
                    E. Taylor
 8. Running Time: 88 minutes
 9. Color Process: Technicolor
10. Video Format: Beta/VHS
11. Description: First of series.
    Collie returns to farm family
    that sold her.
```

You press RETURN to store this record in the computer's data base, and you call up a blank entry form for another movie. You begin filling in the information.

By the time you get to your tenth record, you get tired of entering data. But you keep at it, realizing that you must carefully and consistently enter data in order to be able to retrieve it.

USING YOUR DBMS

Now that you have entered your records into the file, you can put the program to work for you. You can use all of the options listed as commands on the program's main menu. Since you will be using your video file most often to identify movies in your library, let's take a closer look at the way your program lets you select a record from the file—in other words, **search a file**.

Searching a file. You know that your library has several *Lassie* films. What happens when the student council president asks you to recommend the two that you think should be shown at a film festival? You search your file to review the record on each film. You enter:

1. the command "S" to indicate that you want a specific record.
2. the number "3" to indicate that you want to search for it on Field #3, Movie Title.
3. the word "Lassie" to indicate that you are interested in titles that **match** this word.
4. the letter "P" to indicate that *Lassie* is only part of the title field. You are also interested in a **partial match**—titles that include the word "Lassie".
5. enter the number "1" to indicate that your search should begin with record #1.

Coincidentally, record number 1—the first film that you entered in your data base—is *Lassie Come Home*. Your completed record for that film appears on the screen along with the query:

```
Continue search (y=yes, n=no):
```

You enter "y" for "yes" and the DBMS continues searching your library for *Lassie* titles in the order in which they were entered into the file. The DBMS presents, in turn, three more records. You skim each one and choose *Courage of Lassie* and *Son of Lassie*.

For a data base to be useful it must contain accurate and updated information.

Other uses. You can do a number of other things with records in your data base. Occasionally you print the records that have been retrieved. You sort the records and rearrange the order in which information is listed. You update the records, editing, adding, or removing data. In each case you refer to the main menu and then follow the directions on-screen to manipulate and retrieve information.

You find that you use your DBMS for activities like these:

• Adding a listing when the principal donates *Babes in Toyland*.

• Removing the record of *Pride and Prejudice* after the video got jammed in a machine.

• Identifying the director of *The Harlem Globetrotters on Gilligan's Island*.

• Changing your record on *Little Women* when you learn that you have the 1933 version rather than the 1949 film.

• Locating five movies starring Cesar Romero.

• Displaying a list of adventure films produced after 1935.

• Printing an alphabetized bibliography of the musicals in your collection.

A data base helps this company to track projects from beginning to completion.

PUTTING A DBMS TO WORK

Are you convinced that you need a DBMS to help you run your video library? Organize your stamp collection? Keep track of your baseball cards? Here are just a few more examples of how a simple DBMS is helpful in organizing and retrieving information.

At home. One teen-age girl and her brother use a DBMS to help them run a silk-screened clothing business. They buy ready-made T-shirts, sweat shirts, and socks, and paint designs on them. Their friends sell the clothes. The two young businesspeople keep track of sales on their computer, noting how many and what kind of clothing each friend sells. They use this information to help them determine how many and what kind of clothes to silk screen.

In school. A junior high school class uses a DBMS to help them evaluate their television-viewing habits. For several months they keep records of such data as the amount of time spent watching television, the kinds of programs watched, and the amount of violence on the programs. They plan to use the information that they gather in a report on television viewing habits.

At work. The managing editor of a publishing company uses a DBMS to keep track of the books being published. For example, she notes when the manuscript comes in from an author, when it is reviewed by an editor, when it is sent to an

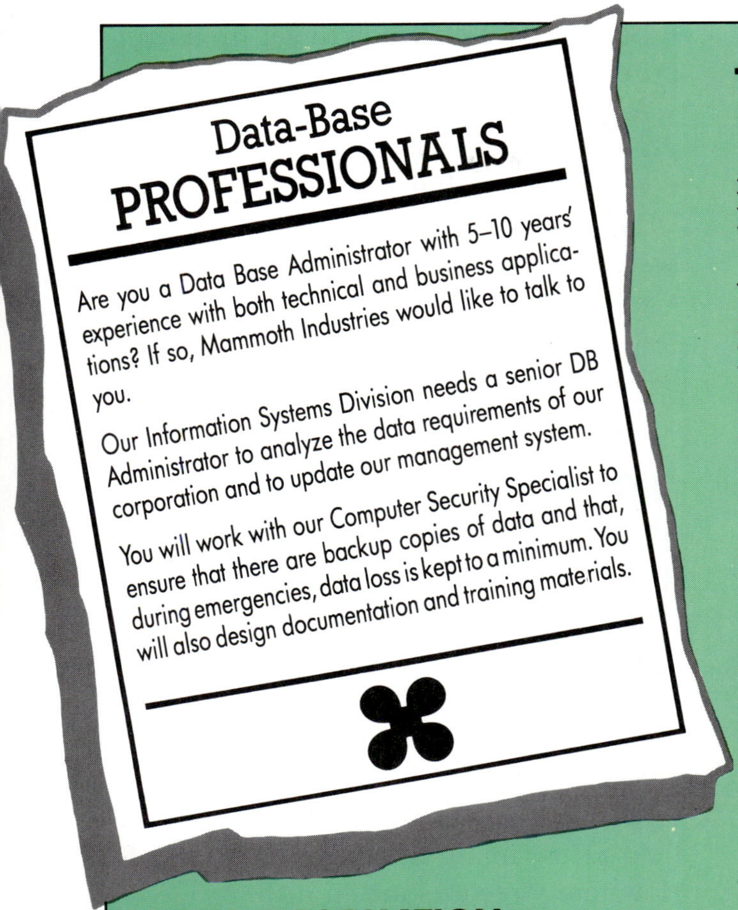
Data-Base
PROFESSIONALS

Are you a Data Base Administrator with 5–10 years' experience with both technical and business applications? If so, Mammoth Industries would like to talk to you.

Our Information Systems Division needs a senior DB Administrator to analyze the data requirements of our corporation and to update our management system.

You will work with our Computer Security Specialist to ensure that there are backup copies of data and that, during emergencies, data loss is kept to a minimum. You will also design documentation and training materials.

THAT'S MY JOB

Carol Klitzner, a Data Base Administrator, has this to say about her job:

"I feel like a master librarian, with a great data base management system that I helped design. I enjoy knowing how all the data are organized, and I enjoy improving the system in ways that allow users to efficiently retrieve the data they need.

"When the system goes down, I'm not happy until everything is straightened out again. I make it my business to see that the system gets up as quickly as possible and that we don't lose any important files."

MORE INFORMATION

Business courses as well as programming courses are helpful in preparing for this career.... More and more corporations and government agencies are installing data-base management systems.... There will be a high demand for people who know how to custom-design DBMS's for specific kinds of organizations.... Salaries are good.

illustrator, and when it is ready to be printed. The editor-in-chief can call her at any time to find out the status of a particular book.

How else might you use a DBMS? A travel agent uses a DBMS to keep track of passenger and flight information. A personnel director uses a DBMS to keep employee records. A shoe store owner uses a DBMS to keep track of inventory. The list of uses goes on and on.

Key Points

- Information in a data base is divided into files, records, and fields.

• To structure a DBMS in a useful way, you must consider carefully the fields of information you want to include in each record.
• After you have created a format for an electronic data base, you enter information in the blank records, field by field.
• When the electronic data base is complete, you can use the DBMS to retrieve specific information instantly and display it on your screen. You can also use the DBMS to sort the information, change it, or print it.

Review Questions

1. What is the relationship of fields, records, and files?
2. What three points must you consider in defining a field?

BUYING A DBMS

While a DBMS has many uses, not all data bases need to be computerized. Before rushing out to buy a DBMS, you should consider both how complicated your data base is and what you'll gain from putting it on computer.

Ask yourself the following questions:

• Is your data base getting too large to handle?
• Do you need to update your files very frequently?
• Do you need many indexes to find the information that you want to retrieve?
• Do you need to retrieve information quickly?
• Do you have the time to set up a computerized data base?
• Will you take the time to keep your computerized data base up-to-date?
• Is the time that you'll save using a DBMS worth the expense of buying the program (and, perhaps, a computer)?
• If you can answer "yes" to each question, you might start investigating commercial programs.

CHOOSING THE RIGHT PROGRAM

Since there are literally hundreds of database programs on the market, it's important to find one that meets your needs. Now it's your turn to start asking questions. Here are just some of the areas of concern:

File size. How many characters are in a field? How many fields are in a record? How many records are in a file?

Data input. How easy is it to enter data? Can you create your own format? Can you revise the format easily?

Program Options. How easy is it to edit, add, or remove data from a file? How quickly can you search for information? In how many ways can you sort, or rearrange, information? Can you design the format of printed reports? Can you print more than one kind of report?

The answers to all these questions should provide you with a data base on data-base management systems. Evaluate your data and you're likely to choose the right program.

REVIEW & APPLICATION

SUMMARY

- A data-base management system (DBMS) is a computer program that allows you to store, retrieve, and manage information electronically.
- With a DBMS program, storing, retrieving, sorting, and organizing large amounts of information is faster and easier than with a manual data base.
- The more information you have in your collection, the more you are likely to benefit from DBMS software.
- A data base is divided into files, records, and fields. A record is a set of related fields, and a file is a set of related records.
- In establishing a data base, you should consider the fields of information you want to include and how much information those fields must contain.
- With a DBMS, you can find and display specific information from your records by searching a file electronically for key words in a field.
- Some DBMS programs can handle more data than others. DBMS programs also differ in how easy they are to use.

VOCABULARY

Match each item in the left column with the correct definition on the right.

a. data base	1. letters, numbers, or combination
b. field	2. a collection of related facts and figures
c. record	3. rearrange the order of listed data
d. format	4. the pattern for entering data in a DBMS
e. sort	5. a collection of fields

REVIEW QUESTIONS

1. What are the four important characteristics of a useful data base?
2. If the fields in a data base contain the years and descriptions of historical events, do the fields contain alphanumeric or numeric data?
3. What are two advantages of a DBMS?
4. What two commands would you give the library computer described in this chapter in order to view data on books describing animals in Africa?
5. What should you read before running a data-base management program?
6. What three steps are involved in formatting a DBMS?

DISCUSSION QUESTION

Why would a data-base management system be useful to a record store? Describe the kinds of fields that might be used in formatting the DBMS.

PROJECTS

C The following program demonstrates the features of a data base. This data base will keep track of your record collection. When you run the program, it will ask you to enter the name of the record and the name of the artist for each of ten records. Then it will ask you if you want to retrieve the records according to title or artist.

```
10 PRINT:PRINT:PRINT
20 PRINT "RECORD COLLECTION
    DATA BASE"
30 FOR I=1 TO 10
40 INPUT "ENTER TITLE: ";T$(I)
50 INPUT "ENTER ARTIST: ";A$(I)
60 PRINT: NEXT I
70 PRINT: PRINT "RETRIEVE DATA"
80 PRINT "   1. BY TITLE"
90 PRINT "   2. BY ARTIST"
100 PRINT "   3. END"
110 INPUT "ENTER CHOICE: "; N
120 IF N=1 THEN GOSUB 300
130 IF N=2 THEN GOSUB 400
140 IF N=3 THEN END
150 GOTO 70
300 INPUT "ENTER TITLE: "; B$
310 PRINT: FOR I=1 TO 10
320 IF B$=T$(I) THEN PRINT
     T$(I), A$(I)
330 NEXT I: RETURN
400 INPUT "ENTER ARTIST: "; B$
410 PRINT: FOR I=1 TO 10
420 IF B$=A$(I) THEN PRINT
     A$(I), T$(I)
430 NEXT I: RETURN
```

Line 40 combines a PRINT statement and an INPUT statement. The line could be written

```
40 PRINT "ENTER TITLE";:
     INPUT T$(I)
```

but it is easier to combine the two statements. The semicolon(;) tells the computer to put the prompt for the input right next to the message.

Look at the PRINT statements in lines 320 and 420. The commas tell the computer to print the two strings on the same line, but in different columns. Enter the program and run it. Input ten records. Then retrieve several different titles and artists.

Further Practice

D Don't lose track of your classmates during summer vacation. Create a format for a data base that includes your classmates' names, addresses, telephone numbers, and birthdays.

D Should your school do away with file cabinets? Consider the advantages of computerized data bases. Describe the data bases that are used or could be used in your school.

Enrichment

C A good test of a DBMS is the ease with which records can be modified. Check out the system that you used to create a data base in the first project. Add a third field—Type of Record—so that you can sort records by type, by title, or by artist.

CHAPTER TEST

Write your answers on a sheet of paper numbered 1 through 9.

MATCHING

1. Match each term to its definition.

a. data	1. rearrange in a particular order
b. sort	2. collection of fields
c. data base	3. facts and figures
d. record	4. collection of facts and figures

MULTIPLE CHOICE

2. Which of the following would lend itself to a DBMS?
   a. a list of four names and addresses
   b. the birthdays of a family of six
   c. all the clients of a large company
   d. your three favorite songs

3. A common type of data base is a:
   a. newspaper
   b. phone book
   c. school ID card
   d. recipe

4. A DBMS is characterized by:
   a. electronic files
   b. movie titles
   c. vacuum tubes
   d. its chips

5. A data base can be used efficiently if it is well organized, up to date, and:
   a. well-defined
   b. complete
   c. portable
   d. digital

6. One advantage of a DBMS is that it:
   a. is very inexpensive
   b. takes no time to set up
   c. replaces transistors
   d. saves time and space

7. An important factor when entering data into a field is:
   a. the importance of the data
   b. the length of the field
   c. the color of the field
   d. all of the above

8. In choosing the right DBMS program, you should consider:
   a. file size, ease of data input, and options
   b. the system used by your library
   c. the system used by a publisher
   d. the computer language you know

9. Here's the file:
   (1) Title
   (2) Director
   (3) Composer(s)
   (4) Year of release
   (5) Stars
   (6) Studio

   Choose the best title:
   a. Movie Musicals
   b. Horror Films
   c. Nature Movies
   d. Books

CHAPTER

8 9 10 11 12

USING a SPREADSHEET

Suppose you and other members of the student council are planning a school fair to raise $4300 for band uniforms. At the fair, you plan to sell whole-wheat muffins, raisin bread, second-hand books, records, and fruit juice by the cup. You also plan to hold a raffle for a video cassette recorder. Luckily, the VCR and the sale items are being donated.

Now you have to figure out how to earn that amount. You must decide two things:

1. How much to charge for each sale item?
2. How many items to sell?

In order to make your calculations, you take a piece of paper and divide it up into rows and columns. Across the top of the paper you write the following titles, each one in a separate column: SALE ITEM, NUMBER OF ITEMS, SALE PRICE, TOTAL. In the rows on the left of the sheet of paper, you list the items that will be sold at the fair: Boxed muffins, Loaves of bread, 45-rpm records, LP records, Paperback books, Raffle tickets, Juice.

What you have created is a **spreadsheet**. This spreadsheet will allow you to experiment and make predictions about sales prices and amounts of the items so that you can determine how to reach your goal of $4300.00.

With pencil and the paper spreadsheet, you and the other students start to plan. Suppose you decide that you will be able to sell 40 boxes of muffins at $2.00 a box. In the column marked "NUMBER OF ITEMS," you enter "40." In the column marked "SALE PRICE," you enter

The amounts in this spreadsheet will have to be rewritten and the total refigured many times before the student council selects the prices that will enable it to reach its goal.

Sale Item	No. of Items	Sale Price	Total
Boxed muffins	40	$2.00	$ 80.00
Loaves of bread	12 (dozen)	3.00 (per loaf)	432.00
45-rpm records	1200	.50	600.00
LP records	450	1.25	562.50
Paperback Books	325	.35	113.75
Raffle tickets	1500	1.00	1500.00
Juice			

"$2.00." Then to figure the total, you multiply 40 × 2.00 and get $80.00.

Next you decide that you can sell 12 dozen loaves of bread at $3.00 per loaf. You enter these figures on the spreadsheet and figure out the total.

You continue making decisions about the number of items and the sale prices you will assign to each item. You decide to sell 1200 45-rpm records for $0.50 each; 450 LP records for $1.25 each; 325 paperback books for $0.35 each; and 1500 raffle tickets for $1.00 each. You figure out the totals for each item and add these to the TOTAL column.

At this point, you take a subtotal before you decide on a price for juice. You add up the totals of all the other items and find that the total comes to $3288.25—not quite your goal of $4300.00. In order to make up the remainder of $1011.75, you'd have to sell over 2000 cups of juice at $0.50 each, which, you decide, is not realistic. What will you do?

The only thing you can do is go back and rework some of the figures, substituting different quantities and sale prices. Each time you change a quantity or price, you'll have to refigure the total and refigure the subtotal in order to know how far you are from meeting your goal. That's a lot of figuring, and you could spend most of a day doing it.

PAPER SPREADSHEETS AND BUSINESSES

The kind of spreadsheet you made up for your school fair is a small version of the kind of spreadsheets businesses have

This handwritten spreadsheet shows the total income for a small company. A paper spreadsheet, pencil, eraser, and calculator, however, are inefficient tools to do financial planning for a large company.

		JAN.	FEB.	MARCH	APRIL	MAY	JUNE
1	SALES	9348.67	10,612.83	10,531.36	8167.49	12,943.80	12,935.55
2	BANK INTEREST	000.00	000.00	174.18	000.00	000.00	176.93
3	RENT	1200.00	1200.00	1200.00	1200.00	1200.00	1200.00
4	SALARIES	4050.00	4050.00	4250.00	4250.00	4250.00	4250.00
5	SALES TAX	747.90	849.02	842.50	653.40	1035.50	1034.84
6	TOTAL MONTHLY	9348.67	10,612.83	10,705.54	8167.49	12,943.80	13,112.48
7	INCOME						
8	TOTAL INCOME	9348.67	19,961.50	30,667.04	38,834.53	51,778.33	64,890.81
9	FOR YEAR						
10							
11							
12							
13							

been using for hundreds of years to keep track of their money and make predictions about their sales and profits.

A typical business spreadsheet might have twelve vertical columns and forty-two horizontal rows. Each column might represent a month of the year. Some of the rows might represent transactions in which the business spends or receives money, and others might show totals for each month of how much money the business spends, how much it receives, how much profit it makes, and other categories of figures. Forty-two rows are usually not enough for a large business to record its transactions on. A complete spreadsheet for such a business might actually consist of dozens of spreadsheet pages.

One of the ways in which a business uses a spreadsheet is to show how each individual transaction or change affects the operation's finances. For example, a change in the price of a product would change the total sales figures for that product, and it would change the profit (or loss) figure for the entire operation.

To keep track of a business's money with a paper spreadsheet, bookkeepers or accountants have to enter transactions on the spreadsheet with a pencil. Later on they use an adding machine or a calculator to determine the effect of the transactions on the totals for income, expenses, and other categories. These calculations would result in more figures to be entered by hand on the spreadsheet. And if bookkeepers or accountants make even a small error, totals will have to be completely refigured. Even something as minor as entering $3250 instead of $3520 can lead to errors that take hours to correct.

Using a paper spreadsheet is usually not difficult for planning a school fair or running a very small business. However, for a very large business with complex financial records, it could take several days to calculate all the effects of a single transaction. If a company were making plans for a new product or big purchase, making financial predictions with a paper spreadsheet could take weeks or even months.

THE ELECTRONIC SPREADSHEET

Since 1979 the **electronic spreadsheet** has been available. An electronic spreadsheet is a program that runs on a computer. How is the electronic spreadsheet different from the old paper-and-pencil

Applications such as electronic spreadsheets can be used by people in almost every type of business.

method? Let's look first at the *similarities* between the old spreadsheet and the new.

First, the electronic spreadsheet has columns and rows, just as the paper spreadsheet does. The columns are identified by letters of the alphabet across the top of the sheet, and the rows are identified by numbers down the left side of the sheet. The rows and columns are otherwise blank, just like those on the paper spreadsheet, so you can label them to represent time periods, kinds of transactions, or other categories. You also can enter numbers on the electronic spreadsheet, like a paper spreadsheet.

When you begin to enter data on an electronic spreadsheet, think of yourself as playing a game, with the spreadsheet as a kind of giant gameboard. In a way, you make up the game—your specific spreadsheet design—by following a few simple rules for entering data.

With an electronic spreadsheet, of course, you enter the data with a keyboard rather than with a pencil. There are many other differences, too, that allow you to plan more carefully—and spend less time at it—than with a paper spreadsheet.

SIZE OF THE ELECTRONIC SPREADSHEET

Remember that the old spreadsheets have about 12 columns and 42 rows. The electronic spreadsheet has over 200 columns and more than 50 rows—sometimes hundreds. On many programs, columns across the top of the sheet begin with "A" and go to "Z" and continue with "AA" to "ZZ," then "AAA" to "ZZZ," and so on. Each row has a number, beginning with 1.

You might wonder how so many columns and rows can fit on a small computer screen. The answer is that they really don't all appear at once. Only about eight or nine columns and about twenty rows appear on the screen at once. When you need to see other columns or rows, you simply scroll across or down to the columns and rows you want to see.

The size of the electronic spreadsheet allows you to make much more complex forecasts than you could with old-fashioned paper spreadsheets. Keeping track of transactions is easier with electronic spreadsheets, too, because you don't have to keep turning pages in a big book as you would if you were using paper spreadsheets.

Spreadsheets have been used for hundreds of years by merchants to record business transactions.

CELLS AND THEIR ADDRESSES

The intersection of a column and a row on an electronic spreadsheet is called a **cell**. On a spreadsheet that has 250 columns and 55 rows, there would be a staggering 13,750 cells! Each has an **address** identified by its coordinates—the letter (or letters) that labels the column and the number that labels the row. Therefore, a cell in column CC, row 13, has an address of CC13. It's important to know the cell locations, because that's how you enter labels and values on the spreadsheet. Instead of writing in labels and values by pen or pencil, you enter them electronically through the computer's keyboard.

THE STATUS AREA

At the upper left-hand corner of the spreadsheet, there is a three-line **status area**. These lines show what you are doing while you are using the keyboard to enter data on the spreadsheet.

The first line shows the location of the cursor.

The second line is the **command line** or **prompt line**. When you enter data on the spreadsheet, you tell the computer how you want the data entered. For example, you might want to label rows or make a column wider than it normally is, or display some of the spreadsheet information on a graph, or move some numbers from one part of the spreadsheet to another part. You can do any of these things by giving the spreadsheet program a command. The command line shows what command the spreadsheet is following at any given time.

The third status line is the **edit line**.

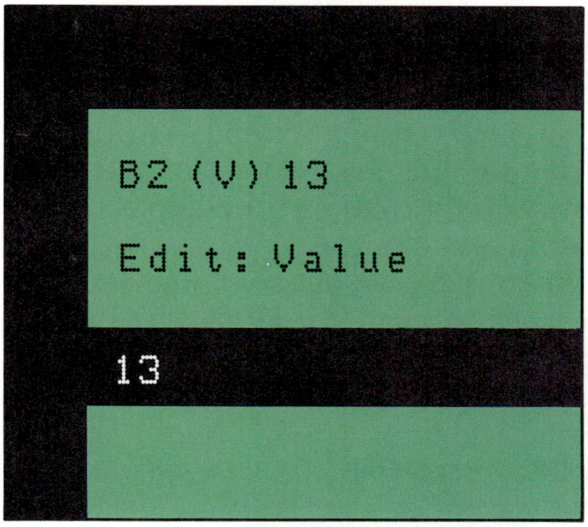

The status area shows in what cell the cursor is, the command you are instructing the computer to carry out, and the data you are entering.

This shows you what information you are entering while you are entering it. For example, if you are at cell B2 and you are entering the number 13, this number would appear in the edit line as well as in the cell.

CONTROLLING THE SPREADSHEET

On an electronic spreadsheet, you have almost total control over the data. You can change the contents of any cell by inserting new information, deleting information, or replacing information. You can give any cell a value (such as 1571.00) or a label (perhaps the name of a month or an account name, such as "Rent" or "Supplies").

One of the biggest advantages of an electronic spreadsheet is that you can also assign formulas to the cells that enable the computer's CPU to make calculations automatically. This can save you a great deal of time. Let's suppose you label cell F3 as the "total" of values entered in cells B3 through E3. Instead of having to use a calculator or mental arithmetic to add the totals for cells B3 through E3, you simply assign a formula to cell F3. That formula is @SUM(B3...E3). The symbol "@" indicates that you are assigning a formula to a cell. The word "SUM" indicates that the function is addition. (In some spreadsheets you might use "+" instead of "SUM".) The parentheses in the formula indicate that everything within them is to be added, and the cell addresses "B3...E3" mean that the values in these two columns and in every cell between them are to be added.

	A	B	C	D	E	F
1						
2						TOTAL
3	00	00	00	00	00	______

```
F3
VALUE
 @SUM(B3...E3)
```

	A	B	C	D	E	F
1						
2						TOTAL
3	00	00	00	00	00	______

The symbols for the formula do not appear in the cell itself; they appear only in the status area. The only thing that appears in the cell is the result of the formula: the total of cells B3, C3, D3, and E3.

You can assign other formulas to a cell, including those for multiplication (*), division (/), and subtraction (−). You can also assign a combination of these functions, such as "@100*(C4-G4)/G3," which means "subtract the value of cell G4 from the value of cell C4, multiply by 100, and divide by the value of cell G3."

Before electronic spreadsheets, recordkeeping was done in large, cumbersome ledger books.

SPREADSHEET POWER

The most powerful feature of the electronic spreadsheet is that it enables the computer to make instant calculations once you enter values and formulas. That means you can make corrections in one value and the spreadsheet will instantly recalculate all other values related to the one you changed. Suppose you had given the formula @SUM(B3...F3) to cell G3, and you changed the value of C3. The value of G3 would automatically change to show a new sum.

	MAY	JUNE	JULY	AUGUST	SEPT	TOTAL
EXPENSES						
Food	20.15	25.00	23.00	21.50	20.00	109.65
Clothing	--	--	--	--	--	--
Transportation	--	--	--	--	--	--

	MAY	JUNE	JULY	AUGUST	SEPT	TOTAL
EXPENSES						
Food	20.15	37.50	23.00	21.50	20.00	122.15
Clothing	--	--	--	--	--	--
Transportation	--	--	--	--	--	--

Remember that if you were working with a pencil-and-paper spreadsheet, you would have to recalculate the total of B3...F3 by hand or by calculator. If you had changed several values, it would take a while for you to recalculate the new total for G3. The electronic spreadsheet automatically—and quickly—recalculates G3 every time you change any value from B3 to F3.

With an electronic spreadsheet, therefore, you can make **forecasts** very easily. In forecasting, you ask "what-if" questions, such as "What if we raised the price of each shirt we sell from $15.20 to $18.50?" To see what effect this would have on other figures, such as Total Income From Sales, you would not have to do anything except change the price of the shirt on the spreadsheet from 15.20 to 18.50. The spreadsheet would automatically show the new total.

ITEM	PRICE	UNITS SOLD	TOTAL SALES
SHIRTS	15.20	200	3040.00

ITEM	PRICE	UNITS SOLD	TOTAL SALES
SHIRTS	18.50	200	3700.00

This is the feature that makes electronic spreadsheets useful to businesses. It allows people to see the effects of a transaction—such as a price change—before the transaction actually takes place. It helps them to avoid problems and to reach the best decisions about ways to make and manage money.

Key Points

- A spreadsheet is a tool for keeping track of transactions and the impact a single transaction has on the financial operations of a business.
- Each cell on an electronic spreadsheet has an address identified by the coordinates of a column and a row.
- In forecasting, you ask "what-if" questions that can be answered by the spreadsheet's power to instantly recalculate.

Review Questions

1. Describe two major ways in which an electronic spreadsheet is different from a paper spreadsheet.
2. What are some types of labels that might be assigned to columns on a spreadsheet?

AN ELECTRONIC SPREADSHEET AT WORK

Electronic spreadsheets are used mainly by business organizations, but many people use them to keep track of their household budgets and to plan projects. In addition to keeping track of money, you could use a spreadsheet to compute population figures, calories, athletic teams' win-loss records, and many other kinds of figures. Here's how you could use an electronic spreadsheet in planning the fair to buy band uniforms.

LABELING COLUMNS AND ROWS

First you would label the spreadsheet rows and columns with the information you have. You'll begin by labeling the rows with the names of the items that will be sold at the fair. To do this, you'll move the cursor to cell A1. You'll label this cell "SALE ITEM." As you type these words, they appear in cell A1 as well as in the edit line at the top left corner of the screen.

```
A1
SALE ITEM
```

Next you'll list the items in column A, rows 3 through 9. You begin with cell A3 (leaving A2 blank so that there's a space between the column label and the first entry). After typing the label "Muffins-boxes," you'll press the cursor-down key and the cursor will move downward to the next cell. Continue to label rows 4 through 9 with: "Bread-doz loaves," "45-rpm records," "LP records," "Paperback books," "Raffle tickets," and "Juice-cups."

```
SALE ITEM
Muffins-boxes
Bread-doz loaves
45-rpm records
LP records
Paperback books
Raffle tickets
Juice-cups
```

Next you'll label columns B, C, and D, as follows: NO. OF ITEMS, SALE PRICE, TOTAL.

```
SALE ITEM   NO. OF ITEMS   SALE PRICE   TOTAL

Muffins-boxes
Bread-doz loaves
```

ENTERING VALUES ON THE SPREADSHEET

In cell B3, opposite "Muffins," you'll enter "40" since that's how many boxes you expect to sell at the fair. Then you'll type in the remaining numbers that represent the amounts for each of the other sale items.

```
   SALE ITEM           NO. OF ITEMS

Muffins-boxes              40
Bread-doz loaves           12
45-rpm records             1200
LP records                 450
Paperback books            325
Raffle tickets             1500
Juice-cups                 700
```

In column C you'll enter the sale price you've decided on for each item. Beginning with cell C3, enter "2.00" (stands for two dollars).

SALE ITEM	NO. OF ITEMS	SALE PRICE
Muffins-boxes	40	2.00
Bread-doz loaves	12	3.00
45-rpm records	1200	.50
LP records	450	1.25
Paperback books	325	.35
Raffle tickets	1500	1.00
Juice-cups	700	1.00

ADDING FORMULAS

For the "TOTAL" column, you'll enter formulas so that the spreadsheet will automatically calculate the sale amount for each item. Begin with cell D3. The formula you'll enter is @(B3*C3). This formula appears on the third status line at the upper left-hand part of the spreadsheet. The sum itself—80.00—appears in cell D3.

```
D3
VALUE
@(B3*C3)
```

SALE ITEM	NO. OF ITEMS	SALE PRICE	TOTAL
Muffins-boxes	40	2.00	80.00

Next you'll need a formula for bread. Notice that the number 12 represents dozens of loaves. You expect to sell each loaf for $3.00 per loaf. This calls for a slightly different formula because you want the spreadsheet to convert dozens of loaves into individual loaves. The formula you will use is @12(B4*C4).

Your next formula will be for records. The formula you will enter is the same as the formula you entered for muffins. Therefore, instead of writing the formula over again, you can simply tell the spreadsheet to copy the formula from cell D3 to cell D5.

```
D3
Command: R
D5
```

Notice, too, that the formula you'll need for computing the total sales of LP records, paperback books, raffle tickets, and juice is also the same as the formula for muffins and 45-rpm records. Therefore, you can direct the spreadsheet to copy the formula from D3 to cells D5 through D9. The computer will automatically set these formulas for the cells you listed and compute the sums. Presto!

```
D3
Command: R
D5...D9
```

Copying formulas from one cell helps save time and prevent errors when filling out the information on a spreadsheet.

Finally, you'll want the spreadsheet to calculate the combined totals of all the sales items. Begin by labeling cell C11 "TOTAL SALES." You'll want the amount to appear as the sum of the figures in column D, so move to cell D11 and enter the formula for the total sales. What will that formula be? Right: @SUM(D3...D9). The sum will automatically appear after you've entered the formula.

```
C11
LABEL
TOTAL
```

SALE ITEM	NO. OF ITEMS	SALE PRICE	TOTAL
Muffins-boxes	40	2.00	80.00
Bread-doz loaves	12	3.00	432.00
45-rpm records	1200	.50	600.00
LP records	450	1.25	562.50
Paperback books	325	.35	113.75
Raffle tickets	1500	1.00	1500.00
Juice-cups	700	1.00	700.00
		TOTAL SALES	

```
D11
LABEL
@SUM(D3...D9)
```

SALE ITEM	NO. OF ITEMS	SALE PRICE	TOTAL
Muffins-boxes	40	2.00	80.00
Bread-doz loaves	12	3.00	432.00
45-rpm records	1200	.50	600.00
LP records	450	1.25	562.50
Paperback books	325	.35	113.75
Raffle tickets	1500	1.00	1500.00
Juice-cups	700	1.00	700.00
		TOTAL SALES	3988.25

CORRECTING MISTAKES

Now suppose you made a mistake, and the sale price for paperback books is not 35 cents but 45 cents. How will you make the change? Simply go back to cell C7 and type the new amount: .45. This will cancel the old figure.

What happens next shows the power of the electronic spreadsheet. Not only will

```
C7
VALUE
.45
```

the total in cell D7 change automatically from 113.75 to 146.25, but the total sales figure in cell D11 will change to 4020.75. If you had been using a paper spreadsheet, you would have had to recalculate the total for the paperback books and the total sales figure for all the items. With an electronic spreadsheet, the totals were recalculated automatically.

SALE ITEM	NO. OF ITEMS	SALE PRICE	TOTAL
Muffins-boxes	40	2.00	80.00
Bread-doz loaves	12	3.00	432.00
45-rpm records	1200	.50	600.00
LP records	450	1.25	562.50
Paperback books	325	.45	146.25
Raffle tickets	1500	1.00	1500.00
Juice-cups	700	1.00	700.00
		TOTAL SALES	4020.75

FORECASTING

In forecasting, you ask the "what-if" questions by changing values on the spreadsheet, obtaining new sums, and getting a different picture of your business situation.

If the goal of your fair is to raise $4300, and at current quantities and prices you would raise only $4020.75, you have two choices: You can either raise the quantity of sale items or you can increase the price of some of the items. Let's suppose you decide to increase the price of muffins to $3.25 a box and the price of 45-rpm records to 55 cents each. What effect will this have on the total sales?

To find out, simply replace "2.00" in cell C3 with "3.25," and replace ".50" in cell C5 with ".55." After you've input the new amounts, you'll notice that the totals in cells D3 and D5 change instantly, and so does the total sale amount in cell D11. The new total is $4130.75—still not enough to meet your goal.

SALE ITEM	NO. OF ITEMS	SALE PRICE	TOTAL
Muffins-boxes	40	3.25	130.00
Bread-doz loaves	12	3.00	432.00
45-rpm records	1200	.55	660.00
LP records	450	1.25	562.50
Paperback books	325	.45	146.25
Raffle tickets	1500	1.00	1500.00
Juice-cups	700	1.00	700.00
		TOTAL SALES	4130.75

Next you decide to increase the price of raffle tickets to $1.25 each. You replace the 1.00 figure in cell C8 with 1.25. The total in cell D8 changes instantly to 1875.00, and the total sales figure changes instantly to 4505.75—just over your goal of $4300.00

The ability of an electronic spreadsheet to let you ask "what-if" questions—and get answers quickly—is perhaps its most powerful feature because it allows planners to make accurate predictions quickly.

D11 (V)@Sum (D3...D9)

	A	B	C	D
1	SALE ITEM	NO. OF ITEMS	SALE PRICE	TOTAL
2				
3	Muffins-boxes	40	3.25	130.00
4	Bread-doz loaves	12	3.00	432.00
5	45-rpm records	1200	.55	660.00
6	LP records	450	1.25	562.50
7	Paperback books	325	.45	146.25
8	Raffle tickets	1500	1.25	1875.00
9	Juice-cups	700	1.00	700.00
10				
11			TOTAL SALES	4505.75
12				
13				

Electronic spreadsheets give the user a powerful and flexible tool for doing rapid and accurate forecasting.

Key Points

• Electronic spreadsheets are used mainly by businesses, but they are useful in many situations that involve working with large numbers of figures.
• To use an electronic spreadsheet, you must label the columns and rows and enter formulas for cells where you want the computer to make calculations.
• By asking "what-if" questions with an electronic spreadsheet, you can quickly forecast what the results might be of a business decision such as a price change.

Review Questions

1. Outside of the business world, in what ways do people use spreadsheets?
2. If you make an error when you enter data in a spreadsheet cell, how can you correct it?

WHEN TO USE AN ELECTRONIC SPREADSHEET

An electronic spreadsheet is very useful for keeping track of a large number of figures, such as for a business. In this kind of situation, the price of a spreadsheet program is more than offset by the amount of time it saves.

For very small or everyday personal record keeping, however, an electronic spreadsheet may not be the best tool. If you're keeping track of how you spend your allowance, for example, you'd probably do just as well—or better—to use pencil, paper, and a hand calculator.

To decide whether or not you need an electronic spreadsheet to solve a problem, ask yourself some questions.

• *Does the problem involve numbers that you can arrange in rows and columns?* If the answer is *no*, a spreadsheet won't help.
• *Do the numbers in one row or column have a numerical relationship to the numbers in another row or column?* Again, using a spreadsheet will help only if the answer is *yes*.
• *How many items am I going to keep track of?* If the number is less than ten, consider using a calculator instead of a spreadsheet.
• *How many different columns will I need?* If you're keeping track of sums for several weeks or months of the year or if you're keeping track of many variables, such as different rates and hours, then an electronic spreadsheet may be better than a paper one.
• *Will I be doing a lot of forecasting?* If you intend to do a lot of forecasting, then an electronic spreadsheet is definitely more useful than paper, pencil, and a calculator—especially for large amounts of data.
• *Are there likely to be many changes in the figures I keep track of?* If there are, and if you're keeping track of a lot of figures, then an electronic spreadsheet is the better choice.
• *Will I need to give copies of different versions of my spreadsheets to different people?* If you do, then you should consider an electronic spreadsheet, since you can change values and use a printer connected to your computer to produce copies very quickly.

There are many tasks for which a calculator is a better tool than an electronic spreadsheet.

CHOOSING AN ELECTRONIC SPREADSHEET

There are several different spreadsheet programs available, but they all function basically the same way. None of them is cheap, and the more sophisticated ones are quite expensive. Unless one of your parents, a friend's parents, or your school has one, you will probably not use an electronic spreadsheet for many years. If and when you do look into getting a spreadsheet (or advise an adult on how to buy one), there are a few points to keep in mind.

First, know what you want to use the spreadsheet for. If you've asked yourself the questions in the preceding section and you've decided that you do indeed need an electronic spreadsheet rather than a paper one, then you probably already have a pretty good idea of what you'll use it for. But it doesn't hurt to check your reasons again before you spend money for the program. In general, an electronic spreadsheet will help you keep track of a large number of facts and figures such as those you'd need in making up a budget for a small business, doing income taxes, keeping track of a large group of animals (such as on a farm or in wildlife research), or following investments in the stock market.

Once you know what you'll use the spreadsheet for, then it's time to look for a specific spreadsheet to meet your needs. When you begin looking, there are a few points to watch for. First, how easy is the spreadsheet to use? Try to find one that is user friendly—that is, one that is not so complicated to use that you become frustrated and give up.

Check to see how easy it is to enter and change data on the spreadsheet. Can you use function keys instead of typing elaborate commands?

Make sure the program has enough rows and columns to handle your job. It's probably a good idea to make sure the program has more than enough columns and rows for your job, in case you decide to tackle a bigger spreadsheet job in the future.

Decide what features are useful to you. Some spreadsheets have a feature called **windows**. Just as you look out a window to see other parts of the world, windows on an electronic spreadsheet allow you to look at other parts of the spreadsheet that aren't displayed on the screen. This can be helpful if you're doing a big spreadsheet job.

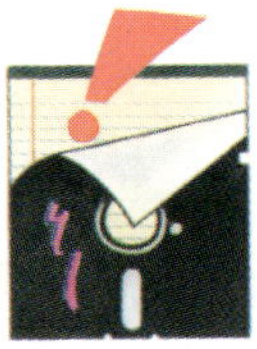

REVIEW & APPLICATION

SUMMARY

- The use of spreadsheets dates back hundreds of years, but electronic spreadsheets have been available only since 1979.
- A spreadsheet consists of columns and rows that are labeled to represent categories of information. The columns and rows intersect to form cells that contain the information.
- On an electronic spreadsheet, you can assign formulas to the cells that allow the computer to make the recalculations for you. This is the electronic spreadsheet's most powerful feature.
- An electronic spreadsheet can include many more rows and columns than a paper spreadsheet.
- With an electronic spreadsheet, you can ask "what-if" questions and easily forecast the results of a proposed financial change, such as raising prices.
- An electronic spreadsheet is very useful for working with a large number of figures. For small amounts of information, a pencil and a calculator might be better.

VOCABULARY

Match each item in the left column with the correct item on the right.

a. edit line	1. enables the computer to make recalculations
b. row	2. displays the information you are entering
c. formula	3. horizontal line of information on a spreadsheet
d. command line	4. shows instruction computer is following
e. cell	5. formed by the intersection of a column and row

REVIEW QUESTIONS

1. When would using a pencil and a calculator to make forecasts be more sensible than using an electronic spreadsheet?
2. How are the columns on an electronic spreadsheet identified? How are the rows identified?
3. How do you determine the address of a cell on an electronic spreadsheet?
4. When you assign a formula to a cell of an electronic spreadsheet, what appears in the cell?
5. How do electronic spreadsheets differ from each other?

DISCUSSION QUESTION

Do you think that business managers who use electronic spreadsheets still need arithmetic skills? Why or why not? Is this good or bad?

P R O J E C T S

C The following program shows simple features of a spreadsheet. The program will ask you to input your allowance, as well as various expenses. You can decide whether these figures will be weekly, monthly, and so on. The spreadsheet will tell you how much spending money you have left over.

```
10 HOME
20 PRINT "SPREADSHEET SAMPLE"
30 PRINT "      A",,"B"
40 PRINT: PRINT "1. ALLOWANCE",B(1)
50 PRINT "2. FOOD",,B(2)
60 PRINT "3. ENTERTAINMENT", B(3)
70 PRINT "4. TRANSPORTATION", B(4)
80 PRINT "   CASH REMAINING", B(5)
90 PRINT: PRINT "WHICH FIGURE
     WOULD YOU"
100 PRINT "LIKE TO CHANGE?"
110 PRINT: PRINT "ENTER 1,2,3,4,"
120 PRINT" OR 0 TO END"
130 INPUT N
140 IF N=0 THEN END
150 PRINT: INPUT "ENTER
     VALUE: "; V
160 B(N)=V
170 B(5)=B(1)-(B(2)+B(3)+B(4))
180 GOTO 10
```

If you are using the Commodore 64, IBM PCjr, or TRS-80 Model III, substitute the clear-screen command for the HOME statement in line 10.

Look at line 160. What sort of statement is it? It's a LET statement, even though the keyword LET does not appear. It could be written

```
160 LET B(N)=V
```

but it's shorter and easier to leave the keyword out. Most computers do not require you to use the keyword LET.

Enter and run the program. Assign values to the different categories. Change some of the values.

Further Practice

D Would an electronic spreadsheet simplify the job of the class treasurer? How would it be helpful to the bookkeeper who is in charge of paying the school staff? Consider whether or not your school needs a spreadsheet program. Who would use the program and why?

D How would you or your friends or relatives use an electronic spreadsheet? Describe how and why an electronic spreadsheet could be used by someone you know.

Enrichment

C Before deciding if you need to get an after-school job, do some forecasting. Make use of the data from the spreadsheet that you created in this chapter. First modify the program to list your earnings and your expenses in twelve columns—one for each month. Have the program print the cash remaining at the end of each month and at the end of the entire year.

CHAPTER TEST

Write your answers on a sheet of paper numbered 1 through 13.

MULTIPLE CHOICE

1. The status area of an electronic spreadsheet contains:
   a. cells
   b. rows
   c. an edit line
   d. all of the above

2. An electronic or paper spreadsheet is divided into:
   a. columns and rows
   b. status lines and edit lines
   c. commands and formulas
   d. "what-if" questions and answers

3. An electronic spreadsheet is better than a pencil and a calculator:
   a. in all situations
   b. for working with a large number of figures
   c. for planning how to use your weekly allowance
   d. for planning a small party

4. Compared with paper spreadsheets, electronic spreadsheets are usually:
   a. larger
   b. faster to use
   c. more expensive
   d. all of the above

5. With an electronic spreadsheet, you can make forecasts by:
   a. asking "what-if" questions
   b. assigning a formula
   c. using a flowchart
   d. adding up your transactions

FILL-IN

6. Some of the rows of a spreadsheet might represent ____________ in which a business spends or receives money.
7. On a paper spreadsheet, the values in the cells must be entered with a ____________.
8. The columns of an electronic spreadsheet are usually identified by ________ across the top of the sheet.
9. The rows of an electronic spreadsheet are usually identified by ______ down the left side.
10. On an electronic spreadsheet, the intersection of a column and a row is called a ____________.
11. At the upper left-hand corner of an electronic spreadsheet is a ____________ that usually contains three lines.
12. When you want to label a column, move some data from one cell to another, or display some spreadsheet information on a graph, you must give a ____________.
13. The location of an individual cell on an electronic spreadsheet is its ____________, identified by its column letter and row number.

CHAPTER

9 10 11 12 13

GRAPHICS

As you watch the computer screen, the outline of a car takes shape. The outline is filled in with color. Headlights, fenders, and wheels appear next. The new chrome seems to glisten in the sunlight. Suddenly the car pivots and starts to drive toward you. It finally turns and drives down a hilly road.

This scene could have been created using state-of-the-art computer graphics. Without the help of models or trick photography, computers can generate three-dimensional shapes that are shaded and can move. The most famous of these computer-generated special effects are those seen in science-fiction movies, but moviemakers aren't the only people creating computer graphics. Computer graphics are used by architects to plan buildings, by astronomers to chart distant stars, by pilots to hone their flying skills, by advertisers to create exciting commercials, and by many others as well. In fact, even the sneakers you wear were probably designed by computer!

You, too, can use computers to create beautiful pictures, doodle, direct a simple animated scene, or put together a chart, map, or graph. It's a lot of fun, and you don't have to be a technical wizard to create great-looking work.

Why not stick with the good old paper-and-pencil method of drawing? What's the advantage of using computers to create graphics? Computers eliminate a lot of tedious, time-consuming work. With computer graphics, as with word-processing software, there's no need to erase or use a new piece of paper—just delete and make changes right on the computer. As a design tool, the computer gives the user control and flexibility unmatched by any other design medium. In fact, in many cases computer graphics enable people to create images of things that are not ordinarily visible—like the inner brain or the depths of outer space.

Computer graphics have come a long way since the first realistic graphics programs were developed by the military in the 1960's. As graphics software for personal computers becomes increasingly sophisticated and user-friendly, its applications will become more and more diverse.

This chapter looks inside the computer to see how graphics are made. It also covers some of the different kinds of graphics you can create with your computer. Finally, it explores some of the ways that computer graphics are being used by professionals.

BEHIND THE SCREENS: HOW IT WORKS

Did you know that when you look at a computer screen you're really looking at thousands of tiny boxes of light? It's easy to picture this if you imagine a piece of graph paper covering your screen. Each box on the graph is called a **pixel**, which stands for *pic*ture *el*ement. Your average television screen consists of about 25,000 pixels. Professional display screens have hundreds of thousands of pixels. Each pixel can be identified by its coordinates. For example, in a grid that starts at 0, if a pixel is in the third column down and the second row across, its coordinates are 2,1.

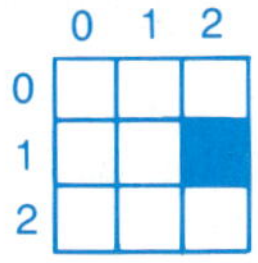

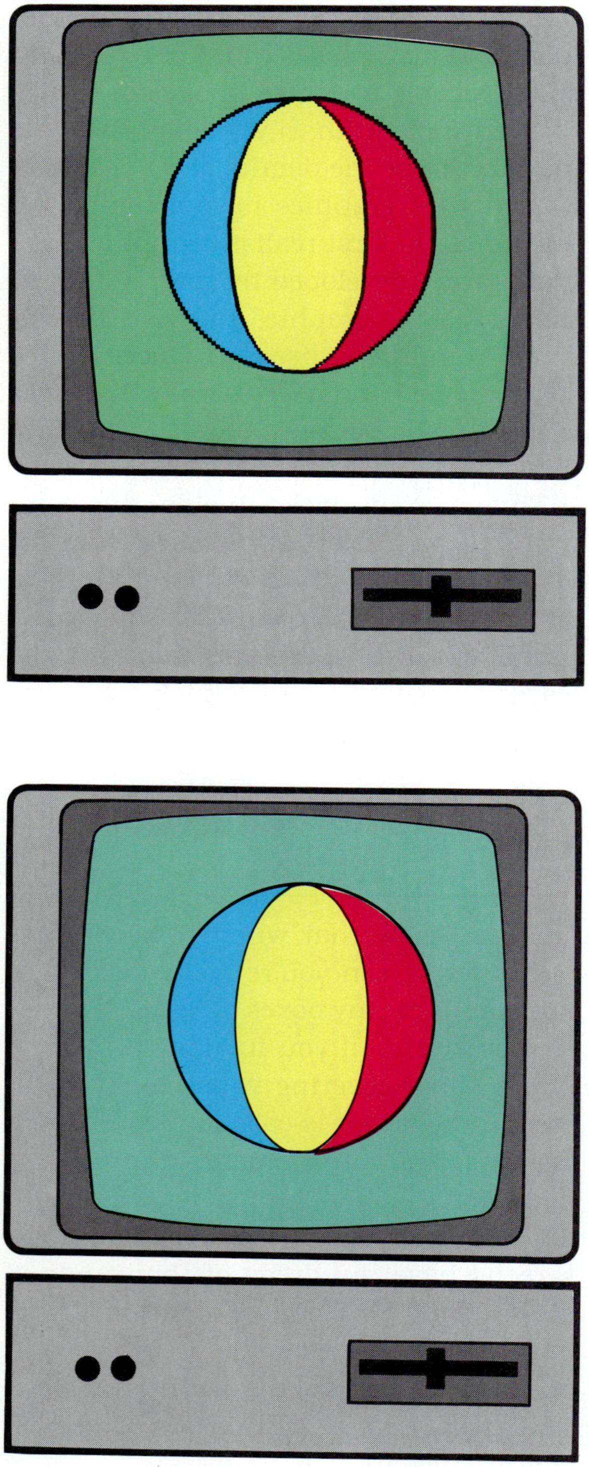

Low resolution graphics have ragged lines like the beach ball at the top, while the smooth lines of the bottom beach ball characterize high resolution.

When you draw a picture on your computer, your computer addresses each pixel, telling it to turn on or off. If you draw the outer frame of a house, the specific pixels that create the shape of that house turn on. In addition, you can control the color and brightness of each pixel.

The quality of the image is called its **resolution**. Low resolution means that the picture you see is jagged, while high resolution means that the picture is sharper and clearer. Resolution is determined in part by the number of pixels on your display screen. The greater the number and the smaller their size, the more blended the boundaries between pixels become and the smoother and more realistic the picture.

Your display screen isn't the only factor that influences resolution. The circuitry inside your computer also helps determine the resolution of an image.

Most microcomputers are designed to create both text and graphics. They operate in two modes: a text mode and a graphics mode. The difference is in the way the computer addresses the pixels. Because a lower resolution is required to display text, in the text mode the computer treats groups of pixels as a single unit. In the graphics mode, in the space where the computer would put one character of text, there might be four, six, eight or more graphic elements.

But even in the graphics mode, personal computers don't necessarily have the capacity to address each pixel individually. Instead they address blocks of four or eight pixels as one unit. This creates a boxy look.

A computer that is designed specifically for creating graphics can address every pixel individually. The Cray X-MP, for example, has the capacity for processing information about two million pixels! Weighing 7.5 tons and containing over two hundred thousand microchips, the X-MP can perform one billion calculations per second. With such a tool at their fingertips, artists can create pictures so realistic in terms of shading, texture, and color that you might think you're looking at a photograph of the real thing.

GRAPHICS YOU CAN CREATE

You can't paint a picture without paint, brushes, and a surface on which to work. When it comes to generating computer graphics, there are also a few essential tools. To begin, you need a computer and a display screen. You also need a program. You can write this program yourself or you can use a commercial graphics program. You need an input device to enter your program into the computer. And if you want a hard copy of your design, you need a printer or plotter.

You can program graphics on any computer. The simplest type of graphics is character graphics, in which you use the characters on your keyboard to draw a picture. With computers that have both a text mode and a graphics mode, character graphics are made in the text mode.

To make a drawing with character graphics, you can write a program in BASIC using PRINT statements. For example, to instruct the computer to draw a pine tree using the letter *X*, this is what you would enter:

```
10 PRINT "          X"
20 PRINT "         XXX"
30 PRINT "        XXXXX"
40 PRINT "       XXXXXXX"
50 PRINT "      XXXXXXXXX"
60 PRINT "     XXXXXXXXXXX"
70 PRINT "    XXXXXXXXXXXXX"
80 PRINT "         XXX"
90 PRINT "         XXX"
100 END
RUN
                  X
                 XXX
                XXXXX
               XXXXXXX
              XXXXXXXXX
             XXXXXXXXXXX
            XXXXXXXXXXXXX
                 XXX
                 XXX
```

Notice the spaces between the initial quotation marks and the start of the tree. That spacing is an important part of the information you must give the computer.

You can use character graphics to make all sorts of designs. You can use lots of regular letter *L*'s to create a giant *L*. You can make a face using *O*'s. You can make invitations or birthday cards—or you might just make fancy designs with letters.

Programming regular graphics is a bit more complicated. First of all, some computers require you to switch into the graphics mode. This is done by using a graphics statement. For some computers, this statement is a simple "GR"; other computers may use different statements. The graphics statement instructs the computer to display graphics on the screen.

In order to draw a picture using BASIC, you instruct the computer to fill in specific pixels by typing in their coordinates.

To draw a rectangle on the screen, you could write a program like this:

```
10 GR
20 COLOR=8
30 VLIN 13,20 AT 17
40 VLIN 13,20 AT 23
50 HLIN 18,22 AT 13
60 HLIN 18,22 AT 20
70 END
```

> This program has four new BASIC keywords:
>
> **GR**— tells the computer to switch to the graphics mode.
>
> **COLOR**—tells the computer which color to use. (In this case, 8 = brown.)
>
> **VLIN**— tells the computer to draw a vertical line.
>
> **HLIN**— tells the computer to draw a horizontal line.
>
> These are BASIC commands on some computers—but not all. To draw a square on your computer, you may need different commands.

Line 10 tells the computer to switch to the graphics mode. Line 20 tells the computer what color to use. The VLIN statement in line 30 instructs the computer to turn on the pixels along the left side of the rectangle—from row 13 to row 20 in column 17. Line 40 lights up the pixels on the right side of the rectangle. The HLIN commands in lines 50 and 60 tell the computer to light up horizontal lines. Line 50 lights up the top of the rectangle—the pixels from column 18 to 22 in row 13. Line 60 lights up the bottom of the rectangle. Finally, line 70 tells the computer that your program has ended.

Now, suppose you want to make your rectangle larger and put a dot inside. How would you do it? Look at this program:

```
10 GR
20 COLOR=8
30 VLIN 13,20 AT 17
40 VLIN 13,20 AT 33
50 HLIN 18,32 AT 13
60 HLIN 18,32 AT 20
70 PLOT 25,17
80 END
```

Lines 10 and 20 remain the same. So does line 30, which is the instruction for the left side of the rectangle. But the right side of the rectangle is in a new position, so its VLIN statement is changed. The two horizontal lines are longer so they, too, need new instructions.

On the computer used in this example, the PLOT statement is used to instruct the computer to turn on one specific pixel. The PLOT command in line 70 tells the computer to light up the pixel at the coordinates 25,17—that's 25 across and 17 down.

With BASIC, you can create many interesting screens. You can even animate them! For example, you could draw a dog, then have it wag its tail . . . jump . . . or walk off the screen.

The commands and methods of programming animation are a little more complex, but the results can be exciting.

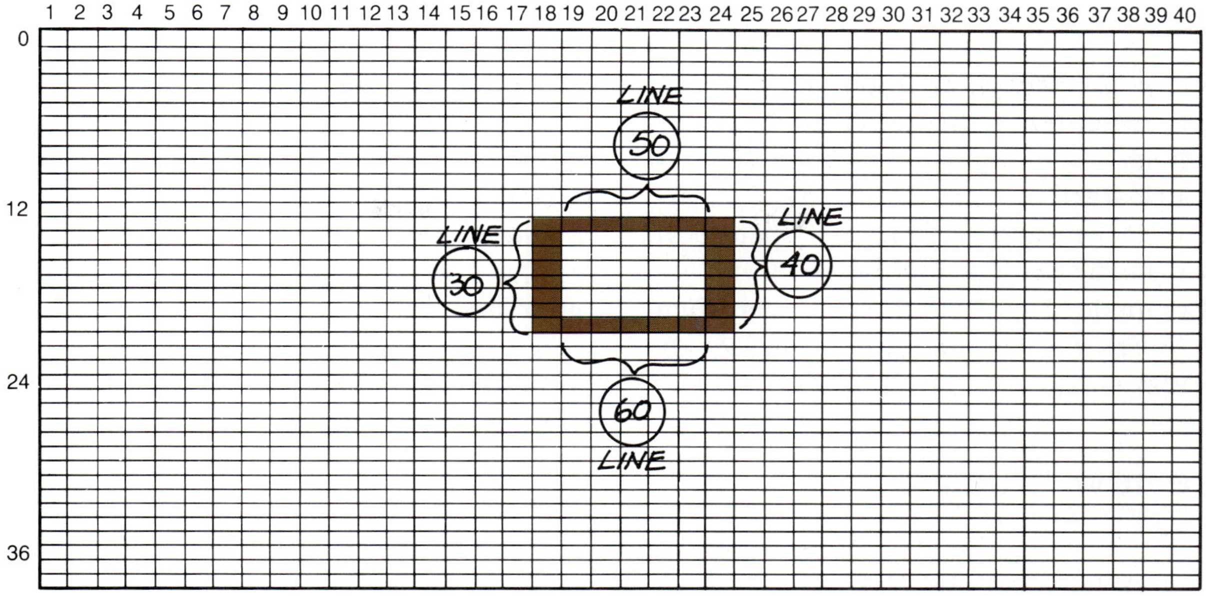

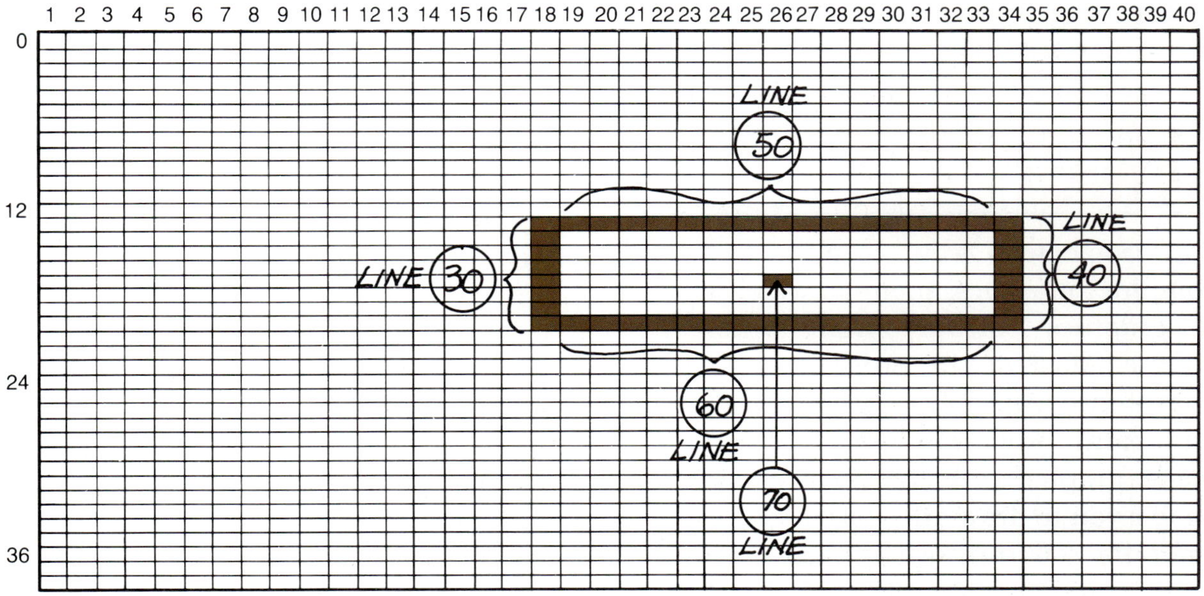

Adding animation to a game or picture can really make it more interesting and more fun.

Key Points

- Computer graphics eliminate tedious, time-consuming work. Computers give designers a lot of flexibility and control.
- Pixels are the basic building blocks of computer graphics. The word *pixel* stands for picture element. When you draw on your computer screen, pixels turn on or remain off.
- Resolution refers to the quality of the

image presented on the display screen. Low resolution means that the picture is jagged, while high resolution means that it's clearer.

• Most personal computers operate in two modes: the graphics mode and the text mode. The difference between them is in the way the computer addresses the pixels.

Review Questions

1. What tools do you need to create graphics on a computer?
2. What factors determine how detailed the image—or resolution—is on your display screen?

USING GRAPHICS SOFTWARE

For people who want help in creating computer graphics, there's a wide variety of graphics software from which to choose. Most of the programs fall into one of two categories: graph programs and paint programs. The first let you make graphs and charts. The second enable you to draw and "paint" with your computer. Within each category, programs vary in terms of ease of use, the options they offer, and flexibility. In addition, some paint programs have a graph option, while some graph programs let you paint.

Let's take a closer look at a sample program from each category.

GRAPH PROGRAMS

Like other application programs, graph programs open with a menu that lists basic options. These generally include create graph, select a graph, edit an existing graph, and print a graph. Graph programs offer a wide variety of formats, including line, bar, pie, and word graphs. You type your data into the computer and select the type of graph on which you want it presented. The computer arranges the information for you.

Let's say that you want to make a chart that shows how much each member of your family uses your home computer. You load the graphics program and this menu appears on the screen:

```
          <<MENU>>
Select:
   1.  Make a Graph
   2.  Select a Graph
   3.  Edit a Graph
   4.  Print
```

You choose the "Make a Graph" option and a screen that asks for your data appears:

```
      <<MAKE A GRAPH>>
```

You enter your facts in the space provided: Mom uses it 21 percent of the time; Dad, 23 percent; your brother Judd, 28 percent; and you, the remaining 28 percent. You title the chart "Family Computer Use."

```
Data page:
Title: Family Computer Use
Subjects
to compare:          Percentage
   1.  Mom               21%
   2.  Dad               23%
   3.  Judd              28%
   4.  Me                28%
```

Now you switch back to the main menu and choose the "Select a Graph" option.

```
<<SELECT A GRAPH>>
Select:
  (P)  Pie
  (B)  Bar
  (L)  Line
  (W)  Word
Press the letter in front of
the option desired.
```

You choose the pie graph format by pressing the "P" key. The computer automatically arranges the information according to the percentages you have provided.

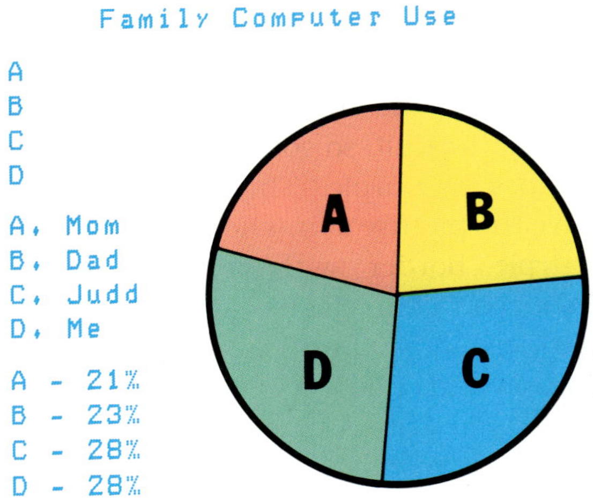

Other options in the program let you fill in the areas with different colors or patterns. And then your chart is ready for presentation.

But wait! Your figures were wrong. Mom uses it 28 percent and Judd, 21 percent. Drawing a new graph is easy. Just return to the data screen and key in your changes. Then press the space bar, and the computer instantly corrects and redraws the graph.

PAINT PROGRAMS

Now let's look at a painting and drawing program. Again, a menu of options appears on the screen.

```
<<MENU>>
Select:
  1.  Paint
  2.  View
  3.  Print
Use the joystick to choose
the option desired. Then
press the joystick button.
```

You can paint—or create—a drawing. You can also view or print out already finished work. You decide to create a zebra, so, using your joystick, you guide the cursor to the paint option and press the fire button. A second screen appears:

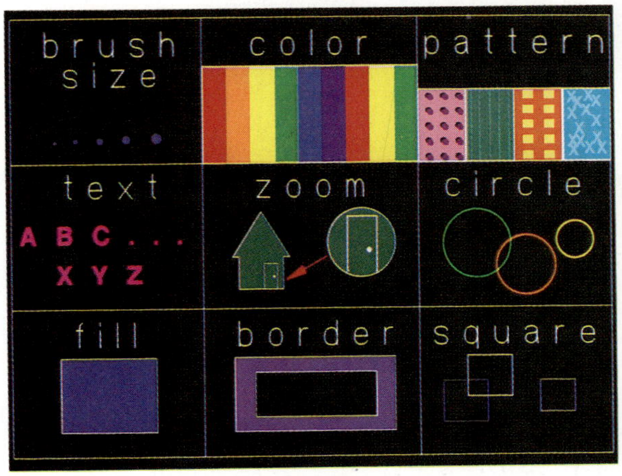

This the palette. It offers you a choice of many colors and four brush sizes. It also gives you a selection of patterns, including solid, dotted, striped, and checkered.

In addition to colors, brushes, and patterns, most programs offer options such as the following:

• *zoom*—enlarges a part of the drawing so that you can paint tiny details.
• *circle*—enables you to make a perfect circle by drawing just two points, one in

The pictured Zebra can be made more interesting by changing such things as the background color or even the color of the Zebra's stripes.

the center of the circle and one on its edge.

• *fill*—allows you to color in whole sections of your picture with a keystroke.

• *text*—lets you add words to a drawing.

Other options let you stretch or repeat shapes, enlarge or reduce parts of the picture, make fancy borders, or even create simple animation. You can switch back and forth between options at any time. When you're finished, you can either save your work or erase it.

Back to the zebra. First let's choose the background color. You decide that the zebra would look great on a red background, so after choosing a brush and the color red, you guide the cursor to the "fill" option and press the fire button. The screen fills with red.

Now you're ready to create the zebra. You begin by drawing its outline in white. Then, choosing the "fill" option, you fill it in. Next you paint the black stripes.

You use the "zoom" option to enlarge the area around the zebra's eyes, and then you add eyelashes.

Back to the "big" picture. You decide it's a little dull, so you change the zebra's stripes to purple. That looks great! To give the picture a finished look, you add a purple border with a plaid pattern. Whoops. That clashes with the zebra's stripes, so you return to the "pattern" option and choose a smooth texture. And there you are—a masterpiece!

INPUT DEVICES

To create graphics, you can use a variety of input devices: the computer keyboard, a joystick, a mouse, a light pen, touch pad, and graphics tablet. There are advantages to each, but it's also a matter of what you're most comfortable using.

A computer keyboard is somewhat awkward for creating graphics. After all, it was designed for typing—not for drawing. It does, however, have certain advantages. For one thing, most people are familiar with the keyboard and know how it works. Since using the keyboard lets you move the cursor one space at a time, it is also a very accurate method of drawing. Using the keyboard, however, is very slow.

Working with a joystick is much faster, enabling you to zip the cursor from one point on the screen to another. In much the same way that you use a joystick for game playing, you choose activities by pressing the fire button. The problem with joysticks is that they offer little control for drawing small details.

If you've never used a mouse, it takes some getting used to. However, the movements involved in using a mouse are more like natural drawing than those required for either the keyboard or a joystick. By sweeping the mouse along the surface of your desk, you can create all sorts of shapes on the display screen. The nice thing about it is that, like sketching on paper, you really draw shapes using the mouse.

The light pen is another useful drawing tool. Shaped like a regular pen, a light pen lets you draw right on the computer screen. As you move the pen over the screen, it electronically activates the pixels underneath.

Two input devices that were designed specifically for creating graphics are touch pads and graphics tablets. Both are flat pads on which you draw using your finger or a special pen called a stylus. Thus it's a lot like drawing with a pencil, paintbrush, or even fingerpaints. The shapes you create are translated into electronic signals that turn on specific pixels on the screen.

Touch pads and graphics tablets differ in how they interact with the computer. A touch pad, like a joystick, sends information to the software. A graphics tablet connects with the computer via a special set of interface circuits that contain built-in graphics programs to supplement the software. Graphics tablets are used by professional computer graphics artists.

You can "draw" on the desktop with a mouse, and the picture will appear on the screen.

Both touch pads and graphics tablets give you a lot of freedom and control over your creations and are fun to experiment with. One good thing to try is tracing a map or photograph right on the tablet. You can then shade and label it, and your work looks great.

PRINTERS

Now it's time for printing out your work. You already learned about letter-quality and dot-matrix printers. For the most

Computer graphics software is a powerful tool in an artist's hands. A simple picture can be easily altered by changing backgrounds, colors, and other details with a touch of a light pen.

Changes can be made using a graphics tablet.

part, letter-quality printers don't print graphics. Dot-matrix printers do print graphics. Another type of printer, called a plotter, produces finer-quality graphics than the dot-matrix. Originally designed for printing charts and graphs, plotters work particularly well with geometric lines and shapes. They print your work on paper by using different-color pens.

More sophisticated and expensive models—like the ink-jet printer, which sprays colored ink on paper, or the laser printer, which actually burns paper with laser light—are used to produce high-quality graphics. But the clearest, most colorful graphic images are produced by taking a picture directly from the computer screen using a graphics camera. These cameras make transparencies (slides) of computer graphics. They have controls that allow for the fine-tuning of brightness, tone, and contrast to produce vibrantly colorful slides. Graphics cameras can be used with any kind of computer, but they cost more than the casual computer artist might want to spend.

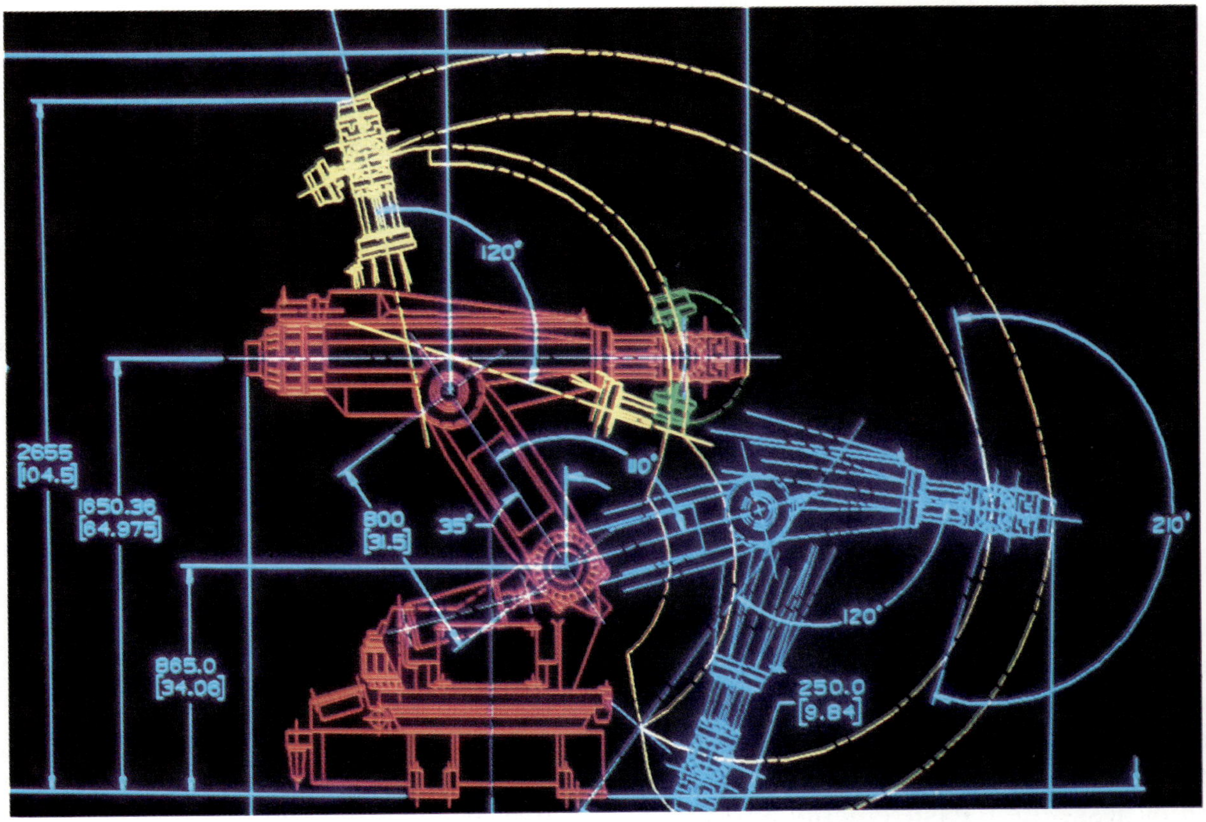

Computers designing computers. The design of this computerized robotic arm is being generated by a computer given instructions by a program that contains the technical specifications.

GRAPHICS USERS

Who uses computer-generated graphics? Everyone from firefighters to molecular physicists. In other words, people in many different professions benefit from computer-generated graphics. People find ingenious new ways every day to put computer graphics to work.

Did you ever wonder what makes your sneakers so comfortable to wear? What gives them all that bounce? The secret is in the design—and more often than not these days, good sneakers are designed by computer. Not just any old computer, but one that's compatible with special **computer-aided design** software, or **CAD** for short.

Sneaker designers, car and airplane manufacturers, architects, and artists are just a few of the people who benefit from using CAD. CAD enables designers to draw, change, and edit three-dimensional plans. The finished design can then be viewed from different angles. What's more, CAD can work with **CAM**, which is **computer-aided manufacture**, to direct the machines that actually make the product.

Unlike paint programs, CAD software stores not only the design but also information about it. Take a new sneaker de-

Future pilots can take off, fly, and land without leaving the ground using computerized simulators.

sign, for example. If you draw the sneaker on a regular paint system, it records the sketch. If you draw it on a CAD system, stored along with the sketch of the sneaker is information about sole thickness, the measurements and material of each piece of the sneaker, and how it should be constructed. If changes are necessary, they can easily be keyed in by the designer.

CAD's usefulness isn't limited to professional designing. A community in Maryland uses a CAD system to help firefighters. Blueprints and other important information about buildings are recorded in the system. In the past, this information was kept in paper files that were difficult to keep up-to-date. Now the information can be up-dated easily, and the computer, stationed on a fire truck, can be consulted as the firefighters rush to the fire.

ANIMATED PIXELS

Another area in which computers are saving people hours and hours of painstaking work is animation. Do you remember any of Disney's films like *Cinderella* and *Pinocchio*? Did you know that each frame of those films had to be created by hand? Animators had to draw a large number of sketches with gradual variations from one to the next.

That was before the days of computer graphics. Now, using a technique called **key frame inbetweening**, the animator creates the first and last frame of a sequence and the computer provides the frames in between. To make Pinocchio's nose grow, an animator could now draw Pinocchio with a small nose, a medium-sized nose, and a very long nose, and the computer would fill in the motion in between.

Animated cartoons are a form of **simulation**. To *simulate* means "to pretend" or "to imitate." For example, the drawings of Cinderella dancing with the prince are meant to look like real people dancing. The same is true for other animated graphics. Today computers are used to simulate scenes that people cannot actually see but believe to exist. For instance, scientists use computer animation to simulate events that are either too small or too far away to capture on film—a hydrogen atom spinning on its axis or a spaceship floating by Saturn.

Another valuable use of computer-generated simulation becomes clear when you consider this scene: the pilot of a commercial jet airliner carrying several hundred passengers is preparing for a landing. The lights of the city come into view and the pilot spots the runway off in the distance. A mile from the runway, the plane encounters unexpected turbulence. The plane dips and then plunges downward. The pilot fails to react quickly enough. The plane crashes.

This is part of a highly effective computer simulation that is used to train pilots. These simulations are similar to, though much more sophisticated than, simulation video games, with which you are probably familiar. First developed for the U.S. Air Force, flight simulators provide pilots with training at controls exactly like those on the planes they fly. The simulations look real and are generated with enough speed to create the appearance of real motion. This training could mean the difference between life and death in critical situations.

Perhaps even more amazing than computers that simulate life are those that watch and listen to the outer reaches of space. These computers work together with radio telescopes, which collect data from the radio spectrum. The computers

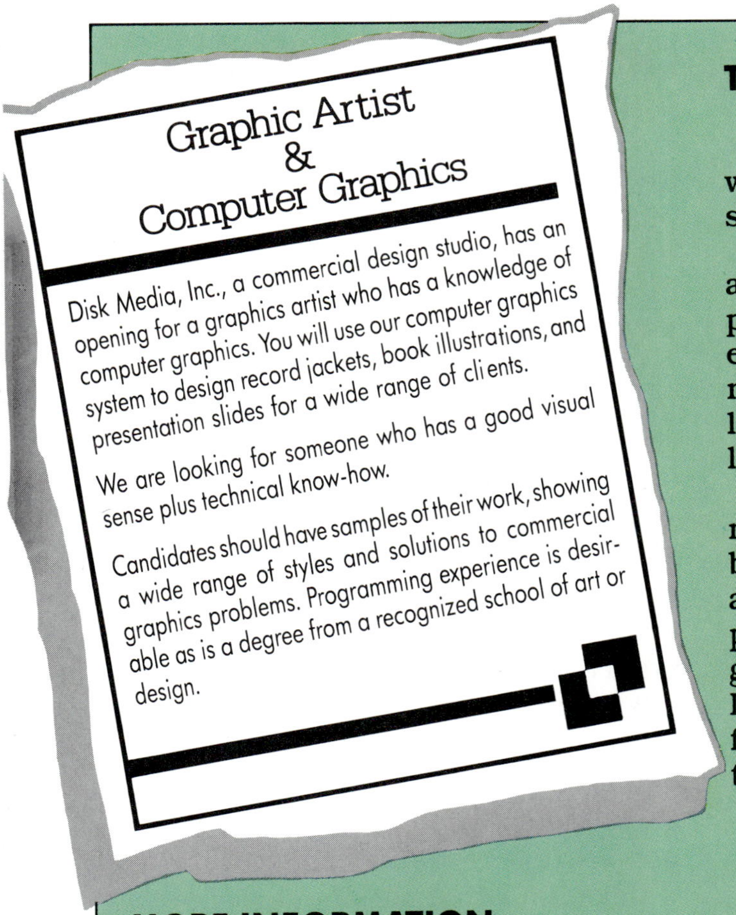

Graphic Artist & Computer Graphics

Disk Media, Inc., a commercial design studio, has an opening for a graphics artist who has a knowledge of computer graphics. You will use our computer graphics system to design record jackets, book illustrations, and presentation slides for a wide range of clients.

We are looking for someone who has a good visual sense plus technical know-how.

Candidates should have samples of their work, showing a wide range of styles and solutions to commercial graphics problems. Programming experience is desirable as is a degree from a recognized school of art or design.

THAT'S MY JOB

Judy Kwan, a computer artist with Burrell Records, has this to say about her work:

"I feel as if I'm working in an area that bridges art and computer technology, and that's very exciting. I'm not only exploring a new field whose capabilities seem limitless, I'm applying what I learn in my work.

"To be a computer artist, you need a pretty strong design or art background. Most of all, you need a good sense of color. For example, the computer I work with can generate thousands of colors, and I have to judge how effective different colors are for each application I design. That's not easy."

MORE INFORMATION

Computer artists usually work flexible hours, determined by the kind of project and its deadlines.... There are many exciting career possibilities in television and in movies, including developing special video effects for music video, news programs, commercials, and science-fiction films.

take this information and translate it into a visual form that scientists can then interpret.

Closer to home are the satellites that orbit the earth collecting information about everything from trout migrations to mineral deposits to earthquakes. These satellites, scanning the land can look below the surface of the earth and pinpoint areas rich in oil or iron ore. A computer then pieces together the bits of data collected by the satellite to form a photograph of the entire area.

Even closer to home are computers that serve as the eyes of medicine. Like computers that create images of space and the earth, those used in medicine are revolutionizing how we see the human body. The days of two-dimensional x-rays have come and gone. Now, using computerized tomography, doctors can produce three-dimensional images of the inner body. In tomography, the computer takes many two-dimensional readings and combines them mathematically. It then manipulates this information to produce three-dimensional images. Often these images eliminate the need for exploratory surgery.

Key Points

• There are two major types of graphics software: graph programs and paint programs. You can also write your own programs to create graphics and animation.
• Six input devices are commonly used for creating graphics: keyboard, joystick, mouse, light pen, touch pad, and graphics tablet.
• Scientists use computer animation to simulate scenes that are either too small or too far away to capture on film. Another valuable form of computer simulation is flight simulation, used by pilots to practice their flying skills.

Review Questions

1. What types of printers can be used to print graphics?
2. How do people benefit from using CAD? How does CAD differ from paint programs? What is CAM?

CHOOSING A GRAPHICS PROGRAM

Now that you've read about creating computer graphics, you probably want to give it a try. Here are a few things to keep in mind when choosing software:

• What type of graphics are you primarily interested in creating? Do you want to paint pictures or make graphs? If you really want to do both, some programs offer a little of each.
• What type of display screen do you use? If it's black and white, make sure you buy a program that works well without color. If it's color, don't waste it by buying a program that produces only black-and-white graphics.
• Paint programs vary a great deal in the options that they offer. Compare programs and select the one that offers the options that best suit your needs.
• Make sure that the input device you plan to work with is compatible with the software you choose.
• If you just want to have fun exploring the world of computer graphics, get the most versatile software in your price range—one with many options.

REVIEW & APPLICATION

SUMMARY

- Computers can generate graphs, charts, and drawings as well as three-dimensional shapes with shading and animation.
- The image on a computer screen is made up of thousands of pixels, which are tiny boxes of light.
- The sharpness of an image on a computer screen depends on the number of pixels the screen has and on the computer's circuitry.
- Most microcomputers can be used in both the graphics mode and the text mode, but computers designed especially for graphics can usually produce higher-quality images.
- You can create your own graphics programs, or you can use ready-made graph or paint software.
- Computer-aided design (CAD) and computer-aided manufacture (CAM) are used by designers, engineers, and manufacturers to create a wide range of products and structures.
- Computer graphics can also be used to create training simulations for pilots and people in other professions and to create realistic pictures of things that we cannot see.
- Many graphics programs are available in stores. In selecting a program, you must consider how you want to use it and what kinds of hardware you have.

VOCABULARY

Match each item in the left column with the correct item on the right.

a. plotter	1. an input device that lets you "draw" on a screen
b. pixel	2. one of thousands of tiny light boxes on a screen
c. resolution	3. a printer for producing high-quality graphics
d. CAD	4. a system used by professional designers
e. light pen	5. the quality of an image on a computer screen

REVIEW QUESTIONS

1. When were the first realistic graphics programs developed, and by whom?
2. How does the quality of an image relate to the number of pixels on a computer display screen?
3. How does a typical microcomputer address pixels differently in the graphics and text modes?
4. What does a VLIN command tell a computer to do? An HLIN command?

DISCUSSION QUESTION

For what kinds of projects would a graph program be more useful? When would a paint program be better?

PROJECTS

C This program creates a simple character graphic animation. The figure takes up a 9-by-6 grid.

```
10 HOME
20 FOR X=1 TO 2
30 PRINT "  123456789": PRINT
40 PRINT "1   -----"
50 PRINT "2  I     I"
60 IF X=1 THEN PRINT "3 (I O O I)"
70 IF X=2 THEN PRINT "3 (I - O I)"
80 PRINT "4  I  J  I"
90 PRINT "5  I  =  I"
100 PRINT "6   -----"
110 FOR I=1 TO 150: NEXT I: HOME
120 NEXT X: GOTO 20
```

If you are using the Commodore 64, IBM PCjr, or TRS-80 Model III, substitute your machine's clear-screen command for the HOME statements in lines 10 and 110.

Enter and run the program.

Further Practice

C Van Gogh was not always satisfied with his first efforts. He often did several versions of a painting. With a computer, he could have revised his first version instead. Revise the graphic program that you created. For "highbrow" art, modify the program to add eyebrows to the face.

D You can not become a great computer artist until you are familiar with the tools of the trade. Design a chart entitled "The Tools of the Computer Artist." List all graphics input devices and describe how you use each one.

D How well do you understand the art of fine-tuning? On paper, demonstrate the difference between low-resolution and high-resolution graphics. First, divide a sheet of paper into half-inch squares and fill in squares to draw the outline of a house. Then draw the same outline using one-eighth-inch squares. Which picture is more realistic?

Enrichment

C Become a master of the art of animation. Keep working on the graphic that you programmed. Modify the program so that your clever creation winks and then smiles before assuming a straight face.

D Joystick, mouse, or light pen? Touch pad or graphics tablet? Every artist has a preference. Which input device would you use? Research your favorite input device and describe in detail how it works.

CHAPTER TEST

Write your answers on a sheet of paper numbered 1 through 10.

MATCHING

1. Match each command or statement with its function.

a. VLIN	1. draw vertical line
b. HLIN	2. switch to graphics mode
c. PLOT	3. draw horizontal line
d. GR	4. turn on a pixel

2. Match each term with the correct function.

a. coordinates	1. draw
b. zoom	2. create charts
c. graph program	3. identify pixel
d. paint program	4. enlarge detail

MULTIPLE CHOICE

3. Which of the following is true of creating graphics with computers?
   a. saves time, work, and materials
   b. gives designers greater flexibility in planning
   c. several different input devices can be used
   d. all of the above

4. As you move a light pen across the screen, it electronically activates:
   a. the keyboard
   b. the CPU
   c. the plotter
   d. pixels

5. The clearest, most colorful graphic images are produced by:
   a. letter-quality printers
   b. graphics cameras
   c. dot-matrix printers
   d. ink-jet printers

6. Before purchasing a graphics program, you should consider:
   a. what type of graphics you want to create
   b. what type of display screen you use
   c. what type of input device you use
   d. all of the above

FILL-IN

7. The number of ____________ on the screen helps to determine the clarity of the images displayed on it.
8. A computer display with low ________ is jagged.
9. To create graphics, you can use a variety of ____________ devices, such as joysticks or graphics tablets.
10. ____________ print computer graphics by using pens of different colors.

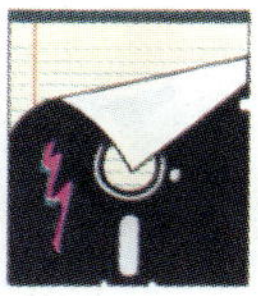

ISSUE: PRIVACY

Today, a good deal of information about people is stored in data banks. The United States government has data banks that contain confidential information about citizens, such as their military records and their social security benefits. One government data bank operated by the Internal Revenue Service stores information about the amount of money people earn each year and the amount of income tax they pay.

Personal information is also stored in smaller computer systems. For example, your school and your doctor may keep computerized records that contain confidential information about you.

Do you have a right to see information about you that is stored in a computer system? Who else has the right to see information about you? These are questions that concern many people.

Many people fear that their privacy might be invaded by the misuse of computerized information. The United States government has passed laws to protect citizens from an invasion of their privacy. The laws determine who has access to information stored in computers. They also restrict the kind of information that computers can store and how long the computers can keep certain kinds of information on file.

One law, the Privacy Act of 1974, gives you the right to see information about you that is kept by the federal government. It also prohibits the government from storing records about your religious or political beliefs. In addition, it prohibits a government agency from giving your records to anyone without a sound reason and without permission from you.

Another law, the Fair Credit Report Act of 1970, gives you the right to see your credit history. A credit history shows how promptly you have paid your bills. It also notes if you have ever been sued.

Your credit history might include mistakes that could create problems for you in getting loans. To prevent this, the law allows you to correct inaccurate information in your credit record.

In addition, the law requires that credit bureaus (companies that keep credit history files) give information about you only to agencies that have a right to know that information. It forbids credit bureaus from collecting information about you that does not affect your credit history, such as how many friends you have.

The law also insures that credit information about unpaid bills is destroyed after seven years. This gives people a chance to improve their credit records. For example, a family that did not pay its bill many years ago might have trouble getting a loan today if the old credit records were still on file.

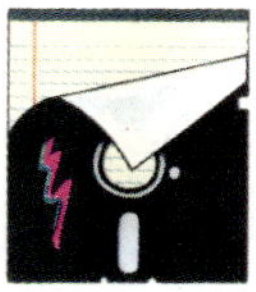

U N I T   R E V I E W

CONCEPTS

- Describe how each of the application programs described in this unit can be used in schools.
- Describe how you could use the four types of application software to prepare a school report on your state capital.
- Do you think CAD expands or limits a designer's creativity? Explain your answer.

CAREERS

- Compare and contrast the careers described in this unit.
- Which of the careers most appeals to you? Why?

ISSUES

- Find out about the electronic funds transfer systems used by banks. How can they be used to monitor people's activities? How can these systems be abused?
- Computers are being used increasingly in the fight against crime. Might this possibly infringe on individuals' rights to privacy? Explain your answer.
- List institutions, organizations, and other groups that might have computer files on people. How are people protected from the misuse of this information?

APPLICATIONS

- Why do you think there is such a wide range in the price of word-processing software, electronic spreadsheets, and data-base management systems?
- Would it make sense for a family to have word-processing software, an electronic spreadsheet, or a data-base management system? Explain your answer.
- List five tasks that can be done more efficiently with word-processing software, an electronic spreadsheet, or a data-base management system. List five tasks that are more easily done with pencil and paper.

TO FIND OUT

- Prepare a computer resource list for your school's PTA. List such resources as books, magazines, and computer camps. If the school has a data-base management system, computerize the list.

UNIT FOUR

COMPUTERS TODAY and TOMORROW

In 1978, two chess champions played a tough five-game match. One player was from Scotland. The other was from the United States. The first game was a draw. The second and third games were won by the Scotsman, David Levy. The American player won the fourth game. Then Levy won the fifth—and the match.

If the loser was disappointed, no one could tell. You see, the American player wasn't a person. It was a computer that had been specially programmed at Northwestern University.

Even though the computer lost that match, many experts believe that within twenty years, there will be a computer chess player so "intelligent" that it will be able to beat all challengers.

In this unit, you'll read about the amazing computer's many uses today and in the future. How will computer technology affect you? The possibilities are limited only by your imagination.

CHAPTER

10 11 12 13 14

COMMUNICATING BY COMPUTER

Here's a trivia question for you. To what product or service does this advertising slogan refer: "Let your fingers do the walking . . . "?

If you said the Yellow Pages, you're absolutely correct. As the slogan suggests, using the telephone and the Yellow Pages to find something that you're looking for is quicker and easier than walking all over town to locate it.

These days, more and more people are finding another way to let their fingers do the walking. They are using computers—not only to obtain information but to send it as well. In fact, an apt slogan for the 1980's might be "Let your fingers do the *talking* . . . "

THE COMPUTER AS A COMMUNICATIONS TOOL

Communicating by computer is almost as easy as punching the keys on a keyboard. Information is sent electronically from one computer—microcomputer, minicomputer, or mainframe—to another, either via telephone lines or through special cables and wires. What kinds of information can be sent? You name it:

- magazine articles
- airline reservations
- bank transactions
- statistics
- news reports
- job listings
- games
- movie reviews
- business correspondence
- football scores
- computer programs
- personal messages
- stock prices
- medical records
- graphic images
- weather reports

You will read more about the variety of information that can be sent by computer later on in this chapter.

ADVANTAGES OF COMPUTER COMMUNICATIONS

Computer communications is playing an increasingly important role not only in offices but also in schools, hospitals, libraries, and homes. People are realizing that sending and receiving information electronically offers several advantages:

1. *Fast, accurate, and direct exchange of information.* Sending and receiving data electronically takes only a fraction of the time needed to send it by mail or messenger. And since the information goes directly to the receiver, the sender doesn't have to worry about lost packages or incorrectly addressed envelopes.
2. *Rapid information processing.* Computers can sort or search through huge amounts of information in a flash. Suppose you were a lawyer who needed a history of all court cases involving the theft of government secrets. How could you get the information? Well, you could go to a law library and search through the reference books. That might take you five hours. You could, instead, use a computer that is electronically linked to a special data bank of legal information. Using that method, you could obtain the information in less than an hour—and never even leave your law office!
3. *Easy handling of large amounts of information.* The amount of data that computers can store and process is enormous. For example, picture a

To do research, this lawyer taps into a data base of a university law library using his computer.

business office crammed full with customer bills and letters. Imagine that there are, let's say, eight stacks of pages, each piled five feet high. That's about *120,000* pieces of paper. If the information contained in those paper mountains were stored electronically on floppy disks, you could easily fit all the disks in just one file cabinet. If the information were kept on hard disks or in a large central computer, you'd need much less space than that. And think how much easier it would be to look for a particular bill or letter electronically than to search through forty feet of paper!

4. *Increased availability of information.* Suppose you're a traveling salesperson working in San Diego, California. Your company's main office is located in Philadelphia, 3000 miles away. You need several pages of financial information that are stored in your company's mainframe computer. Using a portable computer and a special telephone hookup, you can—almost instantly—get the data you need over the telephone. If your company has other salespeople working in Wisconsin, Texas, Oregon, or anywhere else, they can do the same thing. Computer communications makes the information widely and easily available.

Key Points

- Using a computer to communicate is almost as easy as punching the keys on a keyboard.
- Information is sent electronically from one computer to another, either via telephone lines or through special cables and wires.
- Communicating by computer offers many benefits, including:
  —fast, accurate, and direct exchange of information
  —rapid information processing
  —easy handling of large amounts of information
  —increased availability of information

Review Questions

1. What advantages do you think computer communications might have over mail delivery? What disadvantages might exist?

In 1889, most people used a telegraph office to communicate rapidly over long distances.

2. Someone once said that computer communications "puts a mainframe in your briefcase." Explain.

HOW COMPUTER COMMUNICATIONS WORKS

Exactly how do computers "talk" to each other? Basically, there are two ways: computers can be linked by telephone, or they can be connected by cables and wires. Let's look at both methods and see how they work.

TELECOMMUNICATIONS

Have you ever heard the term **telecommunications**? In general, it refers to the sending of information from one place to another by telephone, radio, telegraph, or similar electronic means.

Telecommunications isn't new. The telegraph was invented some one hundred and fifty years ago. And it was more than a century ago, in 1876, that Alexander Graham Bell showed that electrical signals could be used to send spoken words by telephone. What *is* relatively new is the marriage of telephone and computer technologies.

Nowadays, the term *telecommunications* is commonly used to mean the sending of data from one computer to another through telephone lines. Often, such data transmission is called **telecomputing**. The data may be words, numbers, or programs. The computers that are doing the communicating may be microcomputers, minicomputers, mainframes, or a combination of these. They may be located just across the street from each other—or across the continent.

Modems. If you have a computer and want to communicate with another computer by telephone, you need a hardware device called a modem (short for "**mo**dulator-**dem**odulator"). A modem translates (or modulates) your computer input into audio tones. These tones can then be sent through the telephone to the receiving computer. The receiver must have a modem, too, because the tones must be translated back (or demodulated) into computer signals.

There are several kinds of modems. Some are built into the computer. Others can be attached externally. Some modems connect your computer directly to

THE FAST-CHANGING WORLD OF TELECOMMUNICATIONS

1639—The first American postal service is established in Massachusetts Bay colony.

1737—Benjamin Franklin is appointed postmaster.

1789—Congress authorizes a postal service under the Constitution.

1836—The telegraph is invented by Samuel Morse.

1860—The pony express begins to carry mail on horseback between Missouri and California. Each rider was expected to cover seventy-five miles a day. Pony-express service was eventually replaced by long-distance telegraph lines.

1876—Alexander Graham Bell invents the telephone.

1895—Guglielmo Marconi develops wireless telegraphy.

1918—The first regular air-mail route in the United States is established between New York and Washington.

1928—Vladimir K. Zworykin develops the iconoscope. This electronic device led to television for mass viewing.

1933—FM radio is invented by Edwin H. Armstrong.

1940—George Stibitz telegraphs data from Dartmouth College in New Hampshire to a Bell Laboratories calculator in New York. This was the first time that communication and computing were linked.

1961—The Massachusetts Institute of Technology develops the first computer timesharing system.

1960's—American Airlines and IBM develop a seat-reservation system that links telephones and computers. The system took ten years to complete and cost $300 million.

1979—The Source Telecomputing Corporation begins its information-service network.

the telephone system, others, make the connection through the telephone receiver.

Communications software. Besides a modem you need special communications software. This software enables the computer, the modem, and the telephone to work together smoothly. In addition, some communications software allows your system to:

- store telephone numbers and automatically call those numbers at your command. (Some systems can even redial a number automatically if the line is busy.)
- save the incoming information on a disk.
- transmit the incoming information to a printer.

LONG-DISTANCE AND LOCAL NETWORKS

When a number of computer users are linked together, they form a **network**. Usually, a network consists of one powerful central computer and many microcomputers or **terminals**. A terminal has a screen and a keyboard like a microcomputer, but it generally doesn't have its own CPU. It cannot process data; it can only send and receive data. (That's why it is sometimes called a "dumb" terminal.) Microcomputers or terminals that are "networked" together can share the mainframe's computing power and its vast memory.

Such electronic networks have become very common. Suppose that a company has offices scattered across the country.

Connecting the microcomputers in this classroom with a local-area network allows students to share software programs.

Immediate Openings

Telecommunications Technicians

DS&I Corporation needs telecommunications technicians to monitor and service our large telephone and data network. Responsibilities include keeping tabs on our telecommunications lines and identifying problems before they create costly down time or damage.

Candidates will become familiar with DS&I's mainframes, personal computers, and Local Area Network.

Because we maintain around-the-clock surveillance of our equipment, we can offer technicians a choice of shifts.

Candidates must have a high school diploma and vocational training in electronics. Knowledge of communications software is desirable.

THAT'S MY JOB

Roberto DeMorales, a telecommunications technician, says:

"People are really pleased and relieved when I fix the lines to their terminal or phone. They're even more satisfied when they don't lose time because I catch small problems before they develop into catastrophes. Since phone and computer lines are in use all the time, you have to keep on your toes to prevent disaster.

"I'd recommend that people interested in telecommunications take electronics and computer classes in high school. You have to go to technical school anyway to become a technician, but it helps to have some kind of head start."

MORE INFORMATION

Positions in telecommunications technology offer good salaries and good benefits such as insurance, medical coverage, and overtime pay.... Work environments are generally safe and clean.... Promotion possibilities are good, including such advanced positions as shift supervisor and manager of technical services.... Job security is good.

The company can buy one expensive mainframe computer and, through telecommunications, share that computer's power among all its offices. In the same way, other companies can offer everything from airline reservations to theater seats at numerous locations.

However, not all networks use telephone lines for computer communications. Modems and phone lines are great for long-distance connections, but what if the computers to be linked are very near each other? Then they can be joined into what is known as a **local-area network** (**LAN**, for short).

Local-area networks connect their computers or terminals directly by means of cables or wires. The computers or terminals are usually located in the same building or even the same room.

Such an arrangement is popular in business offices and schools. Aside from being convenient, it's also a big money saver. Can you guess why?

The computers or terminals in a networked office can share not only data files and programs but also equipment. For example, suppose that fifty bookkeepers in the accounting department of a firm called the International Record Company use microcomputers. All fifty often need hard copies of their work. Furthermore, all the bookkeepers have a lot of data to store. Should International buy fifty separate printers and fifty individual hard-disk systems for its accounting department? Wouldn't it be easier and less costly to link the microcomputers into a network that includes a small number of printers and hard disks? In many such cases, the answer is yes.

In schools, the networked computer classroom offers additional benefits. By having a number of microcomputers networked to one "teacher station," the teacher can easily work with individual students or with groups of students. Here's how such a system works:

The teacher's computer is connected to ten, twenty, or more student terminals. As few or as many students as the teacher wants can use these stations at the same time. To "plug into" the network, you type your special password into the computer at your terminal. Once your password is accepted, you're all set. Your teacher can have you and all your classmates work on the same file or program, or the teacher can give different assignments to different students. Any time you want you can ask for assistance by typing a "help" command. Your teacher can bring up your screen on the teacher-station computer. Then, the two of you can communicate back and forth via computer.

Key Points

- *Telecommunications* generally refers to the sending of information from one place to another by telephone, radio, or similar means. Today, the term is commonly used to mean computer communication via telephone lines.
- Telecommunications (or telecomputing, as it is often called) requires a modem and communications software.
- A network consists of a number of computers or terminals linked together. A terminal has a keyboard and a screen but does not usually have its own CPU. A local-area network connects its computers or terminals directly by cables or wires rather than phone lines.

Review Questions

1. A modem plays the role of interpreter between a computer and a telephone. Explain.
2. What are some advantages that a network might offer a business? A school?

THE USES OF COMPUTER COMMUNICATIONS

The range of uses for computer communications is broad—and growing. As the cost of computer hardware continues to decrease, more and more people are being linked by networks. Who are these people? They are people in business and industry; students and teachers at schools, universities, and libraries; and home users of all ages.

OBTAINING INFORMATION FROM DATA BANKS

Earlier in this chapter you read how a lawyer could save research time by using a computer to scan a data bank of legal information. There are a number of such **data banks**—also known as **information services**—that you can communicate with by computer. Some are intended only for certain users. Others are open to everyone.

What all these data banks have in common is that they are electronic storehouses of information. Like libraries, they contain vast amounts of information on many different subjects. A data bank's information isn't kept on printed pages, though. It's stored inside a powerful central computer. To obtain this information you don't have to lug home an armful of books. Using a microcomputer, a modem, and a telephone, you can have the information **downloaded**—that is, displayed on your screen, saved on a disk, or printed.

Using a data bank to get information is fast, convenient, relatively easy, and even fun. But data banks are not free. Unlike libraries, the companies that own and maintain information services charge you for the information they provide. Fees range from under $10 an hour to as much as $300 an hour, depending on the particular data bank you're dealing with. Fortunately, computer communications is so fast that you can often find the information you want in minutes.

Communicating with a data bank. Using a data bank in the same way that you would use a library is an increasingly popular method of research. Here is an example that helps to explain why:

Suppose that you're a reporter for a computer magazine. Your boss wants you to write an article about a teen-ager who has written a best-selling computer game. To write your article you need accurate, up-to-date information.

Using your microcomputer, modem, and telephone, you call a data bank that catalogues newspaper articles. You type in the I.D. number and password that you received when you became a subscriber to this particular information service. Once you're **on-line**—electronically connected to the data bank computer—and you have instructed the computer about the kinds of information you are looking for, you type in the name of the teen-ager. Then the computer at the other end searches its electronic files for any articles in which that name appears. In a flash, several recent news articles appear on your screen. Then you type the name of the teen-ager's game, and several additional articles appear. You save the articles that you want on a floppy disk. Later, you can use your printer to make hard copies.

Your data bank research took only three minutes—and you didn't even have to leave the room. Furthermore, you'll be charged for only three minutes of data-bank time—only one twentieth of the hourly rate.

Doing research this way isn't only for reporters, of course. Many students use data banks as an aid in writing reports and doing other homework. For example, there are relatively inexpensive information services that can provide newspaper and magazine articles on just about any subject. There is even a service that has an entire encyclopedia stored in its computer—that's about 10 million words!

Are you thinking that all of this sounds great, but unfortunately you don't have your own computer? Well, here's some good news: libraries are beginning to offer low-cost data-bank communication as part of their reference services.

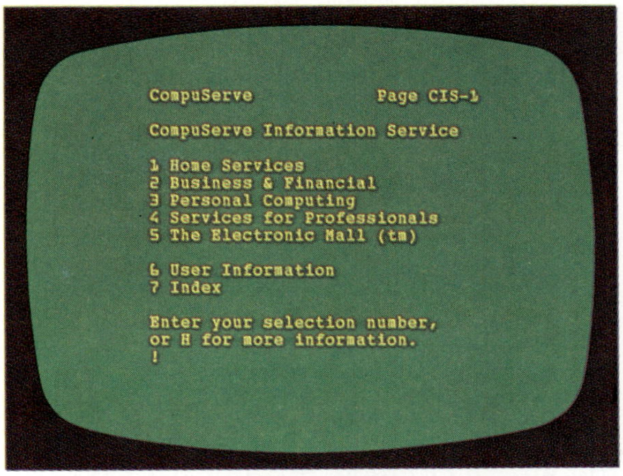

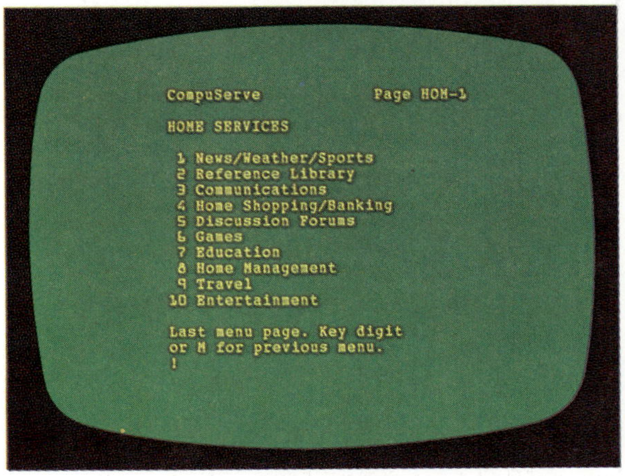

By using communications software, computer users can access commercial data banks to obtain information on hundreds of different topics.

Some well-known data banks. Pick a subject, any subject. Have you got one? Now consider this: there's a data bank that can provide you with information on whatever subject came to your mind. Here is a sampling of some well-known data banks:

- The Source and CompuServe, two of the most popular information services (both have more than fifty thousand subscribers), provide information on a broad range of topics. Users can take advantage of special evening and weekend rates that are less than half of the daytime rate. You'll read about various other services that The Source and CompuServe offer to their subscribers a little later.
- The Dow Jones News/Retrieval Service and Delphi both specialize in business and financial information. For example, the Dow Jones service offers the complete text of the *Wall Street Journal* dating back more than a year. In addition, when a *Journal* reporter sends in a story, the new information is added to the data bank within ninety seconds.
- For specialized information users turn to Dialog Information Services (it includes over two hundred data bases containing mainly scientific, medical, legal, and technical information); LEXIS (for court rulings and legal information); or Medline (for information from 3000 medical journals).
- The New York Times Information Service and NEXIS both specialize in news-related information. For example, NEXIS has the full text of *The New York Times* dating back several years. It also offers *Time*, *Newsweek*, *Sports Illustrated*, *People*, and many other magazines.

TIMESHARING

Jim, Kate, Andy, and Sue are student programmers who are living in four different towns. This morning, at the same time, all four of them are writing programs, but not on their own computers. Instead, they are using terminals that are electronically linked to a mainframe computer located in the university they attend. The mainframe responds so fast that each of the four students feels as though he or she is the only person communicating with the computer.

Jim, Kate, Andy, and Sue are plugged into a **timesharing** system. Their network allows them to share the power of a central computer that is located miles away. They can try out their programs independently, at their own paces.

Timesharing offers computing power and speed not only to students and their teachers but also to many businesses. In fact, there are companies that specialize in selling timesharing as a service. For example, many drugstores use a timesharing service to help process billing and other paperwork.

Key Points

- Data banks, also known as information services, are electronic storehouses of information. They provide rapid access to vast amounts of data.
- Subscribers to a data bank can have information downloaded to their microcomputers through telephone lines.
- A timesharing system enables users to share the power of a large computer that can be located miles away. Each user feels as though he or she is the only one communicating with the computer.

Review Questions

1. How might a data bank help a student who has to write a research paper?
2. How can a small business such as a drugstore afford to use a mainframe computer to process its bills and other paperwork?

ELECTRONIC MAIL

Did you ever have to go out in the rain to mail a letter that couldn't wait? Have you ever received a letter weeks late because it had been mysteriously "lost" in the mail? If so, you will be very happy to know that **electronic mail** is here.

What exactly is electronic mail? It's just what you'd imagine: the sending of messages electronically by computer. Here's how it works:

Suppose that you are a subscriber to The Source or CompuServe. You have ten friends who subscribe as well. A few months ago, you lent one of these friends a record. You want the record back, but you can't remember who has it. Using a microcomputer and a modem, you plug into the information service's network of subscribers. Once you are on-line, you send the same message to all ten of your friends: "Whoever has my Bill Cosby album, please return it."

Your message is stored in your friends' "electronic mailboxes." These mailboxes are nothing like those that are used by the U.S. Postal Service. They are simply storage locations in the information service's computer system. When your friends come on-line, they will check to see if they have any mail. When they do your message will appear on their screens. It's as easy as that. (With luck you might even get your record back!)

Electronic mail is becoming popular in the business world, too. It is fast, direct, and reliable. In addition, storing messages in electronic mailboxes saves time by eliminating "telephone tag": Ms. Green calls Mr. Gold, but Mr. Gold is out to lunch. An hour later, Mr. Gold returns the call, but Ms. Green is at a meeting. The next morning, Ms. Green calls back, but Mr. Gold's line is busy, and so on . . .

Not all electronic mail delivery is tied to an information service like The Source or CompuServe. In fact, organizations already exist that specialize in delivering electronic mail. MCI Mail and EasyLink are two examples. Subscribers to these electronic-mail services can send messages around the world on their computers. In addition, the addressee doesn't even need a computer to receive mail through one of these services. Both will transmit a letter most of the distance electronically, then print and send it the rest of the distance either by mail or by courier.

ELECTRONIC BULLETIN BOARDS

Like an electronic mailbox, an electronic bulletin board provides a place to leave messages. These bulletin-board messages are usually not directed to only one person, however. They are "posted" for anyone to read—sort of like the classified ads in a newspaper.

Electronic bulletin boards are offered through networks such as The Source and CompuServe. In addition, many clubs have their own free bulletin boards. In fact, if you wanted to you could organize a bulletin board of your own. Hundreds of young people with a computer and a modem have done just that.

You can send messages to your friends and never lick a stamp if you use an electronic bulletin board.

What kinds of information can you expect to find posted on an electronic bulletin board? You will find just about anything you can imagine:

- ads for part-time work
- information about a club
- games
- announcements of upcoming events
- items for sale
- personal messages

Some electronic bulletin boards can hold thousands of messages. To make reading the board easier, these messages are usually grouped into categories. For instance, if you wanted to buy a bike, you would check the "For Sale" category.

CONSUMER SERVICES

Probably the area of computer communications that has received the most public attention is consumer services. This area is expected to grow in popularity as more and more people buy home computers.

Many disabled people are able to work from their homes using computer telecommunication.

A wide range of consumer services is available by computer. Here are some of the best-known services:

- *Electronic banking.* Certain banks now make it possible for a customer with a home computer to communicate with the bank's computer. In this way the customer can pay bills or transfer funds from one account to another.
- *Home shopping.* Some services offer computerized home shopping. A detailed listing of products for sale is displayed on your screen. You choose the item that you want and pay for your purchase by credit card.
- *Entertainment.* Information services such as CompuServe and The Source offer everything from recipes and sports information to movie reviews and restaurant suggestions.

TELECOMMUTING

Do you think you would enjoy having a job that let you work at home? For example, imagine not having to go out in cold or rainy weather. Well, by the time you finish your education, a sizable part of the work force may well be working at home two or more days a week. These "telecommuters" will be using home computers and modems to harness the power of their companies' mainframes or minicomputers.

In fact, there are already thousands of telecommuters. By 1990, according to some experts, there will be *millions* of them. Here are some examples:

- A growing number of writers, reporters, and typists prepare their manuscripts at home and then send their work electronically to the office.
- Traveling salespeople use portable computers to obtain information from their company's data bases.
- Some disabled people who have difficulty traveling to an office are able to do computer-related work at home.
- Many parents with child-care responsibilities telecommute. That way, they can stay at home while communicating with the office to receive and submit assignments and have more time with their families.

At the start of this chapter you read about the Yellow Pages slogan "Let your fingers do the walking . . . " Well, guess what? Now there is a data-bank service called Instant Yellow Pages. It lists well over six million businesses across the nation. What next?

REVIEW & APPLICATION

SUMMARY

- The term telecommunications, or telecomputing, commonly refers to the transmission of data from one computer to another through telephone lines and a modem.
- A modem translates computer input into audio tones, which can be sent through the telephone. The receiving computer's modem translates the tones back into computer signals.
- Communications software enables the computer, the modem, and the telephone to work together smoothly.
- A number of computers that are linked electronically form a network.
- Microcomputers or terminals that are networked with a central computer can share its power and its memory.
- Local-area networks link computers or terminals by means of cables or wires rather than phone lines. These computers or terminals are usually in the same building or even the same room.
- Data banks, or information services, are electronic storehouses of information. They give subscribers fast and easy access to huge amounts of information.
- Electronic mail is the sending of messages electronically by computer.
- A growing range of consumer services is available by computer. These services include electronic banking, home shopping, and entertainment.

VOCABULARY

Match each item in the left column with the correct item on the right.

a. telecommuting	1. Links computer with telephone
b. terminal	2. Used for short-distance communication
c. modem	3. Bringing the office home
d. electronic mailbox	4. A "brainless" keyboard and screen
e. local-area network	5. Used for storing computer-sent messages

REVIEW QUESTIONS

1. How can computer communications help a lawyer obtain information about court cases?
2. What does communications software enable a computer system to do?
3. How is a dumb terminal different from a microcomputer?
4. What kind of messages might you find on an electronic bulletin board?
5. How is computer communications helpful to a working parent?

DISCUSSION QUESTION

Do you believe that electronic mail will become the new postal system?

PROJECTS

C This program simulates an electronic mail system. You can use it to write messages to and receive messages from your classmates. Because you're using a microcomputer and not an electronic network, you'll have to write messages in the form of programs. For example:

10 PRINT "I'LL MEET YOU IN THE"
20 PRINT "COMPUTER CENTER AT 2."

```
10 HOME
20 PRINT "ELECTRONIC MAIL"
30 PRINT: PRINT "HOOKUP"
40 PRINT "1. DIALING E-MAIL"
50 PRINT "2. CONNECTION IN
     PROGRESS"
60 FOR I=1 TO 1000: NEXT I
70 HOME: PRINT "WELCOME"
80 PRINT: INPUT "ENTER YOUR
     PASSWORD:"; A$
90 IF A$="345" THEN 110
100 PRINT "ILLEGAL PASSWORD":
     GOTO 80
110 HOME: PRINT "CORRECT
     PASSWORD"
120 PRINT: PRINT "COMMAND
     EXPLANATION"
130 PRINT: PRINT " 1. CATALOG ->
     THIS COMMAND LISTS"
140 PRINT " ALL E-MAIL TITLES ON
     SCREEN."
150 PRINT: PRINT " 2. RUN ⟨TITLE⟩
     -> THIS COMMAND IS"
160 PRINT " USED TO READ YOUR
     E-MAIL MESSAGE."
170 PRINT " EXAMPLE: RUN
     JJ.3-12"
180 PRINT: PRINT " 3. DELETE
     ⟨TITLE⟩ -> DELETES MESSAGE"
190 PRINT " AFTER YOU HAVE READ
     IT."
200 PRINT: PRINT " 4. SAVE
     ⟨TITLE⟩ -> WRITE YOUR
     MESSAGE"
210 PRINT " IN THE FORM OF A
     PROGRAM THAT USES"
220 PRINT " PRINT STATEMENTS."
230 PRINT " USE THE ⟨SAVE⟩
     COMMAND TO PLACE THE"
240 PRINT " MESSAGE IN E-MAIL.":
     END
```

If you are using the Commodore 64, IBM PCjr, or TRS-80, substitute your machine's clear-screen command for the HOME statements in lines 10, 70, and 110. If you are using a Commodore 64, you will also have to change RUN ⟨TITLE⟩ in line 150 to LOAD ⟨TITLE⟩. Then, when the message is loaded, you will have to run it to read it. Look at the IF...THEN statement in line 90. Most computers let you leave GOTO out of the THEN part of an IF...THEN statement. Enter and run the program. Leave and retrieve a message.

Further Practice

D The "office of the future" may be down the block. In several paragraphs, describe an office that uses complete electronic communication.

Enrichment

D Who provides the information you need? Research the cost and services of several consumer networks. Should your class join one?

CHAPTER TEST

Write your answers on a sheet of paper numbered 1 through 9.

MULTIPLE CHOICE

1. Which of the following might use computer communications?
   a. homes
   b. schools
   c. airlines
   d. all of the above
2. The advantages of computer communications include:
   a. fast, accurate, direct exchange of information
   b. lower phone bills
   c. fewer underground cables
   d. all of the above
3. A device that translates computer signals into sounds and sounds into computer signals is called a:
   a. chip
   b. modem
   c. telephone
   d. language processor
4. In a local-area network, computers are linked by means of:
   a. wires and cables
   b. telephone lines
   c. vacuum tubes
   d. none of the above
5. The data that you send from one computer to another can include:
   a. words
   b. numbers
   c. programs
   d. all of the above

ORDERING OF EVENTS

6. List the following steps in the order in which they would occur if you used a data bank.
   a. Tell the computer what kinds of information you want.
   b. Information from the data bank appears on your screen.
   c. Store on a disk any data you want to save.
   d. Type an ID number and a password.

MATCHING

7. Match the items in the left column with the functions on the right.

a. terminal	1. carry data over long distances
b. LAN	2. send and receive data
c. telephone lines	3. store related information
d. data bank	4. carry data over short distances

FILL-IN

8. To send information from one computer to another over telephone lines, you need a __________ as well as __________.
9. If you use electronic mail to send a message to a friend, the message will be stored in your friend's __________.

CHAPTER

11 12 13 14 1

THE VERSATILE COMPUTER

Look at the list below. Do these occupations have anything in common?

- lawyer
- teacher
- designer
- scriptwriter
- farmer
- doctor
- county sheriff
- secretary

They appear to be entirely different occupations, don't they? Yet many of the women and men who hold these jobs have something in common: they use computers in their work.

Of course, not *every* farmer or scriptwriter or doctor uses a computer. And of those who do, most don't use it all day long the way a programmer might, for example. Nonetheless, people in these and many other occupations have come to prize computers for their power, versatility, and speed.

How can one device be so valuable to so many different workers? Here are some of the reasons that people in various professions give:

- Department store manager: "Computers can process and store huge amounts of information. They're fast, efficient, and reliable."
- Construction engineer: "Computers help me plan and manage all kinds of projects."
- High school principal: "Computers make work easier and save time."
- Bookkeeper: "Computers can do the same tasks over and over again without getting bored or tired. And they never complain about long hours!"

Computers are useful to a wide range of people because they can serve many purposes. Let's see just how versatile the modern computer is.

COMPUTERS IN BUSINESS, INDUSTRY, AND AGRICULTURE

Computers have revolutionized the business world. As the cost of computer technology has decreased, more and more businesses have "gone computer." Computers are no longer limited to factories, banks, and big corporations. Small companies, retail stores, law firms, employment agencies, supermarkets, and even many farms now use computers. In fact, according to a recent study, by 1990 four out of every five workers will be using a computer as part of their jobs.

COMPUTERS IN THE OFFICE

In large and small offices alike, secretaries use word processing to write letters and reports. Managers switch on their desktop computers to help them prepare spreadsheets and graphics displays. Accountants and bookkeepers use computer power to help them manage company finances.

Computer systems are used to manage company records, to send electronic mail, and to tie into data banks. Electronic networks link computer users who are located in the same building or across the country.

SIMULATION FOR ON-THE-JOB TRAINING

Do you think that computers make good trainers? In some companies employees master their jobs with the aid of computer-based training programs. Many of these training programs use simulation techniques.

This computer is simulating traffic patterns so that this woman can learn to drive.

In a computer simulation you are put in a role—the job of production supervisor, for instance. In that role you are asked to make realistic decisions. Your decisions may relate to operating machinery, or they may involve a series of job tasks that are to be carried out. If you make the correct decisions, the computer will tell you so. If you make a mistake, you'll "see" the result without anything harmful actually happening. That way, you can learn from your error.

Simulation techniques are used to teach everything from piloting an airplane to running a nuclear plant. For example, some oil companies use simulation techniques to help new workers learn safety procedures. Working with oil and natural gas pipelines can be very dangerous. These lines are under tremendous pressure. A worker's error in judgment can trigger an explosion that will injure many people. Having workers practice their decision making on a computer lets them see the results of their choices without endangering anyone.

ROBOTS AND OTHER MANUFACTURING USES

Computers serve a broad range of manufacturing purposes. For example, if you were a supervisor in a large factory, you might have a computerized control system to help you keep track of continuously running machinery.

Computers are also used to monitor the temperature and pressure of production processes. For example, in a chemical plant or power-generating station, computers may be connected to regulating devices. If the temperature or pressure rises or falls too much, the computer instantly signals the regulating device. The device then makes the needed adjustment—automatically.

Robots. Probably the manufacturing use of computers that you've heard most about is robots. A robot is a computer-controlled mechanical device. Unlike the robots that you may have seen in stores or in movies, industrial robots generally don't look like humans. Instead, they are often large metal boxes with long mechanical arms.

Certain manufacturing jobs, such as automobile assembly-line work, involve doing the same tasks over and over—for instance, tightening bolts or spray-painting a fender. Such repetitive work can get very boring. But a computer-controlled robot doesn't care. Machines keep their "minds" on the job hour after hour—and never need to break for lunch.

Robots can also perform jobs that humans would find hard or impossible to do. They can work in intense heat or freezing cold. They can handle dangerous chemicals, and they can work in polluted air. They can even work in the dark.

Do you think that using robots in place of human workers is a good idea? Many factory owners do. But the people whose jobs are at stake have a different viewpoint. They know that a robot can often do the work of two people. One major car maker predicts that the company will have 15,000 robots working by 1990. The robots will take away about 30,000 jobs from people unless the company finds other work for them. However, the company argues that this will allow it to produce a car for less money and make it possible for the company to compete against foreign-made cars.

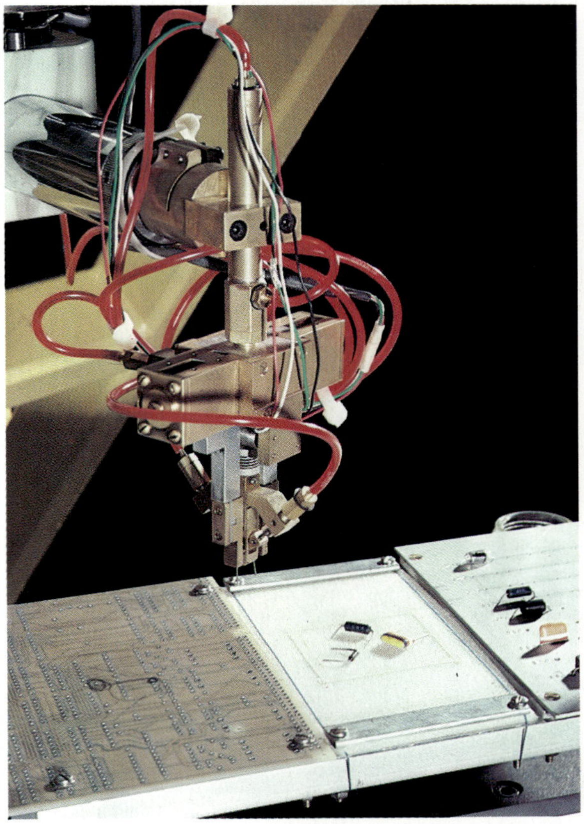

A robotic arm is picking up electronic parts in a university computer lab.

Key Points

• Workers in a wide range of occupational fields have come to prize computers for their power, versatility, and speed.

• As the cost of technology has decreased, businesses of all kinds have "gone computer."

• In business and industry, computers are used to perform various office tasks, to do on-the-job simulation training, to operate control systems in factories and manufacturing plants, and to control industrial robots.

Review Questions

1. In what way might a secretary use a computer? How might a company manager use it?
2. For what kinds of jobs might robots be better suited than human beings?

COMPUTER-AIDED DESIGN

Have you ever thought about how much time and work go into designing something large and complex like an airplane, a ship, a building, or a bridge? Designing something of that sort is an enormous job. A team of designers and engineers spends months calculating, drawing, and revising complicated plans.

Optical scanners are being used in supermarkets to speed check-out and to track inventory.

Today, with the aid of computers, designers can spend less time drawing and calculating and more time designing. For what kinds of designs are computers being used? Here are two examples:

• Car makers use computers to study how different designs affect car performance. Using such devices as electronic pens and tablets, an automotive engineer can quickly and easily sketch design changes on a computer screen. The computer can zoom in for a close-up of one part of the drawing or rotate the sketch to get a different view. Using simulation techniques, engineers can "road-test" many proposed designs without having to build a test model for each one. This saves both time and money.

• Engineers and architects use computers to plan the design of office buildings, shopping centers, and similar large projects. They create a detailed visual model. Then they have the computer perform calculations of size, shape, weight, and so on. After studying the computer's figures, they revise the original design. For example, they may decide that a stronger construction material is needed to support the building's weight. They then run a revised model through the computer and study the results. More design changes follow. They repeat this process until they have the best possible design.

COMPUTERIZED SUPERMARKETS

It's 1979. Your older sister has a part-time job as a checker at your local supermarket. As customers line up their purchases on the counter, she reads the marked price on each item and rings it up on her cash register. Sometimes an item doesn't have a price on it, so she has to ask her supervisor what the price is. This slows down the check-out process. Once she has rung up all the purchases, the register calculates the total.

Now it's six years later and you have the job that your sister used to have at the supermarket. Things have changed. Now, as customers line up their purchases, you pass each item over an **optical scanner** in the check-out counter. The scanner reads the **Universal Product Code** that is printed on each item. This series of bars and numbers tells the store's computer what product has been purchased. The item's price, which is stored in the computer's memory, is flashed on a small screen for the customer to see. Once you have run all the purchases over the scanner, the computer almost instantly displays the total. The check-out process is much faster than it used to be.

Aside from speeding up check-outs, computers help supermarket managers by keeping track of inventory—the number of items the store has in stock. As Universal Product Code numbers are scanned and read into the system, the computer records which items, and how many, have been sold.

Before long computers may be playing an even larger part in supermarket operations. In Japan there is a supermarket that uses modern technology to do most of the tasks that people have always done. Robots operate the parking-lot gate, greet customers entering the store (6000 a day), and announce special sales. Even the meat department is run by a robot that processes each customer's order in less than a minute. Shopping wagons have built-in calculators to help customers tally their purchases. A computer controls the store's lighting and air conditioning. Optical scanners speed check-out and monitor inventory. There's even a room where customers' children can view videodisc programs.

COMPUTERIZED BANKING

In the previous chapter, you read how some banks let their customers use microcomputers to bank at home. That's just one of many roles that computers play in the banking world.

Banks use powerful computer systems to handle a wide range of tasks:

- processing checks
- keeping track of customer accounts
- processing deposits and withdrawals
- computing loan interest
- transferring funds from one account or bank to another

In addition, most major banks now have computerized **automatic teller machines** located outside the bank. Do you dislike waiting in line at the bank? Do you sometimes need to make a withdrawal after banking hours? Automatic teller machines let you make deposits and withdrawals, or even pay your bills, twenty-four hours a day. All you need is a plastic bank card, which you insert into the machine. Once you type in your identification number, you're ready to do your banking.

COWS AND COMPUTERS?

An Iowa farmer needed to decide which of his many heifers to keep for breeding and which to sell. Using a microcomputer, he typed in a variety of physical details about his cows. In no time at all, the computer produced a list of the best heifers in the herd.

Although computers on the farm are more the exception than the rule, many farmers realize the value of computers as a work tool. With a computer, farmers can quickly and easily make calculations about such things as crop-planting schedules and fertilizer use. Computers can also help farmers do financial projections and keep livestock records.

Some farms even use sophisticated electronic feed systems. These systems use computers to monitor how much food each animal eats. This information

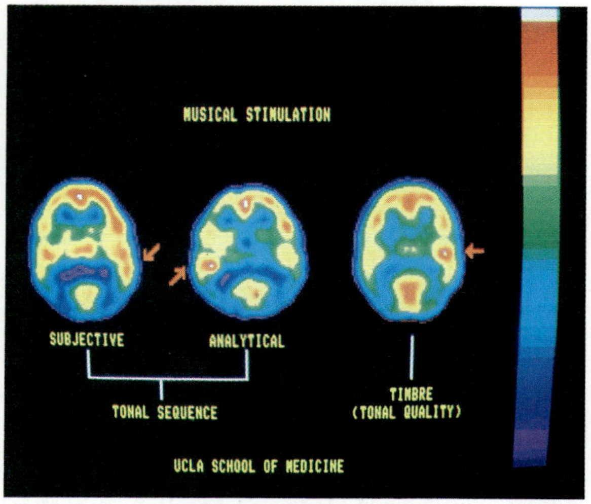

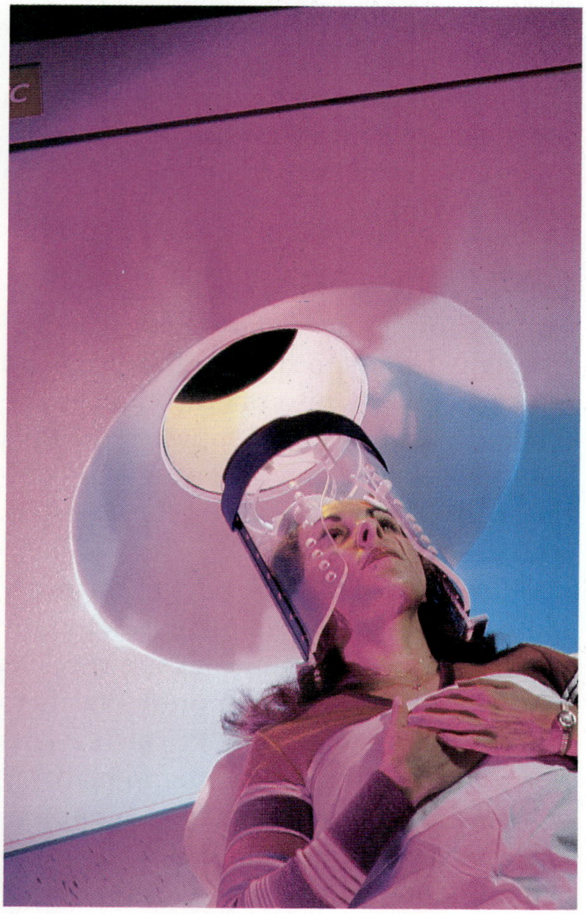

This woman is having pictures taken of her brain by a computerized CAT scanner. Scientists use CAT scan images to study different stimuli, such as music, on the brain.

tells farmers which animals need more food. It may also tell them that a particular animal is sick because it's "off its feed"—that is, not eating.

COMPUTERS IN HEALTH CARE

Just as the versatile computer serves various purposes in business and industry, it performs many functions in the health-care field. Doctors, nurses, medical secretaries, researchers, pharmacists, and other professionals in the field all find the computer an important work tool.

TELL THE COMPUTER WHERE IT HURTS

How often have you been sick in your life? Maybe you've had colds, chicken pox, or a stomachache. If you saw a doctor, you were probably treated quickly and effectively.

But medicine is a complex science. There are countless diseases, each with its own set of causes and symptoms. Moreover, dozens of illnesses have the same or similar symptoms. This can make it hard for a doctor to determine exactly what's wrong with a patient.

Computers can help. For example, some doctors now use computers as an aid in diagnosing—that is, in figuring out what's wrong with a patient. The patient is given a series of medical tests. Data from these tests is then put into a computer. In a few minutes the computer indicates which tests have abnormal results. The computer may even suggest possible diagnoses. Of course, the doctor must make the final decision, but the computer speeds the process. Also, because a computer can store in memory much more data than a person can, an unusual illness may be identified more quickly with a computer's help than it would without it.

Computer-aided machines also help doctors provide fast and efficient health care. For instance, a device called a **CAT scanner** takes close-up pictures of body organs. By the way, *CAT* has nothing to do with four-footed house pets. It stands for "computer-aided tomography." Tomography is an x-ray process.

THE COMPUTER AS MEDICAL ASSISTANT

Carl Jacobs had a heart attack last night and was rushed to the hospital. He survived, but he's still in the intensive-care unit. There, he's connected to a computerized device that constantly monitors how his heart is working. If Carl's heart should suddenly slow to a dangerous level, the computer will signal doctors and nurses for help.

Claire Reynolds went to the drugstore this morning to fill a prescription that her dentist gave her for pain. Claire's drugstore has a computer system in which each customer's medical history is stored. Before the pharmacist filled Claire's prescription, he checked her history. The computer indicated that Claire was already taking another medication prescribed by her family doctor. When combined with the dentist's pain pills, that medication could cause serious side effects. The pharmacist called Claire's dentist, and a different medication was prescribed.

These are just two examples of how

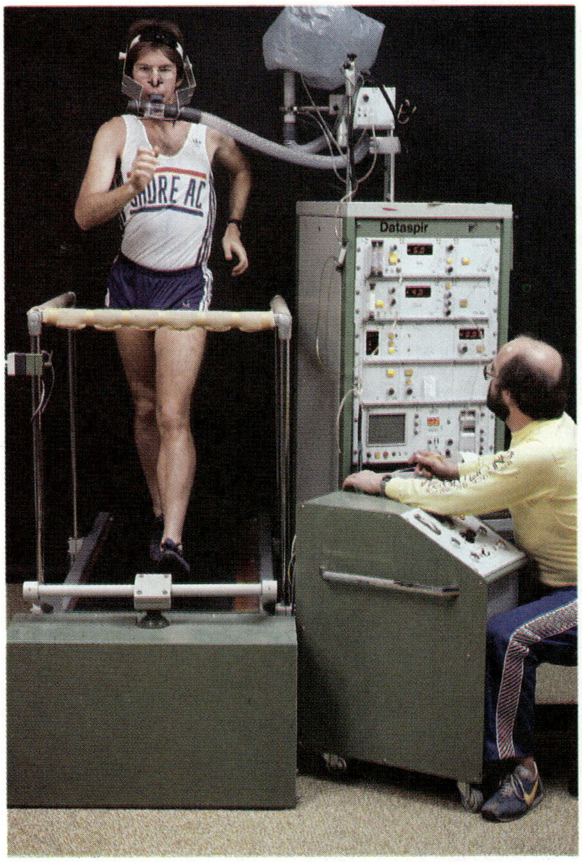

Computers help monitor this runner's respiratory system as he jogs on a laboratory treadmill.

computers assist health-care workers. There are numerous other ways in which computer power is being put to use in hospitals, clinics, private offices, and laboratories. Here's just a sampling:

- Computers play a key role in medical research. For example, they are used to calculate how the pollution in an area contributes to the disease rate of the people who live there. Computers are also used to study the effects of impact on different parts of the body—how a car crash might affect a person's spine or head, for instance.
- Computerized medical data banks en-

able health-care workers to keep up with the latest research.

• Computer networks are used to match up organ donors with patients who need organ transplants.

• Computer-simulation techniques are used to train health-care professionals. The computer simulates a patient who requires immediate treatment. Based on the given symptoms, the trainee must figure out what to do. If the trainee makes a mistake, the computer points out the error.

• Computers are used to create maps that show the spread of an epidemic.

• Computers are used to keep records ranging from patient bills to medical histories to inventories of supplies. By reducing the amount of time-consuming clerical work, computers give health-care workers more time to spend with their patients.

HELPING DISABLED PEOPLE

One of the most promising areas of computer technology concerns disabled people—those who are paralyzed, blind, deaf, or otherwise handicapped. Computers are expanding the options of disabled people, both at home and on the job.

Custom-made electronic devices enable severely handicapped people to use computers to communicate, to feed themselves, and even to play video games. For example, people whose arms are paralyzed can work a computer with their feet by using a "tread switch," which resembles a sewing-machine pedal. People whose arms and legs are paralyzed can use a device that is held in the mouth or attached to the head.

Computer-produced speech, or voice synthesis, enables blind people to perform tasks that were once impossible for them to do alone. Thanks to computers, they can use their sense of hearing in place of their sense of sight. For people who are partially sighted, there are devices that produce enlarged text on a special monitor.

Key Points

• With the aid of computers, designers of large-scale projects save hours of drawing and calculating time.

• The speed and power of computer technology has enabled supermarkets, banks, farms, and other businesses to run more efficiently.

• Computers in the medical field aid health-care workers in diagnosing and treating patients. They also play a key role in medical research.

• Computers are expanding the options of disabled people both at home and on the job.

Review Questions

1. How can computer simulations help engineers who are involved in designing automobiles?
2. Computer technology has brightened the future for disabled people. Explain, giving specific examples.

COMPUTERS IN EDUCATION

Chances are good that many of the schools in your community—from day-care centers to colleges—are using computers. If you did a survey, you might find examples such as these:

• three-year-olds using computer programs to learn to distinguish between shapes
• elementary school students using computers to learn how to read and write
• teen-agers using computers to prepare for college entrance exams
• university students using computers to see what happens when temperatures in a nuclear power plant rise above the danger mark

Why are computers becoming such popular teaching aids? The computer has endless patience. It will repeat the same instructions five times, ten times, even one hundred times—and never yawn. A computer also lets you learn at your own pace—not at the pace of that student across the aisle who is so much quicker (or slower) than you to understand new information. And when you are sitting by yourself at the computer, you have that computer's undivided attention. In addition, many instructional software programs are as enjoyable as they are educational.

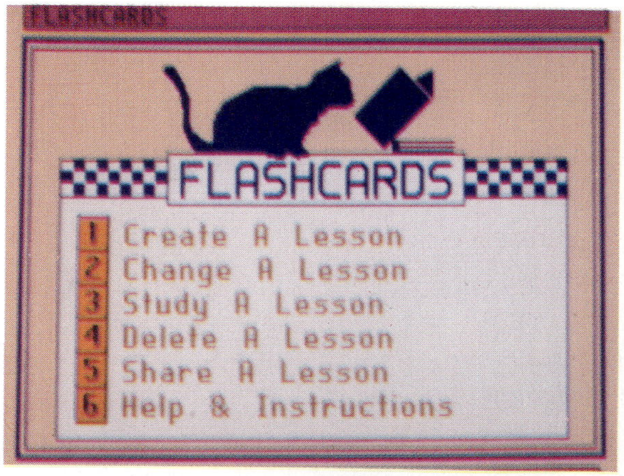

You don't have to raise your hand to get this "teacher's" attention, just push a button.

COMPUTER-ASSISTED INSTRUCTION

Computer-assisted instruction (**CAI**, for short) is the term commonly used to describe the process of people learning through the aid of a computer. It's a term that covers a variety of situations.

The computer "teacher" may be a microcomputer, or it may be a terminal that is part of an electronic network (you read about classroom networks in Chapter 12). The material that is taught may be presented under a teacher's step-by-step control, or it may be prepackaged in a software program that you, the learner, control.

The actual instruction may take various forms. It can be text to be read, practice exercises to be completed, problems to be solved, or questions to be answered. Simulations let you carry out experiments that are too dangerous, expensive, time-consuming, or otherwise impossible. For example, you might dissect a frog, rule ancient empires, or travel west in a wagon train. You learn by gathering information, making decisions, and then seeing the results of your decisions.

COMPUTERS IN THE PRINCIPAL'S OFFICE

Schools use computers for more than teaching, however. Administrators use computerized systems to schedule classes, print report cards, and store student records. Guidance counselors use computerized data bases to provide students with information about colleges and careers. Teachers use computerized spreadsheets to maintain and update records of their students' grades and attendance. Athletic coaches use comput-

The long arm of the law need only reach as far as its computer to obtain crime-stopping data.

erized programs to keep track of sports equipment, game schedules, and team records.

COMPUTERS IN LAW ENFORCEMENT

Here is some bad news for criminals: the "long arm of the law" is now computerized. The computer's speed, power, and ability to process huge amounts of data are helping law-enforcement officers do their jobs more effectively.

POLICE DATA BANKS

Because of their ability to store large amounts of information, computers are now being used to keep records on criminal activity. Electronic data banks of crime-related information are readily available to state and local law-enforcement agencies across the country. The Federal Bureau of Investigation (FBI) operates a nationwide police-information data bank known as the National Crime Information Center.

The following kinds of information are stored in law-enforcement data banks:

- the names and arrest records of known criminals
- information about stolen property
- information about wanted or missing persons
- information about cars (including license-plate numbers), guns, and even boats

With the aid of computers, a small crime can often lead to the arrest of a major criminal. In one case police officers stopped a driver for making an illegal turn. When the car's license-plate number was checked by computer, the police discovered that the vehicle had been stolen in another state. It turned out that the driver was wanted for a bank robbery. He was immediately arrested.

COMPUTER DETECTIVES

Aside from their use in information networks, computers also play an important part in detective work. For example, computers in police crime laboratories are used to analyze and compare substances that are found at the scene of a crime. The computer's findings are often used as evidence in court.

Computers are also used for "crime-mapping." Data concerning the crimes that have been committed in a certain area is fed into a computer. The computer then produces a map that shows whether there are any patterns to the crimes. Using such information, law-enforcement officials may decide that a neighborhood requires more protection.

Artistic talent combined with a computer, a graphics tablet, and graphics software can greatly expand a person's creativity.

COMPUTERS IN THE ARTS

A few decades ago the only people who used computers were scientists and mathematicians. Today, computer users include writers, artists, musicians, and many other people in the arts. The "creative computer" is helping people to write books, draw cartoons, compose songs, and create the special effects you see in science-fiction movies.

WRITERS AND WORD PROCESSORS

Not long ago, two best-selling authors, Stephen King and Peter Straub, decided to team up and write a novel together. The only problem was that King lived in Maine and Straub lived in Connecticut. What did they do? King and Straub worked together electronically, linking their word processors by modems and phone lines. Their joint effort, *The Talisman*, was published in 1985.

More and more professional writers are using word processing to improve the quality and speed of their work. Not only novelists like King and Straub but journalists, technical writers, scriptwriters, textbook authors (like the ones who wrote this book), and many others now use computers. Word processing takes the drudgery out of editing and revising. It also saves hours of retyping time. In addition, there are special software programs available that help writers check their work for spelling and punctuation errors.

Furthermore, once they have a microcomputer, writers can also use their machine to communicate with data banks. This saves them additional time when doing research. Finally, writers use their computers to keep records, handle paperwork, and send out bills.

THE ARTISTIC COMPUTER

In the hands of an artist, the computer becomes a drawing tool. Illustrators, designers, cartoonists, and movie makers find that computer technology gives them a new means of creative expression. Using such devices as graphics tablets, light pens, and plotters, artists create colorful drawings, graphs, maps, and charts.

Why are computers popular with professional artists? You've probably already guessed. Using a computer, artists can make changes and corrections quickly and easily. Do you want that boy to be wearing a red shirt instead of a blue one? Do you want that car to be a convertible instead of a hardtop? That's not a problem. Electronic revisions take far less time than changes made by hand. Similarly, different versions of a complex drawing can be produced in a few minutes, without having to redraw the picture from scratch.

Do you see similarities between a writer and an artist when it comes to using computers? Even though one works with words and the other with pictures, both enjoy the speed, flexibility, and convenience of developing their creations by computer.

THE MUSICAL COMPUTER

Diane is a teen-ager who has always loved music. In addition to her guitar and her flute, she also has an electronic **music synthesizer** that's connected to her home computer. The synthesizer has a pianolike keyboard that Diane plays as she composes music. She can record her musical compositions on a disk and then have the synthesizer play them back. Because the synthesizer can imitate the sounds of different kinds of instruments, Diane can hear her composition played in a variety of ways. If she wants she can even have her computer print out sheet music showing the notes that were played.

Like Diane, a growing number of composers, performers, and music teachers use computers in their work. Computers and synthesizers allow musicians to:

- produce the sounds of a wide range of instruments—as well as some uniquely electronic sounds.
- experiment with musical compositions played at different speeds, rhythms, and pitches.
- store musical compositions on disks and make changes easily and quickly as often as desired.

Key Points

- Computers are being used as teaching tools in a growing number of schools, colleges, and homes.
- Computer-assisted instruction is commonly used to describe the process of people learning through the aid of a computer.
- The computer's speed, power, and ability to process huge amounts of data help

law officers work more effectively.

- Today's computer users are not just scientists and mathematicians. They are also people who work in the creative arts.

Review Questions

1. Why might a newspaper reporter want a personal computer?
2. "A computer can only be as creative as its user." Explain.

COMPUTERS IN THE HOME

Can you imagine living without electricity? Most of us take electric power for granted. Do you want toast? Just switch on the toaster. Do you want to hear the latest weather forecast? Then turn on your radio or television set. Do you need to vacuum the house? Just plug in the machine and go. When you think about it, without electricity most of our modern-day comforts and conveniences wouldn't be possible.

Can you imagine living without computers? If you answered, "Sure I can," you had better slow down a second. You may think that computers are not an important part of your home life. But you may be surprised. For several years computer technology has been "sneaking" into our homes—not just in the form of desktop computers but in the form of the "unseen computer." Before long, the unseen computer may become as essential to our comfort as electricity is now.

THE UNSEEN COMPUTER

What exactly is the unseen computer? It's a tiny microprocessor that is hidden in objects around your home. Most people have at least one or two in their house or apartment. Some people have many more than that. You don't believe it? Then look at the following list. Any one of these items listed may contain a microprocessor:

Music synthesizers are used for every kind of music from classical to country and western.

- digital clocks
- microwave ovens
- radios
- calculators
- washing machines
- cameras
- stereos
- telephone answering machines
- television sets
- thermostats
- telephones
- dishwashers
- dryers
- sewing machines
- typewriters
- exercise machines

And this is just the beginning. For example, there are computerized doorbells that you can buy. They don't just go "ding-dong," either—they play music.

Now look around you. What devices do you imagine will be computerized in the future? You're probably right . . .

HOME COMPUTERS

Most people do not have personal computers in their homes—yet. However, as costs continue to decline, more and more families will buy home computers. A decade ago, handheld calculators cost $60 and people were wondering whether they really needed one. Today, more powerful calculators cost about *one-tenth* that amount, and even young children are using them!

As you read, no invention in history has dropped in price as rapidly as the computer. No doubt, a decade from now microcomputers will be as common as calculators.

For what tasks will families use home computers? The possibilities are endless. For example, today some people use personal computers to control their home's heating and air conditioning. Others have computerized lawn-watering systems. Microcomputers are used to turn lights on and off at programmed times. They're even used to run home-security systems.

With a home computer and the right software and peripherals, you can do just about anything:

- play games
- keep track of stamp collections
- use word processing for letters, reports, and the like
- communicate with electronic networks and data banks
- compute your income tax
- plan nutritional meals
- teach yourself Spanish, history, or just about any other subject
- keep financial records
- play music
- calculate a monthly budget
- draw pictures
- plan a personal exercise program
- write your own programs

This list could go on and on—and it will continue to grow in the years to come.

COMPUTERS: THE SOLUTION TO ALL PROBLEMS?

Are you getting the feeling that we should be using computers for every task and hobby? Then don't. Always keep in mind that no matter how sophisticated a computer is, it is still only a tool. How—and whether—to use it depends on the situation and on the user.

It is not always easier or better to do a task with a computer. For example, most families can handle their financial matters with no help from computer hardware and software. Similarly, most computerized appointment calendars, address books, and recipe files waste more time than they save. A word-processed letter will never seem as personal as one that's handwritten. And a computer "teacher" will never be as helpful or as friendly as a human teacher.

The point is that you don't need to use a computer for everything. Personal computers should *be* personal. That is, they should meet your specific needs. Computers are versatile, powerful, and fast. But like any other tool, they are not the solution to all problems.

REVIEW & APPLICATION

SUMMARY

- The computer's versatility, power, and speed make it a useful tool for workers in business and industry, agriculture, health care, education, law enforcement, and the arts. People in these and other fields use computers to do word processing, keep records, do research, hook up to networks, handle financial matters, train new employees, and monitor various processes.
- Computer simulations allow learners to take on a role and make realistic decisions in that role.
- Robots—computer-controlled mechanical devices—are increasingly being used to perform repetitive or dangerous tasks.
- More and more stores are using optical scanners to read the Universal Product Code printed on items. This system speeds the check-out process and allows for computerized inventory control.
- Electronic data banks in fields ranging from medicine to law enforcement make huge amounts of information readily available across the country.
- As prices drop, more families will buy home computers. These computers will serve a broad range of purposes, from self-education to entertainment to personal record keeping.
- As sophisticated as it is, the computer is still only a tool. Its usefulness depends on the situation and on the user.

VOCABULARY

Match each item in the left column with the correct item on the right.

a. CAT scanner	1. Learning by role playing
b. optical scanner	2. Computer-controlled mechanical device
c. simulation	3. Takes close-up x-ray pictures
d. robot	4. Reads Universal Product Code
e. computer-assisted instruction	5. Learning through the aid of a computer

REVIEW QUESTIONS

1. How might a computer simulation teach you to operate machinery?
2. How would the use of computers affect the work of an architect who is designing a shopping center?
3. How can an optical scanner speed up the check-out line at a supermarket?
4. What are some of the ways in which a farmer might use a computer?
5. What is an unseen computer?

DISCUSSION QUESTION

Some people feel that computers are taking over our lives. Do you agree or disagree with this feeling? Why? Do you think that "the computer invasion" is good, bad, or a little of both? Why?

PROJECTS

This program can be used to calculate the total number of calories you consumed at breakfast this morning.

```
10 CN(1)=150: CN(2)=230:
    CN(3)=80: CN(4)=60
20 CN(5)=45: CN(6)=120:
    CN(7)=100: CN(8)=60: TC=0
30 HOME: PRINT "COUNTING CALORIES"
40 PRINT "1, 1 CUP OF MILK"
50 PRINT "2, 1 CUP OF YOGURT"
60 PRINT "3, 1 EGG"
70 PRINT "4, 1 LINK OF SAUSAGE"
80 PRINT "5, 1/2 GRAPEFRUIT"
90 PRINT "6, 1 CUP JUICE"
100 PRINT "7, 1 CUP OF CEREAL"
110 PRINT "8, 1 SLICE OF TOAST"
120 PRINT: PRINT "TOTAL
     CALORIES="; TC
130 PRINT: INPUT "ENTER
     NUMBER OF ITEM, OR 0
     TO END: "; N
140 IF N=0 THEN END
150 PRINT: PRINT "1, SAME AMOUNT"
160 PRINT "2, DOUBLE AMOUNT"
170 INPUT "3, 1/2 AMOUNT "; AM
180 IF AM=1 THEN TC=TC+CN(N)
190 IF AM=2 THEN TC=TC+2*CN(N)
200 IF AM=3 THEN TC=TC+.5*CN(N)
210 GOTO 30
```

If you are using the Commodore 64, IBM PCjr, or TRS-80, substitute your machine's clear-screen command for the HOME statement in line 30.

Enter the program and run it. Input several different breakfasts.

Further Practice

Expand the program so that it contains more items. You can get the calorie counts from an encyclopedia or textbook.

The potential of computers to save time, effort, and money was first recognized in the workplace. Describe how computers are used today in the field or occupation of your choice.

Enrichment

Do you have a hearty appetite? Or do you leave food on your plate? Serving sizes can vary greatly depending on who's doing the eating. Modify the program so that it can handle three times the amount and one third the amount.

What's universal about the Universal Product Code? Do some research to find out what information the Universal Product Code stores and how it works.

So you want to be a doctor. Or would you prefer interior design? Whatever career you choose, you are likely to use computers in some way. Describe how computers might be used ten years from now in a career that interests you.

CHAPTER TEST

Write your answers on a sheet of paper numbered 1 through 14.

MULTIPLE CHOICE

1. Computers are used by:
   a. doctors
   b. farmers
   c. designers
   d. all of the above
2. To record prices of groceries, a supermarket cashier would use:
   a. a modem
   b. a printer
   c. a CAT scanner
   d. an optical scanner
3. The use of robots in industry:
   a. increases production costs
   b. increases the number of employees needed
   c. may decrease the number of manufacturing jobs for people
   d. none of the above
4. Teachers can use computerized spreadsheets to:
   a. administer tests
   b. teach spelling
   c. keep records on grades and student attendance
   d. assign homework
5. People do *not* use home computers to:
   a. play games
   b. plan budgets
   c. write letters
   d. get cash from a bank

FILL-IN

6. A _____________ puts you in a role in which you are asked to make realistic decisions.
7. A computer can _____________ a set of instructions as many times as you want, which allows you to learn at your own pace.
8. _____________ can perform jobs under conditions that would be difficult or impossible for human beings.
9. With an automatic teller machine, you can make a bank deposit or withdrawal by inserting a _____________ into the machine.
10. Computerized medical _____________ enable health-care workers to keep up with the latest research.
11. _____________ enables blind people to use their sense of hearing in place of sight to use computers.
12. In police _____________, computers are used to analyze and compare substances that are found at the scene of a crime.
13. More and more novelists and other professional writers are using _____________ to improve the speed and quality of their work.
14. A composer might play tunes on the pianolike keyboard of a _____________ that is connected to a computer.

CHAPTER

12 13 14 1 2

COMPUTERS in the FUTURE

WHERE DO WE GO FROM HERE?

There's no question about it—computers will play a major role in human life in the future. By the year 2000 these machines are likely to be as common as the telephone is today. Is that good or bad? Before you decide, think about some of the benefits and problems of the telephone today.

The telephone links people in a communications network that extends around the world. The phone makes it possible for you to have a great deal of information right at your fingertips. Without budging from your home, you can order groceries, theater tickets, and books. You can get recipes, jokes, and stock market quotes. You can call a library and find out the author of a book someone recommended to you. You can get the weather report or the time of day. And, of course, you can speak to your Uncle Henry in Florida, Alaska, or London, England.

Along with the benefits of the telephone, however, there are also some problems. Some people get crank calls at strange hours of the night. Some people receive huge phone bills for long-distance calls they never made. The computer, like the phone, is a wonderful invention, but people are worried that computers may be misused.

This chapter looks at some of the newer developments in computers and at how computers are likely to be used in the future. It also looks at some of the questions that need to be asked as computers become more powerful and more important.

SUPERCHIPS—THE COMPUTER'S ENGINE

The two most important parts of the telephone are the transmitter and the receiver. The transmitter changes the human voice into electronic signals. The receiver reverses this process.

At the heart of today's and tomorrow's computers is the superchip. As you know, a chip, or microprocessor, is a small piece of silicon containing electronic circuits.

The first chips, introduced in the 1960's, had hundreds of electronic circuits. Today's superchips have 100,000 or more circuits. A single very-large-scale integration (**VLSI**) chip has more computing power than ENIAC, the huge computer of the 1940's that filled an entire room. And the VLSI chip is only about 1/1500 the size of this page.

In just a few years, ultra-large-scale integration (**ULSI**) chips will emerge as the next generation of computer powerhouses. Each of these chips will contain up to a million circuits.

LIGHTWEIGHT POWER

VLSI and ULSI chips make computer power extremely easy to carry around. By the year 2000 computers as powerful as today's mainframes may be no bigger than a pocket calculator.

What does the small size of computer chips mean for people? What kinds of things will it make possible? For one thing, just about everybody will be able to afford a computer of some kind. The amount of raw material that goes into making a VLSI or ULSI chip is about the same as that in a smaller-capacity chip.

The film for a maze of integrated circuits must be carefully inspected before being miniaturized.

Consequently, the VLSI or ULSI chip offers more power for the same—or less—money. Furthermore, the small chip size means that computers and their storage capacity can be contained in very small spaces, such as in a wristwatch or even a shirt button.

IDENTITY ON A CHIP

In the near future you'll no longer need a key to unlock a door. You'll simply say "Open Sesame" or "Open Starship" and a computer chip embedded in the door will recognize your voice and the key word. The computer will then release the latch that allows you to open the door, whether the door is to your house, your car, or your room.

THE CASHLESS SOCIETY

Imagine yourself as a working adult in the early twenty-first century. Instead of receiving your salary in cash or as a check, you'll receive a "credit" to your personal account, which will be controlled by a computer in a bank. To make purchases and pay fares, you'll use the personal superchip embedded in your wristwatch or ID ring, card, or button. This superchip will contain more than enough information to identify you in a unique way—the sound of your voice, your physical description, your date of birth, the names of everyone in your family, your address, your central credit account number, your blood type, your place of employment, your income, and so on.

When you wish to make a purchase, you'll select the items you want and pass your ID device over a sensor that will read the appropriate information. The sensor will check that you have enough credit in your bank account to pay for the purchase or that you are a good credit risk. If it approves the purchase, the cost of the item will then be subtracted from your account.

When you ride a bus or subway or pay a toll, you'll just brush your ID device past a sensor and proceed without waiting. The sensor will record the time, date, and amount of the fare or toll. You'll never have to carry coins or paper money again.

Suppose somebody steals your ID device? Don't worry. The chip identifies you as uniquely as your fingerprint. When you're not wearing it—or if someone else tries to wear it—it becomes inoperative. If you lose it or if someone takes it, it will beam its whereabouts to a central computer that will help you get it back.

CHIP COMMUNICATION

With a personalized superchip, you will be able to communicate with almost anyone almost anywhere. A network will connect the computers by radio waves—in much the same way that "beepers" and cordless phones work today. You might be at a football game, for example, and get a call from your cousin who unexpectedly came into town for a visit—but had no idea where you were.

SMART MACHINES

Superchips will change the way we communicate, and they'll also change the way machines operate: machines will become smarter. For example, most of the appliances around the house will have superchips that will enable them to work automatically. A sewing machine, for instance, will have a chip that is programmed to stitch a specific pattern—all the user will have to do is supply the fabric and tell the machine which pattern to sew.

Vacuum cleaners with superchips will be programmed to automatically vacuum carpets on a regular basis—once a week or once every two weeks or however often the owner decides. The temperature in homes and offices will be maintained automatically, year-round, by superchips in the control units of air conditioners and heating units.

Smart machines—like this sewing machine—are becoming more and more a part of our daily lives.

Automobiles with superchips will be programmed to reach specific destinations without a driver's intervention. By means of superchips, a car in the future will be able to adjust its rate of speed, turn on its headlights and windshield wipers, and open its trunk—all at the sound of the driver's voice.

BOOKS WITHOUT PAPER

Identity devices and smart machines are only a few of many applications for superchips. Others may also bring about surprising changes in the way we live.

Remember, a superchip's feature is that it provides an enormous amount of data processing and storage in a remarkably tiny and inexpensive package.

In the near future you may no longer have to go to a bookstore to buy a book. Why? When you want to read the latest best-seller, you'll order a book "chip."

That's right. A single superchip can contain one or more books, each 200 or 300 pages long. You'll insert the chip into a chip reader that will project a printed image, paragraph by paragraph, on your computer screen or on a large flat wall screen. If the book has pictures, they, too, will be projected onto the screen with lifelike exactness. Instead of a bookcase, you'll have a book-chip case—one that will hold a whole library of information in a space the size of—well, one of today's paperback books. You'll be able to afford lots of books, too, because they'll be much cheaper than they are today.

And if you don't feel like reading the book for yourself, you can have your computer read it to you, because in the future computers will be able to talk.

Key Points

- Superchips containing hundreds of thousands and even millions of electrical connections are the engines of today's and tomorrow's computers.
- The small size of superchips will make it possible for everyone to have a personalized identification chip that can be worn in a wristwatch or ring, or on a card. This ID chip will help make the cashless society possible.
- Superchips will make it possible to store books on a chip and to greatly reduce the size of libraries.

Review Questions

1. Why will computers become smaller in the future?
2. What effect will superchips have on how we shop?

ARTIFICIAL INTELLIGENCE

Can a machine be as intelligent as a person? A few years ago most people laughingly dismissed such a possibility. Today it has to be taken seriously because scientists and engineers are indeed developing computers that can "think" in ways that humans do.

The field of computer science that is concerned with developing intelligent computers is known as **artificial intelligence**, or **AI** for short. Researchers working in this field are trying to give computers the characteristics associated with intelligence in humans: the ability to infer, reason, solve problems, understand language, and so on. The AI field

An AI program to identify aircraft is being developed. Stored diagrams are matched by the computer with the actual aircraft.

has already begun to bring about many important developments in computer technology.

The three principal areas of artificial intelligence that are being developed simultaneously are expert systems, robotics, and voice synthesis and recognition.

WHAT IS AN EXPERT SYSTEM?

You probably know someone who is an expert on a subject. One of your teachers may be an expert on football; a friend may be an expert on science-fiction movies. These people are experts because they know a great deal about their subject. They are able to answer questions that require knowledge of their subject.

Suppose your friend who's a science-fiction movie expert is playing a game of "20 Questions" with you. You say, "I'm thinking of a science-fiction movie that is titled after a specific year." Your friend might ask, "Is the year before 1985?" You answer, "No," and your friend now knows the movie is not *1984*. Next your friend asks, "Is the year after 2009?" You answer, "No," and your friend now knows the movie is not *2010*. Finally your friend asks, "Is the movie written by Stanley Kubrick and Arthur C. Clarke and directed by Kubrick?" You answer, "Yes," and your friend correctly guesses that the movie is *2001: A Space Odyssey*.

In order to ask good questions and get the right answer, your friend needed to have some knowledge about science-fic-

ISSUE: Who's in Control?

Although many people will no doubt want to have their own personalized ID chip, some may not. Some people may see these chips as dehumanizing—turning the wearer into a code or an account number. They feel the rights of people could be abused by governments that made everyone wear an identity chip and then closely monitored people's behavior—in order to limit their freedom.

On the other hand, some people believe that we can be prepared to face the problems that technological progress brings. They think that when new inventions are developed and put to use, new laws can be created to safeguard people's rights. For example, when people misused the telephone by wiretapping, laws making wiretapping illegal were passed to protect people's right to privacy.

tion movies. In addition, your friend needed to be able to ask good questions and to match your responses against his or her knowledge. You apply logic in order to arrive at the correct answer. The rule might be something like this: If a science-fiction movie named after a specific year was written by Arthur C. Clarke and Stanley Kubrick and directed by Kubrick, the movie was *2001*.

This is the same way that today's expert systems work. They have received their name because they imitate people who are experts. An expert system has three basic parts. It has a very large data base, the ability to ask questions, and a set of rules that allow it to use the data to arrive at conclusions. Some expert systems can also explain the method they used in reaching their conclusions.

EXPERT SYSTEMS TODAY

Several different kinds of expert systems are already in use in business and industry. The American Telephone and Telegraph Company, for instance, has a system known as ACE (for Automated Cable Expertise) that can locate problems in telephone cables. In just over an hour the system can track down a problem and recommend a way to fix it. Before ACE was adopted, it took a team of technicians more than a week to do the same job.

In hospitals around the country, expert systems help physicians diagnose and treat illnesses. A typical system is fed a large amount of data on certain kinds of illnesses. It is also programmed with the rules that doctors follow in determining what illness a patient has by observing the patient's symptoms. The system also has the ability to question either the physician or the patient about the illness. A system might ask, for instance, "Has the patient had a sore throat lately? Has the patient had a persistent fever?" Depending on the answers it gets, it asks further questions or offers a diagnosis.

To be reliable, an expert system—like any human expert—must have all the data that is relevant to a problem. Otherwise its conclusions may be wrong. For example, assume an expert system on lung diseases does not include information on emphysema, a serious disease that makes breathing difficult. If the system is used to diagnose a person who is

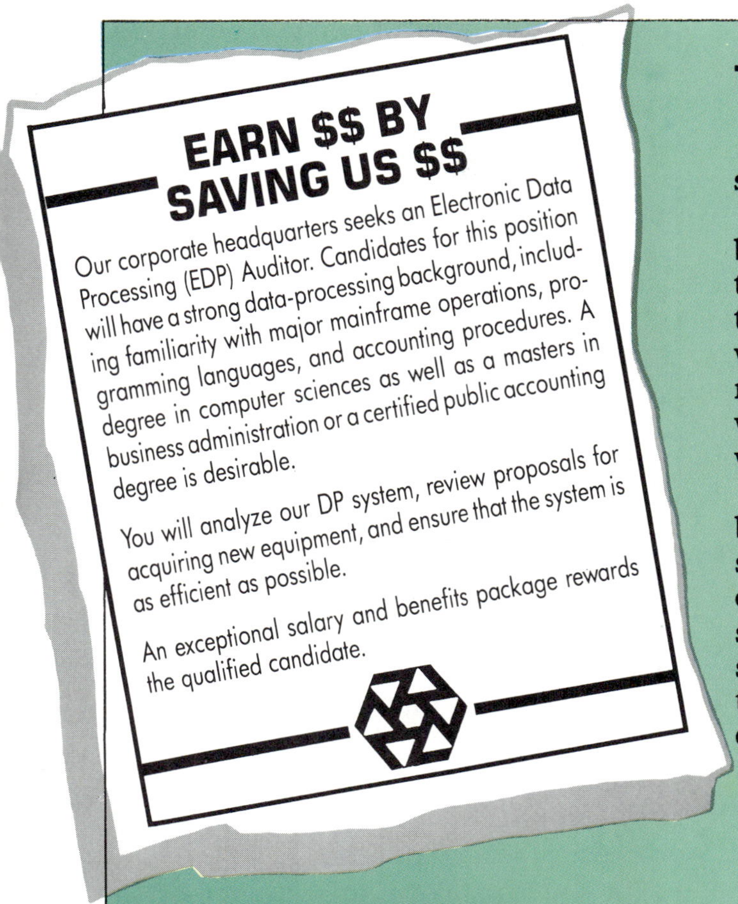

THAT'S MY JOB

Helen Breen, an EDP auditor, says:

"I have many more responsibilities now as an EDP auditor than I had as a programmer. I like that. I really know what is going on with the system—who's programming, which data are more secure, where we are cost-effective, and where we need improvement.

"It is a tremendous responsibility. If someone in the computer security group discovers that a computer pirate has entered the system, I'm the one who is responsible for straightening things out and for making sure it doesn't happen again."

MORE INFORMATION

EDP auditing is a good career move for senior programmers and analysts.... The number of jobs is likely to increase as corporations seek to control DP spending.... Salaries are at the top of the DP ladder.... This position can lead to a job in corporate management.

having breathing difficulties, it may suggest that the person has asthma. It won't mention emphysema because it won't have any knowledge of the disease.

MORE ADVANCED EXPERTS

Most expert systems today are used in science, business, and industry. By the 1990's expert systems will be even more widely used in these fields. But by then expert systems will also be common in homes and schools.

You're probably already familiar with educational software that indicates whether your answer to a question is right or wrong. Before too long programs will also tell you how you arrived at the wrong answer. These programs will contain specific information on the processes people follow in reaching a conclusion. For example, suppose you were given the following problem: If grapefruit are 49 cents each and apples are three for 81 cents, how much would you pay for 3 grapefruit and 2 apples? Suppose your answer was $1.52. The computer will tell you this is incorrect and will remind you that you are buying 3 grapefruit. It will have looked at $1.52 and determined that the most probable way for you to have arrived at your incorrect answer was to have added the cost of 2 grapefruit and 2 apples.

EXPERTS THAT THINK

At their current state of development, computers using artificial intelligence more or less *mimic* human intelligence. Actually they are just doing some pretty simple operations but at incredible speed. The machine that helps diagnose a patient's illness, for example, is matching a certain input against data that it has been programmed to recognize—the symptoms of certain diseases.

In the future engineers and scientists hope to produce machines that do more than just imitate the way the human brain operates. They are developing computers that use human logic and parallel processing.

For example, suppose someone says to you "Only birds have feathers," and "A penguin has feathers." If you did not already know what a penguin is, you would then be able to say without hesitation that a penguin is a bird. This kind of logic allows humans to acquire and analyze knowledge. Future computers with AI will use this kind of logic to learn new information. These computers will also be able to ask for information they need in order to solve a problem. The expert system described earlier that was not programmed to recognize emphysema, for example, will be able to ask for information about other illnesses for which it does not have data.

Parallel processing will also make computers behave more like the human brain. In your mind you can usually process two or more kinds of information at once. For instance, you can look at an object and tell several things about it—let's say you see a man with dark hair, wearing a yellow jacket, jogging down the street.

Most of today's computers can focus on only one thing at a time. They might see the same person and take awhile to recognize that it is a man. To determine that the man has dark hair and is wearing a yellow jacket and is jogging down the street would take three more separate processes for a computer.

The ability to take in all four—or more—kinds of information at once makes the human brain much faster than a computer in certain ways. Scientists and engineers hope to make computers faster and more "intelligent" by giving them the ability to do parallel processing.

Key Points

- Expert systems are in use in hospitals where they help diagnose illnesses.
- Expert systems are able to find problems, or "troubleshoot," much faster than humans.
- In the future computers with artificial intelligence that use logic and parallel processing will be able to "think" in ways that humans think.

Review Questions

1. What is the aim of the field known as artificial intelligence?
2. What are three important aspects of an expert system?

ROBOTICS

The second major application of artificial intelligence is in the area of robotics. A robot is a mechanical device controlled by a computer that does a job the way a person might do it. Simple robots do repetitive jobs such as welding objects on an assembly line. Advanced robots today are able to do more sophisticated jobs, such as vacuuming a house or mowing a lawn.

INDUSTRIAL ROBOTS

There are about 6000 robots in the United States today. About 1500 robots have been produced each year in this country. Soon that rate will grow to 60,000 or more per year, and by the year 2000 there will be about a million working robots. Most of these robots will be used in industry, in plants where they do jobs formerly done by people.

The robots you learned about in Chapter 13 are really not the "thinking" kind. Their movements are precisely controlled to do heavy-duty, repetitive, and sometimes dangerous work. These robots are programmed to make a set of movements over and over. If a car frame should happen not to appear before a robot welder, the robot arm would go through the welding motions anyway. A human supervisor must watch these robots to make sure they function correctly.

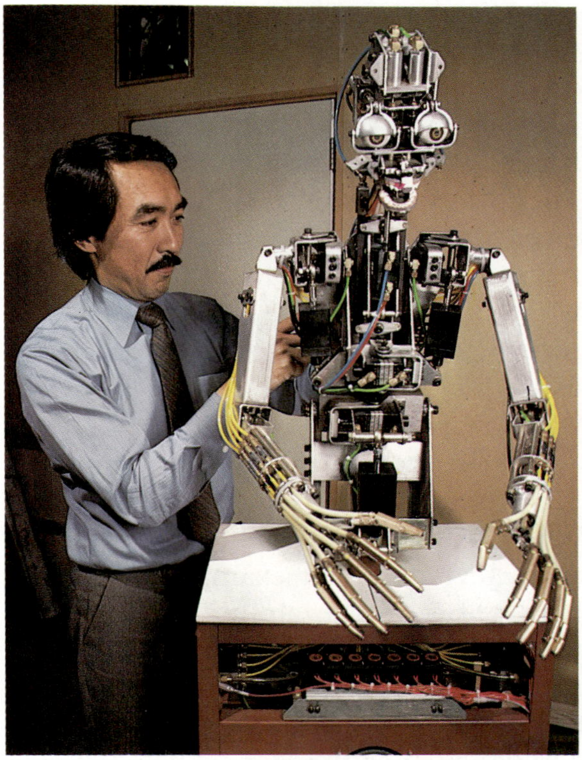

No, it's not a creature from outer space, but a computerized robot being tested in a lab.

Robots of the future will be smarter. They will be able to think for themselves. An industrial robot assigned to a welding job will know enough not to weld if the car frame does not appear in the right position. It will also be able to figure out what parts need welding.

EXPERIMENTAL ROBOTS

Factories are not the only places where robots can be helpful to people. Scientists and engineers are working on robots that will work in homes and offices, helping people with tasks such as carrying heavy packages, keeping watch for burglars and fires, preparing food, cleaning house, walking the dog, mowing the lawn, and so on.

Because of developments in artificial intelligence, these robots will know a great deal. They will have a large base of data about their owners, and they will have the ability to do many kinds of jobs. They'll be able to understand spoken language, and they'll be able to speak directly to their users. Like industrial robots of the future, they'll also be able to recognize objects by sight and touch because they'll be equipped with vision and touch sensors.

One area where robots will be increasingly useful is in helping disabled people. In the future robots will be able to replace seeing-eye dogs, for example. These robots will have the ability to see where they are going and to safely guide their masters. They'll be able to make decisions about objects that might be dangerous, such as moving cars and stairs, and they'll have one big advantage over their warm and furry predecessors: They'll be able to talk. Their masters can ask them questions such as "What's wrong? Where are we heading? What street is this?" and the robot guides will be able to tell them.

THE GIFT OF SIGHT

How does a robot learn to see? Scientists and engineers are working on ways to make robots able to recognize shapes of objects. This area of research is called **vision analysis**. In vision analysis, a computer or a robot guided by a computer has a sensor that picks up the light reflected by an object, such as a coffee cup.

The computer then changes the visual image into a string of numbers. Next the computer searches its memory for a similar set of numbers that identify the shape as a cup. (The computer can only recognize shapes that it has been programmed to recognize.)

In some experiments for the food industry, vision systems have been developed that enable robots to inspect crackers, rejecting those that are burned. How does a robot tell a burned cracker from a

ISSUE: Watching the Experts

Expert systems offer tremendous advantages. They make specialized knowledge available to a large group of people. They give us more experts where experts are needed. Because computers are able to process information much faster than people can, expert systems also give us the advantage of speed in analyzing data and in making decisions.

But some people see a danger in too much reliance on computers. What happens if there's a power failure? they ask. They are concerned that, by relying on computers too much, we will lose our ability to solve problems for ourselves without machines.

On the other hand, because computers do not make mistakes if they are programmed and operated correctly, expert systems also give us the advantage of reliable information. An expert system can save a patient's life or help a company increase its profits. And with computerized expert systems spreading the knowledge of human experts, the human experts will be free to make new discoveries.

regular one? The robot first sees the cracker as a series of dots, like a blowup of a newspaper photograph. It assigns a value to the dots—for example, a high number to dots in the light-shaded area and a low number to dots in a dark-shaded area. If there is a high percentage of dark-shaded areas on a cracker, the robot recognizes the low numbers and rejects the cracker.

This procedure alone takes about 60,000 to 70,000 numbers. For a more complicated job, such as seeing a table leg, doorway, or dog, the robot would have to have enormous brain power—enough to store millions of numbers. This kind of power will be possible with USLI chips.

Vision analysis is being used to produce a computerized braille for the blind.

Key Points

- A robot is a mechanical device, controlled by a computer, that carries out tasks the way a human might.
- By 1990 the United States will be producing between 20,000 and 60,000 robots per year, and there will be more than a million robots working in industry by the year 2000.
- Robots of the future will be able to "think" using artificial intelligence and the ability to recognize objects by sight and touch.

Review Questions

1. What advantages will robots bring to blind people?
2. How does vision analysis work?

VOICE SYNTHESIS AND VOICE RECOGNITION

Chicago's O'Hare Airport is one of the busiest in the world. It handles millions of passengers and millions of pieces of baggage each year. Computers, of course, keep track of planes and passengers at the airport. And computers also keep track of baggage—by recognizing the human voice.

At different airline terminals within O'Hare, baggage handlers shout out the destination of each passenger's bag as it rolls along a conveyor belt. A computer then routes the baggage to the correct plane or arrival terminal, cutting down on the number of bags that are lost or misplaced.

This is just one of the ways in which **voice recognition**—a computer's ability to recognize the human voice—is working to make life easier for humans today.

TALKING AND LISTENING COMPUTERS TODAY

You've probably already heard computers talk to you in certain games and toys. These applications are known as **voice synthesis**—the ability of computers to mimic the sound of the human voice.

Although some computers can recognize and imitate the human voice today, their abilities are rather limited. They recognize only a few hundred words at most, and each word often has to be repeated in order for the computer to really understand it. The same is true with talking computers: Their vocabulary is very small compared to the average human's vocabulary. This situation, however, is rapidly changing.

TALKING AND LISTENING COMPUTERS TOMORROW

In the future computers will be able to scan a printed page such as a newspaper or book and read it aloud in a flowing, humanlike voice. Similarly, in the future a person will be able to dictate a letter to a computer and the computer will convert the spoken words into a printed letter. Before computers are able to talk fluently and listen with full understanding, there are a few obstacles to overcome, however.

UNDERSTANDING HUMAN SPEECH

To recognize human speech, a computer first has to convert the speech sounds into electrical signals. Then the computer scans the electrical signal and converts it to a series of numbers—1's and 0's. This is known as *digitizing the sound wave*. The computer then compares the patterns of numbers to other patterns that have been stored in its memory. When the new pattern exactly matches a stored pattern, the computer "recognizes" or "understands" the word.

Most humans do not have a problem understanding the same word spoken by two or three different people, unless one has a very heavy accent. Humans are able to screen out the characteristics of the person's voice and concentrate on what is being said. Computers, so far, do not have this ability. To most of today's computers the same word spoken by three different people is really the same as three different words.

Another problem facing computer designers is the fact that humans talk fast and mumble. How many times a day do you hear—or say—"Huh? What'd ya say? I can't hear you," or "Would you repeat that, please?" If *you* have trouble hearing or understanding what someone else says, imagine what a computer goes through as it tries to make sense of something like "Well, it's like . . . uh . . . I mean . . . whaddyadoinnextweekend-doyouwantgotoamovie?"

Computers also have trouble distinguishing between words and phrases that sound the same. For example, most native speakers of English pronounce "the sky" and "this guy" in the same way. Another person will know which meaning is meant by listening to the other words in the sentence. Scientists and engineers are attempting to program computers with the same ability.

PRODUCING HUMANLIKE SPEECH

To produce humanlike speech, a computer must be programmed with words or parts of words. Some computers analyze the sound of a human voice, store those sounds as digital patterns, and then reproduce them as necessary, word for word. This is the kind of system you've heard in computerized toys and talking dolls.

Other computers store linguistic rules along with digital patterns of words and word parts. The rules enable the computer to combine digitized words or word parts into sentences.

The actual sound of the word is produced when the computer converts the digital pattern to an electrical signal that matches the sound wave produced by the word when a human speaks it. The electrical signal is amplified and fed to a small speaker, which then vibrates and produces a sound that resembles a human voice.

There are two big problems in designing talking computers. First, they need enormous amounts of memory in order to produce even a small number of words. Second, scientists do not completely understand all the rules that govern the way humans speak. Without such an understanding, it is impossible to program a computer to produce the subtleties and range of human speech. Nevertheless, scientists and engineers are making a lot of progress in developing computers that are capable of talking and understanding human language. They've already produced a computer that can translate certain written words of Japanese into written English and vice versa. Who knows? In the future, you may have your own personal translator, a computer you can take with you when you travel to foreign countries.

Key Points

- Computers with the ability to recognize and produce a modest amount of human speech already exist.
- To recognize human speech, a computer digitizes the sound of the human voice, then compares the digital pattern to patterns stored in its memory.
- To reproduce human speech, a computer uses linguistic rules for combining digitized words or word parts. The digital pattern is converted to an electrical signal, amplified, and fed to a speaker, producing a human-like sound.

Review Questions

1. What is the difference between voice recognition and voice synthesis?
2. What are some of the problems facing developers of computers in attempting to instruct them to speak and understand human language?

COMPUTERS—WHERE ARE THEY HEADING?

Developments are occurring so rapidly in the field of computers that the future is impossible to predict. Yet certain trends seem obvious. Because of superchips and artificial intelligence, many products, such as cars, radios, and televisions, will be produced entirely by robots in automated factories. Also, computers will be smarter, more powerful, and cheaper.

COMPUTERS AND EVERYDAY LIFE

Computers are already having a dramatic effect on our lives. They've made it possible to send people into space, to have concert-hall sound reproduction in our living rooms, and to use credit cards instead of cash to make purchases. In the future you can look forward to many more conveniences and changes in everyday life.

THE PAPERLESS OFFICE

In the office and home of the future, there will be less paper to push around. People will communicate by electronic mail within the office and between offices. Instead of dictating a letter to a secretary, you'll dictate the letter to your computer. The machine will print your letter on its screen, and you will have a chance to edit it. Then you will instruct the computer that you want to send the letter to Mr. or Ms. X in Chicago at the Y Corporation. The computer will automatically look up the mail code for that location and person and will send the letter electronically. You can instruct the computer to wait for a reply or you can instruct it to give Mr. or Ms. X the date by which you'd like a reply.

In the office of the future, you will not need to go to a file drawer full of papers in order to get a document. You will just tell your computer to get the document. You might say something like "I'd like to see the contract with Mr. Buzzy, please." The computer might ask, "Do you mean the one you signed on February 28 this year or the one you signed December 23 last year?" You will make your choice and the computer will display the correct document on its screen.

In fact, with all the electronic communication that will be available in the future, people won't have to go to the office at all, unless they want to. Read over this section again. Nowhere does it say that you're in the office. You could be sitting at home, using your computer to communicate with the office computer.

FEWER WORK HOURS

The average work week today is around thirty-five hours. In 1965 it was about forty-one hours; in 1880 it was about sixty-five hours.

By the year 2000 the average work week will be closer to twenty hours. Why? Because many of the routine, time-consuming tasks will be taken over by computers. It will be possible to do more work in less time, and people will have more leisure time.

Don't forget, too, that in the future people may also have their own personal robots to take care of household chores that now take a lot of time.

THE JOB MARKET

Computers with artificial intelligence will have an effect on the job market. For one thing, fewer people will be needed in manufacturing and industry because robots will be able to do the work faster and cheaper.

Jobs in manufacturing will decrease to about 3 percent of the total market, but jobs in technical fields will increase. There will be more jobs in fields such as engineering, computer programming, technical sales, and computer repair.

There will also be more jobs in health care, counseling, and entertainment.

Some people fear that computers and robots will raise the unemployment rate. The truth is that machines *do* eliminate certain kinds of jobs. However, they also create new jobs because they make it possible to produce more and better goods and services. When the quality and quantity of goods increases, prices drop. That means that more people can afford them, which means, in turn, that more goods have to be produced. If more goods have to be produced, more people must be employed to produce them. This has happened throughout history since the late 1700's, when a machine called the spinning jenny made it possible for one person to spin sixteen separate yarns at a time instead of just one.

SPREAD OF SPECIALIZED KNOWLEDGE

One of the problems with human experts is that there are not enough of them. As our need for information grows, we need more experts. Artificial intelligence will help solve this problem by making expert knowledge available to people who are not experts.

As you know, expert systems are programs that have both a large knowledge base and the ability to ask questions and make inferences. These systems can be programmed with specialized knowledge. For example, an expert system might be programmed with the knowledge of someone who, let's say, knows how to repair video cassette recorders (VCRs). That program can be duplicated and sold to anyone who wants to repair his or her own VCR.

Key Points

- Electronic mail will reduce the amount of paper used in offices.
- Computers will enable more people to work at home.
- Video games will become increasingly more sophisticated.

Review Questions

1. What effect will computers have on the number of hours people work? Why?
2. Why are computers not likely to increase the rate of unemployment?

The development of new computer technologies is limited only by our imaginations.

ISSUES: Questions for the Future

With all the mind-boggling developments that are taking place in the field of computers, many questions arise. There are no clear-cut answers to any of these questions. It is possible only to look at what is happening now and make reasonable guesses about what will happen. New discoveries and inventions are being made all the time. Any one of them may turn the whole computer revolution in a different direction. The only thing that is absolutely certain is that computers will be around for a long time to come.

WILL COMPUTERS BECOME SMARTER THAN HUMANS?

Scientists and engineers are making computers smarter, it's true. Even today, any computer can perform calculations and retrieve information from its memory many times faster than any person. It's very likely that the work being done in artificial intelligence will produce computers with pretty high IQs, which means they'll probably be able to do even more things faster than—or as well as—people. Computers may eventually be able to learn by using such senses as smell, touch, and taste. But will computers become smarter than people? That's anybody's guess.

WILL COMPUTERS GET OUT OF CONTROL AND DOMINATE PEOPLE?

In the movie *2001: A Space Odyssey*, a powerful computer named Hal assumed more authority than it should have. Some people wonder if that situation could ever really happen. Well, computers *are* becoming smarter and more powerful. In the future they'll even be able to program themselves to do certain jobs, and they may even be able to make copies of themselves by directing other computers in factories. As we continue to make computers smarter, we'll have to build in safety features that prevent computers from getting out of control.

WILL COMPUTERS HELP US ACHIEVE A FAIRER SOCIETY?

At the present time computers are still pretty expensive. Not everyone can afford one. Some people are concerned that families with computers will have an advantage over those that don't have computers and that our society will become divided between people who are computer literate and those who are not.

Whenever a new invention comes along, it is indeed the more privileged families that get it first. However, like the automobile, telephone, radio, and television, the computer will eventually find its way into most people's lives.

Computers, therefore, will probably not make society any more or less fair than it is now with regard to the distribution of cars, phones, and televisions.

REVIEW & APPLICATION

SUMMARY

- Superchips, including very-large-scale integrated (VLSI) and ultra-large-scale integrated (ULSI) chips, will enable computers of the future to be compact, powerful, and inexpensive.
- Developments in the field of artificial intelligence will produce computers able to act in ways that are similar—if not identical—to those of human intelligence.
- Robots of the future will do household chores and help disabled people.
- Computers of the future will be able to speak and understand human language.
- Parallel processing will enable computers to handle more than one type of data at once. This will make computers even more intelligent than they are today.

REVIEW QUESTIONS

1. Name four products or advantages that will result from the use of superchips.
2. Name two areas in which expert systems are already in use.
3. How does a computer recognize human speech?
4. How is the actual sound produced in a computer that is programmed to reproduce human speech?
5. Name three fields in which there is likely to be an increase in the number of jobs because of increased use of computers.

VOCABULARY

Match each item in the left column with the correct item on the right.

a. ULSI	1. a program that acts like a human expert
b. VLSI	2. converting light from an object into digital signals
c. AI	3. containing as many as 100,000 circuits
d. vision analysis	4. containing as many as a million circuits
e. expert system	5. field concerned with making intelligent computers

DISCUSSION QUESTIONS

1. Computers are being used in many ways to help people know more and work less. If you were a scientist or an engineer, what kind of job would you want to design a computer to do? Tell how superchips and artificial intelligence would help you.
2. Describe how you might design a computer that has a sense of smell or taste. Tell how this computer might be used.

PROJECTS

C As you have read, it is very difficult for computers to deal with human languages because of such things as verb forms, syntax differences, and words that are spelled the same but mean different things. Codes, however, are very easy for computers to handle. This program encodes and decodes messages.

```
10 DIM M1$(50), M2$(50,20)
20 PRINT: INPUT "TYPE 1 TO
    ENCODE, 2 TO DECODE       "; C
30 IF C=1 OR C=2 THEN 50
40 GOTO 20
50 PRINT: INPUT "HOW MANY
    WORDS"; X
60 PRINT: PRINT "ENTER
    MESSAGE, ONE WORD AT A TIME"
70 FOR D=1 TO X: INPUT
    M1$(D): NEXT D
80 FOR Z=1 TO X: FOR Y=1 TO
    LEN(M1$(X))
90 FOR Q=1 TO 26
100 IF C=1 THEN READ A$, B$
110 IF C=2 THEN READ B$, A$
120 IF MID$(M1$(Z),Y,1)=A$
     THEN M2$(Z,Y)=B$: Q=26
130 NEXT Q: RESTORE: NEXT Y:
     NEXT Z
140 FOR Z=1 TO X
150 FOR Y=1 TO LEN(M1$(X))
160 PRINT M2$(Z,Y);
170 NEXT Y: NEXT Z: END
500 DATA A,!,B,#,C,$,D,%,E,&,F,'
510 DATA G,(,H,),I,+,J,-,K,3,
     L,6,M,@
520 DATA N,*,O,/,P,>,Q,<,R,?,S,C
530 DATA T,.,U,Z,V,;,W,4,X,F,
     Y,9,Z,S
```

Look at line 30. What do you think OR means in BASIC? The same thing it means in English. In this case, the computer will skip to line 50 if either C=1 or C=2 is true. If neither one is true, the computer will skip to the next line.

Enter and run the program. Encode and decode several messages.

Change line 30 to

```
30 If C<>1 AND C<>2 THEN 20
```

Now delete line 40 and run the program again. Does it still work? AND means the same thing in BASIC as in English. The computer will loop up to line 20 only if both C<>1 and C<>2 are true. If either one is not true, the computer will skip to the next line.

Further Practice

D The invention of the telegraph helped to unify the nation. The invention of the car helped to create suburbs. Which of the changes that the computer brings is most important? Why?

Enrichment

D It's time to add a branch to the family tree. Use your library to gather information on fifth-generation computers. Find out who is developing these computers, when the computers will be ready, and what capabilities the computers will have.

CHAPTER TEST

Write your answers on a sheet of paper numbered 1 through 9.

MATCHING

1. Match each term to its definition.

a. robotics	1. Correspondence by computer
b. cashless society	2. Understanding human speech
c. paperless book	3. Superchip containing text
d. voice recognition	4. Exchange of goods without paper money
e. electronic mail	5. Science of humanlike devices

MULTIPLE CHOICE

2. At the heart of today's and tomorrow's computers is a:
   a. CRT
   b. peripheral
   c. superchip
   d. keyboard
3. A chip is a small piece of:
   a. silicon containing circuits
   b. metal containing batteries
   c. plastic containing wires
   d. wood containing electrodes
4. Small chip size means that computers will be:
   a. less powerful
   b. more expensive
   c. harder to build
   d. contained in small spaces
5. Superchips are characterized by their:
   a. large storage and processing capacity
   b. silicon and sensitivity
   c. ability to conduct electricity
   d. cost and compliance
6. Developing computers that can think is the aim of a field known as:
   a. expert systems
   b. robotics
   c. voice synthesis
   d. artificial intelligence
7. One advantage of an expert system is that it:
   a. can work faster than humans
   b. makes decisions on impulse
   c. does not need a large data base
   d. can program itself
8. One day, computers with artificial intelligence will:
   a. control people
   b. be large but inexpensive
   c. use human logic and parallel processing
   d. be small but expensive
9. By the year 2000, most robots in use in the United States will be in:
   a. health care
   b. agriculture
   c. business
   d. industry

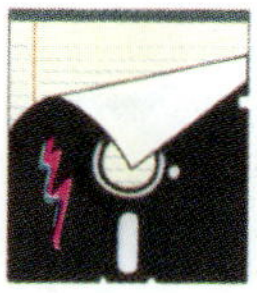

ISSUE: CITIZENSHIP

In a democratic society, citizens have certain rights and responsibilities. In the United States, for example, citizens over the age of 18 have the right to vote. Voting is more than just a right, however. It's also a responsibility. People feel an obligation to evaluate the issues and cast a vote for the candidate of their choice. No one is *forced* to vote, of course. However, most people feel that voting is a duty that they owe to their society—and to themselves.

As you've read in this book, computer technology has brought with it many benefits. But it has also introduced new problems, ranging from computer-caused unemployment to computer crimes.

Today, people are focusing more and more attention on their rights and responsibilities in the computer age. Like voters in an election, people are evaluating the issues and expressing their personal feelings through word and action.

What are some of the rights and responsibilities people are thinking about? Here are some examples. As you read them, think about where *you* stand on the issues.

Privacy: People want their privacy protected. If financial, medical, or other personal information about them or their family is stored in a data bank, they don't want unauthorized people to have access to this data.

Protection: People in business want their products and ideas protected against theft. Software developers, for example, want to receive payment for copies of the programs they've created and copyrighted. Similarly, executives don't want outsiders to gain access to confidential information stored in company computers.

Right to Know: People want the right to know what information is kept in their records. For example, suppose that a financial institution has an electronic file about an individual. Unless the individual has the right to see those records, he or she can't be certain they are correct.

Computer literacy: In order to deal with advancing technology, people want to become informed about computers and understand both the computer's benefits and its limitations.

Speaking out: People want to express their viewpoints on software piracy, illegal data-bank entry, and other timely issues that concern them. To do so, they write letters to local, state, and federal officials. They join computer clubs and user groups in order to share ideas.

Respect for others: People become sensitive to the rights of others. They do not copy software programs without permission. They take financial responsibility for telecommunications costs.

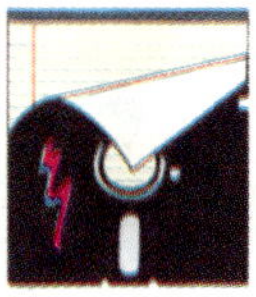

UNIT REVIEW

CONCEPTS

- What does the term *computer literacy* mean? Do you feel you are computer literate? Explain your answer.
- Why do you think the current era is called the Information Age? What role do computers play?

CAREERS

- Which computer careers discussed in this book are most appealing to you? Why?
- What high school courses are necessary to prepare for a career in computers?
- Does a person need more than a high school degree for a career in computers? Explain.

ISSUES

- List several reasons for the proliferation of computer crime.
- What responsibilities does society have toward people who lose their jobs due to changing technologies?
- What information should be available to each of the following employers about a prospective employee? What information should be withheld? (a) Main Street Department Store, (b) Central School District, (c) FBI

APPLICATIONS

- Choose a subject area and discuss how computers can be used in the classroom to make learning easier. What aspects of the course are better handled by the teacher?
- What questions should a parent ask when evaluating an educational software program for use in the home?

TO FIND OUT

- Do retailers in your community hire students to help sell computers and software? Interview managers of appropriate stores. Also talk with employees to learn about their responsibilities, salaries, and working environment.

GLOSSARY

A

ABACUS The oldest known mechanical aid for calculating, consisting of beads strung on wires or wooden rods.

ADDRESS The location of an individual cell on an electronic spreadsheet identified by the column letter and row number.

ALPHANUMERIC Consisting of letters and numbers, or of letters only.

ANALOG COMPUTER A computer that calculates by measuring the continuous change in some physical quantity, such as temperature or air pressure.

APPLICATION SOFTWARE A program that enables a computer to do a specific job, such as word processing.

ARITHMETIC UNIT The part of a computer's central processing unit that adds and compares numbers.

ARRAY A way of storing data in a program.

ARTIFICIAL INTELLIGENCE (AI) Field of computer science concerned with the development of computers that have the ability to infer, reason, solve problems, and understand language.

ASSEMBLY LANGUAGE A computer language that uses mnemonic code and is close to the machine language of the computer.

AUTOMATIC TELLER MACHINE A machine located at a bank or other convenient location that allows people to make cash withdrawals or deposits and do other banking business.

B

BASIC Most widely used computer language; stands for *B*eginner's *A*ll-purpose *S*ymbolic *I*nstruction *C*ode.

BINARY NUMBER SYSTEM A number system based on only two numbers, 0 and 1.

BIT Short for *bi*nary digi*t*: a 1 or a 0, either of the two digits in the binary number system.

BRANCH One of the possible pathways along which a program may proceed.

BUFFER A special part of a computer's memory for temporary storage of information.

BUG A mechanical flaw in a computer system or an error in a program.

BYTE A unit of measurement for the memory capacity of a computer; equals one character.

C

CARTRIDGE A plastic box that contains a permanent program and has read-only memory.

CASSETTE A small reel of magnetic tape in a plastic case, which can be used to store programs and data.

CAT SCANNER A computer-aided machine that takes close-up pictures of body organs through an x-ray process; CAT stands for *C*omputer-*A*ided *T*omography.

CELL The intersection of a row and column on an electronic spreadsheet.

CENTRAL PROCESSING UNIT (CPU) The part of the computer that interprets and follows instructions and sends the results to the user, the computer's memory, or both.

CHARACTER A letter, number, or other symbol; a space is also considered a character in terms of computer storage.

CHIP A thin wafer, about a quarter of an inch square, that plugs into a computer board and contains an integrated circuit; usually made of silicon.

COBOL A computer language developed for large computers and some microcomputers; designed for business use.

COLD START Turning on a computer.

COLOR On some computers, keyword that when combined with a number, tells the computer which color to use in graphics.

COMMAND LINE (PROMPT LINE) A line in the status area of an electronic spreadsheet that shows what command is being performed.

COMMUNICATIONS SOFTWARE Enables a computer, modem, and telephone to work together; sometimes stores information, automatically dials telephone numbers, or transmits incoming information to a printer.

COMPILED LANGUAGE A computer language that must be translated by a compiler into computer code before a program can be run.

COMPILER Program that translates a compiled language into code that can be read by the computer.

COMPUTER-AIDED DESIGN (CAD) Relating to software that allows a user to create designs using a computer.

COMPUTER-AIDED MANUFACTURE (CAM) Relating to software that allows a computer to direct machines that manufacture products.

COMPUTER-ASSISTED INSTRUCTION (CAI) The process of people learning through the aid of a computer.

COMPUTER LANGUAGE A set of words, symbols, and commands that a computer can "understand."

COMPUTER LITERACY Knowing about computers, knowing how to use them, and being aware of their benefits and drawbacks.

COMPUTER TRESPASSING Breaking into a computer system and using it without permission.

CONTROL UNIT The part of a computer's central processing unit that determines what action the arithmetic unit will take.

COPY (TEXT) Output that consists of characters.

COPY PROTECT To protect software against unwanted or illegal duplication.

CRT A computer display screen; stands for *C*athode-*R*ay *T*ube.

CURSOR A spot of light on the display screen that indicates the exact place at which the user is entering data or giving commands to the computer.

D

DAISY WHEEL In some printers, a wheel-like device that has letters, numbers, and characters on the ends of its spokes.

DATA 1. A general term for the pieces of information that a computer processes. 2. Keyword that tells the computer that information is to follow.

DATA BANK (INFORMATION SERVICE) Electronic storehouse of information accessed by using a microcomputer, modem, and telephone.

DATA BASE A collection of related information.

DATA-BASE MANAGEMENT SYSTEM Software designed for record keeping; allows the computer to sort through files of stored data and retrieve specific information.

DATA PROCESSING The use of computers to sort, add, rearrange, or otherwise manipulate information.

DEBUG To locate and correct errors in a program or defects in hardware.

DEDICATED COMPUTER See SPECIAL-PURPOSE COMPUTER.

DEDICATED WORD PROCESSOR A computer designed specifically for writing, editing, and printing text.

DIGITAL COMPUTER Calculates by counting.

DISK DRIVE The device that reads and writes on a floppy or hard disk.

DISKETTE See FLOPPY DISK.

DISK OPERATING SYSTEM (DOS) A program that controls the storage of information on disks and makes it possible for the computer to use programs.

DOCUMENT or **(FILE)** Anything written with a word-processing program.

DOCUMENTATION The printed information provided with or created for software which explains how to use it.

DOT-MATRIX PRINTER A printer that forms characters by using pins to strike an ink ribbon against the paper.

DOUBLE-DENSITY DISK Disk used with a disk drive that reads 80 tracks.

DOUBLE-SIDED DISK Designed to be used with a disk drive with two read/write heads, one for each side of the disk.

DOWNLOAD To transfer information electronically from a data bank or a computer to another computer.

E

EDIT LINE A line in the status area of an electronic spreadsheet that shows what information the user is entering.

ELECTRONIC MAIL Sending and receiving messages electronically by computer.

ELECTRONIC SPREADSHEET A computer program that allows the same types of data entry as a paper spreadsheet but automates the process of calculation, storage, and printing.

END Keyword that instructs the computer that it has reached the end of a BASIC program.

ENTER A key found on some computers used to enter information into the computer.

ENDLESS LOOP A loop in a program that never ends.

ERROR MESSAGE Information displayed on the screen by the computer to indicate that something is wrong and the program cannot continue.

EXPERT SYSTEM Computer system characterized by a very large data base, the ability to ask questions, and a set of rules that allow it to use its data to arrive at conclusions.

F

FEEDBACK In interactive communication between a computer and its user, the computer's response.

FIELD A single category of information in a data base.

FILE 1. A document written with a word-processing program. 2. A collection of related records in a data base.

FILENAME Title given to a word-processing document to identify it.

FLOPPY DISK (DISKETTE) The most common storage device used with microcomputers; a flexible disk made of thin plastic and magnetically coated; it is protected by a jacket that has openings to allow the disk drive to read or write information.

FLOWCHART A diagram used to plan a program.

FORECAST To make financial predictions based on "what-if" questions, often with the aid of an electronic spreadsheet.

FORMAT 1. To prepare a blank diskette for use. 2. In word processing, to set up the physical appearance of a document to be printed. 3. A listing of fields to be included in each record of a data base.

FOR...NEXT Loop used to repeat part of a program a specified number of times.

FORTRAN A computer language similar to BASIC, used mostly for scientific applications.

FUNCTION KEY Generally, any key on the keyboard that does not produce a letter, number, or special symbol.

G

GENERAL-PURPOSE COMPUTER A computer that can do a variety of tasks, such as calculating and word processing.

GOSUB Keyword that sends the computer to a subroutine.

GOTO Keyword that tells the computer to skip to a specified line.

GR On some computers, a keyword that tells the computer to switch to the graphics mode.

GRAPHICS Non-text output in the form of pictures, charts, or graphs.

GRAPHICS TABLET A flat, tabletlike input device that allows the user to draw a picture or design with a special pen; the drawing appears immediately on the computer screen.

H

HARD COPY (PRINTOUT) Text or graphics printed on paper.

HARD DISK A round, pancake-shaped, magnetic storage device that is permanently sealed in a case and can store much more data than a floppy disk.

HARD-SECTORED A disk that is divided into a fixed number of sectors.

HARDWARE The physical equipment of a computer, such as the screen, the keyboard, and the storage device.

HIGH-LEVEL Relating to computer languages that are far removed from machine language.

HIGH-RESOLUTION GRAPHICS Graphics that have high-quality resolution, producing sharp and clear images.

HLIN On some computers, a keyword that tells the computer to draw a horizontal line.

HOME COMPUTER (PERSONAL COMPUTER) Usually a microcomputer, consisting of a keyboard, a television-type screen, and a unit containing a microprocessor.

I

IF...THEN Program statement that instructs the computer to look at an expression in order to determine what action to take next.

IMMEDIATE MODE Method of operation in which the computer does one task at at time.

INITIALIZE 1. To set the starting value for a variable. 2. To format a diskette.

INPUT 1. Data and instructions given to a computer to enable it to do a specific job. 2. Keyword that tells the computer to stop and wait for the user to enter a value to be stored in a variable.

INPUT/OUTPUT (I/O) DEVICE A peripheral that can perform both input and output functions.

INTEGRATED CIRCUIT Thousands of tiny, interconnected electrical circuits contained in a computer chip.

INTERACTIVE Referring to the back-and-forth, two-way communications that takes place between user and computer.

INTERFACE UNIT A device that provides the necessary electrical and mechanical connections to enable two pieces of hardware to work together.

INTERPRETED LANGUAGE A computer language that is translated line by line by an interpreter as the program runs.

INTERPRETER Program that translates an interpreted language into computer code line by line as a program is being run.

J

JOYSTICK A device that permits the user to move a picture, line, word, or cursor on a display screen.

JUSTIFIED Relating to text in which one or both margins are straight and even.

K

KEYBOARD A device resembling the keyboard of a typewriter, through which a computer can receive input.

KEY FRAME INBETWEENING Animation technique in which the animator creates the first and last frames of a sequence and the computer fills in the frames in between.

KEYWORD The word in a program statement that tells the computer what to do.

KILOBYTE A unit of measurement for the storage or memory capacity of a computer; equals 1024 bytes; usually referred to a "K," as in 64K memory.

L

LANGUAGE PROCESSOR Translates computer language instructions into the electronic impulses used by the computer.

LEFT$(X$,n) Function that tells the computer to take the leftmost *n* characters in X$.

LEN Function that tells the computer to return the number of characters in (or LENgth of) the string variable in parentheses.

LET Keyword that instructs the computer to store numeric or string data in a variable.

LETTER-QUALITY PRINTER A printer that uses metal or plastic letters to strike an ink ribbon, producing typewriter-quality text.

LIGHT PEN A pen with a light-sensitive detector; it is used by touching its tip to the display screen.

LINE SPACING The amount of space between printed lines.

LIST Command that instructs the computer to display the program lines currently in memory.

LOADING The process of putting operating instructions into RAM.

LOCAL-AREA NETWORK (LAN) A number of terminals or microcomputers, usually located in the same building or room, connected by cables or wires.

LOGIC ERROR Mistake in a program that often won't prevent the program from running but will usually cause the program to give the wrong output.

LOGO A structured computer language that usually uses a turtle as the cursor; used to create graphic designs.

LOOP In a program, a series of steps that the computer repeats.

LOW-RESOLUTION GRAPHICS Graphic images whose resolution is not as sharp as that of high-resolution graphics.

M

MACHINE LANGUAGE A language used directly by the computer untranslated.

MAINFRAME A large, powerful, and expensive type of computer that can store vast amounts of data and can perform many tasks at the same time.

MEGABYTE A unit of measurement for the memory capacity of a computer; equals about one million bytes.

MEMBRANE KEY A type of key that looks as if it were printed on a flat surface; it does not have to be pushed, merely touched.

MEMORY A computer's ability to store information electronically; the information can be recalled, erased, or changed.

MENU A list of operations that a computer can perform in relation to a software program.

MERGE To instruct the computer to combine information from two or more files.

MICROCOMPUTER Small computer with enough power and storage capacity to meet the personal needs of many different kinds of users; also called personal computer, home computer, or desktop computer.

MICROPROCESSOR A microcomputer's central processing unit, especially when contained on a single chip.

MICROSECOND A millionth of a second.

MID$ (X$,n1,n2) Function that tells the computer to take n2 characters from X$, starting with character #n1.

MINIATURIZATION The process by which the design of an integrated circuit is reduced photographically to fit on a chip.

MINICOMPUTER A computer that is generally smaller than a mainframe computer and larger than a microcomputer; can store large amounts of information and perform more than one task at once.

MODEM Short for "modulator-demodulator"; a hardware device that enables computers to communicate with each other by telephone by translating computer input into audio tones and then translating the tones back into computer signals.

MODULAR DESIGN A program divided into modules in the planning and programming stages.

MODULE A self-contained unit that performs a task that is needed to accomplish a larger task.

MONITOR Display screen designed specifically as an output device for a computer.

MOUSE An input device consisting of a small box with one or more buttons; as the user moves the box around on a desktop, the cursor moves around the screen correspondingly.

MUSIC SYNTHESIZER A pianolike keyboard connected to a computer, which allows the user to compose, perform, and play back music.

N

NANOSECOND A billionth of a second.

NETWORK A number of computer users linked together; usually, a powerful central computer and many microcomputers or terminals.

NEW Command that clears the computer's memory.

NUMERIC Consisting of numbers only.

NUMERIC KEYPAD A group of keys resembling the keys of a calculator that are used to input numbers.

NUMERIC VARIABLE A memory location that holds numbers.

O

OBJECT CODE Machine language that the computer can understand directly.

OCR (OPTICAL CHARACTER READER) A device that scans a typewritten or printed page and converts the letters or numbers into electronic signals that can be read by the computer and recorded on tape or disk.

OFF-SCREEN FORMATTING The storing of format commands in memory; format is not displayed until the document is printed.

ON-LINE Electronically connected, as with a mainframe or other computer through the use of microcomputer, modem, and telephone.

ON-SCREEN FORMATTING The on-screen display of document format.

OPERATING SYSTEM Program that provides the instructions that enable the computer to handle tasks necessary for it to work.

OPTICAL SCANNER Input device used to read the Universal Product Code printed on product packages.

OUTPUT Information the computer produces as a result of processing.

P

PASCAL A structured computer language that requires all variables to be defined before beginning the program.

PERIPHERAL Any hardware device that is connected to a computer in order to make the computer easier to use or to expand the computer's capabilities.

PERSONAL COMPUTER (HOME COMPUTER) Usually a microcomputer, consisting of a keyboard, a television-type screen, and a unit containing a microprocessor.

PIXEL One of the tiny points or boxes of light that make up a computer screen; stands for *pic*ture *el*ement.

PLOT On some computers, a keyword that instructs the computer to light up a pixel.

PLOTTER An output device that controls the movements of one or more pens over a piece of paper and can produce intricate hard-copy drawings.

PORT The place on a computer or peripheral where connecting cables or wires can be attached.

PRINT Keyword that instructs the computer to put letters, numbers, or symbols on the screen.

PRINTER A mechanical output device that can print text and, sometimes, graphics on paper.

PRINTOUT
See HARD COPY.

PROGRAM Set of instructions given to a computer, telling it what to do.

PROGRAMMING Creating instructions, or programs, for a computer.

PROGRAM MODE Method of computer operation in which the computer can be instructed to carry out a series of steps in a specific order.

PROMPT LINE See COMMAND LINE.

Q

QWERTY LAYOUT The arrangement of keys on a typewriter keyboard; refers to the sequence of letter keys at the far left just below the number keys.

R

RANDOM ACCESS Direct access to any data stored; compare SEQUENTIAL ACCESS.

RANDOM-ACCESS MEMORY (RAM) The temporary memory of a computer which holds the software and other input data in use.

READ Keyword that tells the computer to assign the next item in the data statement to D$.

READ-ONLY MEMORY (ROM) The permanent memory of a computer.

READ/WRITE HEAD Disk drive head that "reads" the information recorded on a disk or "writes" new information on the disk.

RECORD A collection of fields in a data base.

REM Stands for remark; keyword used for making comments in a program.

RESOLUTION The quality of the image on a display screen.

RESTORE Keyword that tells the computer to start over with the first item in the first DATA statement.

RETURN 1. Keyword that tells the computer that a subroutine has ended and to return to the main program. 2. A key found on some computer keyboards, used to enter information.

RIGHT$ (X$,n) Function that tells the computer to take the rightmost *n* characters in X$.

ROBOT A computer-controlled mechanical device.

RUN Command that tells the computer to carry out program instructions.

S

SECTOR One of 10 to 16 fan-shaped areas radiating out from the spindle hole of a disk, established by the operating system when the disk is formatted.

SEMICONDUCTOR A material that will conduct electricity in some circumstances but not in others.

SEQUENTIAL ACCESS
Access to data only in the order in which it was stored; compare RANDOM ACCESS.

SILICON CHIP See CHIP.

SIMULATION Use of computers to imitate real or imagined situations for training purposes.

SINGLE-DENSITY DISK Disk used with a disk drive that reads 35 or 40 tracks.

SOFT COPY The text and graphics that appear on a screen.

SOFT-SECTORED Relating to a disk that is divided into sectors by the disk operating system and can be formatted for use with different operating systems.

SOFTWARE Set of instructions that tells a computer what to do.

SOFTWARE PIRACY Illegal copying and sale of copyrighted software.

SOURCE CODE The original program before it has been compiled or translated into machine code.

SPECIAL-PURPOSE COMPUTER (DEDICATED COMPUTER) A computer designed for one particular purpose.

SPREADSHEET Tool used in financial forecasting, consisting of an arrangement of rows and columns.

STATEMENT In programming, an instruction.

STATUS AREA Located in the upper left-hand corner of an electronic spreadsheet, several lines that give the user information about data being entered.

STEP Function used with a FOR...NEXT loop that tells the computer what number to count loops by.

STORAGE DEVICE Device for storing data, such as a floppy disk.

STRING VARIABLE A memory location that can store characters such as letters.

STRUCTURED PROGRAMMING
Programming using top-down structure.

SUBMENU A list of choices that may appear on the screen following a choice on the initial menu.

SUBROUTINE A self-contained unit in a program that accomplishes a specific task.

SYNTAX The way in which letters, numbers, symbols, and words are put together to form a computer language.

SYNTAX ERROR A mistake in a computer language, such as an error in spelling or punctuation.

SYSTEM DISK A disk upon which the operating system is stored.

T

TERMINAL Input/output device that consists of a screen and keyboard but generally does not have a central processing unit.

TEXT (COPY) Output that consists of characters.

THROW-AWAY CODE Program lines in BASIC that fill in parts of a program so that other parts can be tested; replaced by actual program lines when the program is completed.

TIMESHARING Sharing the power of a central computer among a network of electronically linked users.

TOP-DOWN STRUCTURE Program organization entailing modular design, planned from the "top" with the most general module and worked "down" from there.

TOUCH-SENSITIVE SCREEN A display screen that can be used as an input device because it responds to the user's touch.

TRACK One of 35 to 80 concentric circles into which a disk is divided by the operating system when the disk is formatted.

TURTLE The cursor in Logo, which can be commanded to move and draw a line behind it.

U

ULSI CHIP A computer chip envisioned to contain up to a million circuits; stands for *U*ltra-*L*arge-*S*cale *I*ntegration.

UNIVERSAL PRODUCT CODE A series of bars and numbers printed on packages that can be read by an optical scanner.

USER-FRIENDLY Describing software or hardware that is easy to use.

V

VARIABLE A location in the computer's memory where information that can vary is stored.

VISION ANALYSIS Ability of a computer or computer-guided robot to recognize shapes of objects by converting a visual image into a string of numbers and comparing that string to other sets of numbers stored in memory.

VLIN On some computers, a keyword that tells the computer to draw a vertical line.

VLSI CHIP A computer chip that contains 100,000 or more circuits; stands for *V*ery-*L*arge-*S*cale *I*ntegration.

VOICE-RECOGNITION DEVICE Input device that allows the user to communicate with a computer by speech.

VOICE SYNTHESIS Computer-produced speech that imitates the human voice.

W

WARM START Resetting a computer without turning it off.

WINDOW The ability to view simultaneously parts of a file other than the contents of the current screen display.

WORD PROCESSING A computer application that resembles typewriting but allows instant correcting of errors, moving text to different locations, and other editing functions.

WORD WRAP The automatic movement of a word too long to fit on a line to the next line.

WRITE-PROTECT NOTCH Notch cut into a floppy disk which, when covered with a special tab, prevents the writing or erasing of data.

INDEX